SCHIZOPHRENIA

Yrjö O. Alanen

SCHIZOPHRENIA
Its Origins
and
Need-Adapted Treatment

Yrjö O. Alanen

Foreword
Stephen Fleck

Introduction
Murray Jackson

translated by
Sirkka-Liisa Leinonen

London
KARNAC BOOKS

First published in English in 1997 by
H. Karnac (Books) Ltd.
58 Gloucester Road
London SW7 4QY

British Library Cataloguing in Publication Data

A C.I.P. record for this book is available from the British Library

ISBN 1 85575 156 9

Edited, designed, and produced by Communication Crafts

Printed in Great Britain by BPC Wheatons Ltd, Exeter

10 9 8 7 6 5 4 3 2 1

To my co-workers

CONTENTS

PREFACE AND ACKNOWLEDGEMENTS

The starting-point of this book is to promote a concept and therapy of schizophrenic psychoses based on an integrated psychodynamic approach to this disorder. The theories of schizophrenia are still quite contradictory, due to researchers' often one-sided views of its causes. The progress of the treatment of schizophrenic psychoses has also been greatly hampered because of a lack of integrative starting-points. I think that few schizophrenic patients are currently receiving the kind of treatment that they need.

I begin by looking back on my first experiences as a psychotherapist with schizophrenic patients, an activity that I have now been engaged in for 40 years. The second chapter consists of general theories of the nature of schizophrenia and its impact on public health. In chapter three, a short review of contemporary research of the aetiology of schizophrenia is presented, followed by an attempt at an integrative synthesis of the origins of schizophrenia based on research findings and my own experiences and views. The chapter may also function as a theoretical background to the therapeutic approach described in the final chapters of the book.

Chapter four is a brief discussion of the current state of the treatment of schizophrenia. Main attention is given to the studies of psychological approaches. Chapter five focuses on the development and principles of the comprehensive psychotherapeutic approach called "need-adapted treatment of schizophrenic psychoses", which was developed by myself and my colleagues working in Turku, Finland, and which has stimulated a great deal of interest and applications in the Scandinavian countries. According to our experience, the success of the treatment is greatest when it is based on an integrative understanding of the individually determined and changing therapeutic needs of each patient as well as those of the patient's closest interpersonal network, generally his/her family. The follow-up results described in this chapter suggest that our approach is effective in reducing chronicity and disability arising from schizophrenia.

Chapter six complements the description of our approach clinically. I first summarize my experiences in family and individual therapy with schizophrenic patients as well as in the psychotherapeutic hospital community suited for their treatment. The application of the need-adapted approach in practice is then illustrated by three concise case reports, one written in collaboration with my colleague, specialist nurse Irene Aalto, and one with psychiatrist Jyrki Heikkilä. In chapter seven, I discuss the effects of predominant social policies on treatment and rehabilitation, and I present my views on the development of treatment activities within the community psychiatric context.

This book was first published in Finnish 1993. The English edition has been revised by leaving out a more comprehensive review of schizophrenia investigation, adding information based on later research, and enlarging the clinical material. I wish to express my cordial thanks to my friends, Stephen Fleck, M.D., and Dr. Murray Jackson, for their collaboration. Both of them read patiently through the manuscript and, based on their abundant experience, gave me invaluable advice with regard both to subject matter and to language. I am also very grateful to Brian Martindale, M.D., for his constructive criticism and advice.

I dedicate this book to my co-workers, both at the Turku clinic and elsewhere. The Turku Schizophrenia Project was a team project developed actively over the years by many researchers and clinicians, of whom I wish to mention the psychiatrists Jukka Aaltonen, Ritva Järvi, Anneli Larmo, Klaus Lehtinen, Ville Lehtinen, Vilho Mattila, Viljo

Räkköläinen, Raimo Salokangas, Simo Salonen, and Hilkka Virtanen, the psychologists Juhani Laakso and Aira Laine, the ADP operator Anne Kaljonen, and, last but not least, ward nurse Riitta Rasimus and the staff of Ward 81, who took the main responsibility for the inpatient treatment of psychotic patients, expanding to therapeutic relationships even outside of the hospital. My special thanks are due to Irene Aalto and Jyrki Heikkilä for their valuable contribution to chapter six, as well as to art therapist Marja Karlsson, who provided me with the cover picture of this book—a painting by a young schizophrenic patient.

In addition to my Turku colleagues, I am indebted to the coworkers who participated in the activities of the Finnish National Schizophrenia Project as well as in the Inter-Scandinavian NIPS Project. Among the latter, I want especially to honour the memory of the late Dr. Endre Ugelstad, from Norway. Endre's contribution to the planning and realization of the NIPS Project was crucially important.

The original translation of my manuscript into English was made by Sirkka-Liisa Leinonen. I thank her, as well as the Academy of Finland and the Turku University Foundation for the economic support that made the translation possible.

Finally, I will express my greatest gratitude to my loving and loveable wife, Hanni, for her understanding support throughout the uncounted working hours involved.

Turku, Finland
August 1997

FOREWORD

Stephen Fleck

Professor of Psychiatry and Public Health (Emeritus)
Department of Psychiatry, Yale University School of Medicine

Professor Alanen's work may be the most comprehensive treatise on schizophrenia in 25 years—that is, since Manfred Bleuler's *Die Schizophrenen Geistesstörungen* (Bleuler, 1972). Alanen's volume begins and ends with accounts of patients and their treatments, illustrating first the benefits and constraints of dyadic psychotherapy with schizophrenics and the beginning realization of the significance of familial disturbances. The case reports at the end of the book illustrate "need-adapted treatment" developed in Turku under the author's auspices and guidance documenting the need for and implementation of flexibility in approaches adapted to each patient and adapted further to the patient's particular situation or human context, as well as to the course of the illness. Psycho-active drugs are used sparingly, usually at low dosage, and never as THE treatment.

The four chapters between these case reports reflect our travels and travails over the last four and one-half decades in particular, and they do so with considerable erudition. The evolution of the serendipitously discovered psychopharmacological treatments and the ensuing exploration of the biological substrate of psychoses that dominates the research field today have been paralleled by the development of community psychiatry and rehabilitative treatments. However, with regard to research funds, the latter has remained a step-child.

Dr. Alanen covers these developments and investigations, as well as psychoanalytic theories and approaches, in great detail and eventually he offers an integrated view of the development of schizophrenia—a systems-oriented approach encompassing the bio-psychosocial gambit from genetics to environmental factors. It is a well-reasoned model and a constructive contrast to what Uttal (1997) has called "neuro-reductionism". Necessary reductionistic research-based practices have become a major impediment to comprehensive treatment, let alone to continuity of care in many places. Research necessarily involves narrow diagnostic and rigid treatment procedures, which unfortunately have contaminated non-research clinical practice (Fleck, 1995).

Alanen's comprehensive, painstaking, and balanced account of relevant findings re schizophrenia, however fragmentary they might be, are combined with the aura of a truly caring physician. Thus "need-adapted treatment" evolved—each patient and context being treated and helped according to her or his particular individual and familial needs. This model has spread throughout Finland and to some of the neighbouring countries, and we can only hope that these attitudes and programs will move west and serve as an antidote to the current U.S. practice of profit-oriented managed care. It is allegedly more economic to fit a patient into a service—even "speciality clinics" (as briefly as possible)—than it is to shape services to each patient's needs and to those of the significant others. In the final chapter Alanen points out the socio-political aspects of schizophrenia, indicating that short-term and limited treatments may not be "economic" in the long run, aside from the humanitarian minuses of short treatments. The knowledge to render comprehensive and individually tailored treatment and services is here, even as our understanding of schizophrenia remains incomplete. As for the future, patients, healers, and investigators alike might heed Faust's observation: "Fortunate he who can yet hope to emerge from this sea of errors" (Goethe, 1808; transl. S.F.).

INTRODUCTION

Murray Jackson

Psychiatrist and psychoanalyst
Maudsley Hospital and King's College Hospital (Emeritus)

First published in Finnish in 1993 and now in a new English version, this book offers a comprehensive account of the work of Professor Yrjö Alanen, a distinguished psychiatrist and psychoanalyst who, together with his colleagues, has been active both in clinical practice and in psychiatric research in the field of schizophrenia in Finland for the last 45 years.

This work has been very successful; it has received wholesale support from the Finnish government and has generated a sophisticated level of psychobiological and psychoanalytical understanding and a comprehensive nation-wide approach to treatment that is both rational and humane. Although the influence of this "need-adapted" approach has spread to many centres throughout Scandinavia, it is relatively unknown in the United Kingdom. Despite the fact that the author has in recent years addressed the British Psychoanalytic Society and published in the *British Journal of Psychiatry*, it has produced little sign of serious interest in the work, let alone recognition of its profound implications.

"Schizophrenia" is the psychiatric classification of a group of severe and persistent mental disturbances characterized by the disruption of the processes of rational thinking and perceiving, which usually leads to delusional beliefs and hallucinatory perceptions in the auditory and visual field. The author's view of schizophrenia is that although it is a highly complex and insufficiently understood phenomenon, it is essentially a reaction to life crises by individuals who are psychologically and biologically less well equipped to meet expectable developmental challenges, deprivations, and adversities than are non-psychotics. Study of the life history of such individuals provides evidence for the view that the root causes of this vulnerability are to be found in the psychological and social experiences of infancy and childhood. Whilst recognizing that everyone emerges into the world with differing biological equipment, the author makes clear his view that although the biological aspects are of undeniable relevance in research and treatment of schizophrenia, they are frequently given disproportionate emphasis, often at the expense of psychodynamic understanding.

The Finnish approach was originally centred on treatment with individual psychotherapy, but subsequent understanding of the theory and practice of family therapy methods came to take priority. At first the obvious benefits of this approach seemed impressive; gradually the limitations of its exclusive use also became clear. This led to the "need-specific" approach, whereby the needs and capacities of the individual patient are evaluated from the moment of first contact, and treatment modalities of family therapy, both systemic and psychodynamic, individual psychoanalytically oriented psychotherapy, other psychological treatments, and psychoactive medication are offered as and when believed to be appropriate to the patient's condition at any particular time. This is a far cry from most current psychiatric practice, and it is continuing to evolve.

Mental health professionals in particular will find the text applicable to their own interest and expertise. The detailed accounts of epidemiological and other research findings include that of other workers, and attempts to measure and quantify those factors amenable to such an approach receive an even-handed critique. Those with psychoanalytic or cognitive–behavioural interests will find much food for thought, and the "need-adapted" approach can be recognized as providing the necessary support for further exploration and development of their own particular skills. All will be interested in the account of work currently being pursued in Turku, where evidence is accumulating that the implementation of psychotherapeutic and family methods from the first moment of contact with first-episode patients can greatly reduce and in many cases totally obviate the need for neuroleptic medication. Those interested in developing methods of early intervention by the use of small psychosis teams will be interested to learn of their widespread use throughout Finland, and more recently in Sweden. Supporters of collaborative international interdisciplinary research will find an admirable model described in the account of the NIPS (Nordic Investigation of the Psychotherapy of Schizophrenia) Project, and of long-term care and rehabilitation of the chronically ill in the work of the Sopimusvuori Project.

This new and detailed account of the Finnish contribution will now be available to a wider audience, and the author's unassuming and non-partisan approach to the claims of various perspectives and treatment methods will allow the reader to come to his own conclusions about their merits and limitations. The appearance of this book is especially welcome because it arrives at a time when the pressures of the market economy are generating potentially destructive inter-disciplinary competition and polarized "anti-psychiatric" and "anti-analytic" stereotyped attitudes. Although the search for brief and effective methods of treatment in psychosis is in itself praiseworthy, it opens the door to a "fast-food" psychiatric approach that does great disservice to the practice of good clinical psychiatry, ultimately adds to the burden of work of over-stressed psychiatrists, and undermines the recognition of the fact that the majority of schizophrenic patients need expert help for long periods of time. It also introduces the danger that low standards of clinical practice may gradually become accepted as the norm.

The appearance of this important book will be welcomed by all those struggling to deepen their understanding of psychotic mental illness and to alleviate the suffering of those unfortunate victims of psychosocial and biological deficiencies and deprivations whose fate has led them into the confusing and often terrifying world of major psychosis, and into the alienating diagnosis of "schizophrenia".

SCHIZOPHRENIA

CHAPTER ONE

Three patients

The attitude towards schizophrenia and schizophrenic patients is always a notably personal matter. I have repeatedly noticed this among researchers and psychiatrists: no matter how scientific and objective we wish to be, our theories of the nature and treatment of schizophrenia, shaped, as they are, by our psychiatric training and experience, are also influenced by our personalities and life histories. The attitude towards schizophrenia is often influenced by ideological considerations.

I begin this book by relating my own experiences with schizophrenic patients. I hope this will also introduce the reader into the world of schizophrenics—through the gate I used myself.

The first schizophrenic I know of having met was a young woman who was kept in confinement in the mental department of the Kurikka local authority home, waiting for a bed to be vacated in the district mental hospital. That was in the late 1940s, when I had started medical studies and went to see the local authority home with my father, the municipal officer of health for this rural community in Finland. Knowing my interest in psychiatry, he indicated the patient to me as a schizophrenic and encouraged me to get acquainted with her.

The cell was gloomy, its only "furniture" being a ragged sleeping bag with straw squeezing out of the tears. There was a small shuttered window near the ceiling. I was probably brought a chair, but whether the patient was, I do not remember. I only remember that she was sitting on her bag, her hair tousled, making strange faces from time to time. But she was interested in meeting me and spoke volubly, though in a way that was difficult to understand. Her speech revealed glimpses of problems related to her family, strange references to homosexuality, and many other things.

At that time, I was myself struggling with identity problems, though much less momentous than hers. Conflicts of family relationships and the personal pressures caused by them were of topical significance for me, too. The things this young woman was saying interested but also horrified me. It seemed obvious to me that what she said was not randomly incoherent, but reflected her problems, though in an uncanny and shocking way.

My father took a more objective attitude. He said he considered the illness hereditary, referring to the abnormality of the whole family. I do not remember whether he said that some other members of the family were also mentally ill, but I knew myself that the patient's brother was considered odd and was called "Smarty Santanen". The girl's fate aroused pity in me: would she have to spend the rest of her life isolated in a hospital?

Another factor that influenced my preliminary conceptions of schizophrenia was more theoretical. Though a medical student, I also studied psychology at the university and was interested in art. In his book on developmental psychology, Heinz Werner (1948) compared the artistic productions of children, primitive people, and mental patients. He concluded that the art of the mentally ill is produced at a level that is lower than the "upstairs" logic of an adult in a high-culture community but which, nevertheless, exists in his dreams and subconscious mind. Picasso and other twentieth-century pioneers of modern art had been seeking stimuli on that more primitive level of expression to which we all have internal access, provided we have not been blocked by external and internal constraints implicit in our culture. I believe that the emergence of modern art and the psychological understanding of schizophrenia are not coincident by chance alone (even if the appreciation of art seems to have progressed more rapidly).

As I advanced in my studies, I found myself to be naturally oriented towards psychiatry, which also signified a permanent solution for a central part of my identity problem. While a student at the University Clinic in the Lapinlahti Hospital in Helsinki, I began, encouraged by my teacher Martti Kaila, to work on a doctoral thesis on the mothers of schizophrenic patients (Alanen, 1958) and simultaneously to learn about how to understand and treat these interesting patients. Never since that time have I lost this interest.

The first experiences of psychotherapeutic work are especially important for the professional development and orientation of a psychiatrist. I shall describe three patients who taught me much. (Their names have been changed.)

Sarah, my first patient

Sarah, a 25-year-old seriously schizophrenic language student, was my first long-term patient belonging to the schizophrenia group. When I first met her (in 1953), I was just beginning my psychiatric training and was only one year her senior.

Sarah had suddenly become delirious while studying at a university summer school away from home. Her parents told me that when they had been informed of their daughter's illness and had gone to see her, she had told them she was a medium and tried to hypnotize them, making rebuffing gestures with her hands. In the hospital Sarah told me that she had been used for experiments for the psychology courses simultaneously going on in the summer school. They had begun to hypnotize and train her in a group of ten people. She said she was now a clairvoyant, a medium able to converse with both spirits and many people far away, who were taking turns to speak through her brain. Later on these voices coalesced into one, which she called her "Guide". The Guide lived inside Sarah but was a separate person from her. She was able to hear the Guide's voice within herself and to talk to it. The Guide was also able to write, using Sarah's hand.

Although the illness manifested itself suddenly, it was the end-point of a long process of development. Sarah had always been withdrawn: she preferred to live in a fantasy world of her own and tended to cut herself off from her companions. Over the preceding couple of years she had developed a morbid fear of examinations and lecturers. She made no progress in her studies. She had also begun to isolate herself at home, studying at night and getting up in the afternoon, avoiding her parents.

The summer school had been her last attempt to resume her studies in a new environment, but eventually it led to a break in her precarious psychic integration.

I met Sarah and her Guide about three months after her admission. By that time she had been given both insulin and electroshock therapy, and her psychosis appeared notably alleviated. Even so, she continued to be seriously ill, preferring to isolate herself, talking to herself and laughing with her voices. I interviewed her for my research, inquiring about her childhood memories and her relationship with her parents. She gave matter-of-fact and calm answers but kept looking out of the window and partly covering her face with her hand. Her narration was colourless and conventional. She showed some bitterness at her mother, but as soon as she expressed such bitterness, she began to defend her again. She emphasized having been a conciliatory, good girl at home, and she said that her homelife had actually been "quite ordinary".

Having conversed with the patient for an hour, I asked her whether she still had the other person, the Guide, within her. What happened was quite astonishing. Sarah said: "Let your Guide speak now", and then began to recite in a deep, monotonous, theatrical tone: "Miss K—Sarah herself—is not ill, she is a unique creature, she is a medium. There is another person in her, but Miss K does not know who this other person is; she is not quite certain whether she is a medium or a schizophrenic. The Guide thinks this is idle speculation." The Guide continued, saying that it had long been dissatisfied with Miss K's "smooth words", and that it was annoying to watch such different personalities as Mr and Mrs K—Sarah's parents—having to live together. Sarah now began, in her own voice, to blame the Guide for ridding her from her responsibility towards her parents, and there followed an animated dialogue between her and the Guide. In the role of the Guide, Sarah walked about in the room, gestured theatrically, laughed, and even began to sing.

Sarah's mother belonged to the series I was collecting for my doctoral thesis, and I met her soon after this. I described her as follows (Alanen, 1958, p. 175):

> When I questioned this mother (M) about the patient's child-hood, she willingly led the conversation to her own childhood home, saying that "there, if anywhere, one would have found complications". M's own father, to whom she was attached, was an alcoholic and had shot himself when M was 16. Following this, M had had to leave her school, against her own wishes, and take a job in order to be able to help her mother, with whom she

had strained relations, in supporting the younger children. Since that time M's attitude towards life was dominated by powerful, martyr-like resentment. "When life runs evenly, I always think that some blow is soon coming from somewhere." ... She married a businessman of labile temperament, nervously hasty, with hypomanic traits, who at times used a great deal of alcohol. The patient (P) described her father saying that there is always some kind of air "of an imminent catastrophe" about him. M had felt frustrated as she had to be alone great deal. The first child came after a year's marriage; it was a girl, and the mother regarded her as beautiful; her attitude towards her has always contained more attachment than her attitude towards P, a second girl. P was born 4 years after her sister; but this time the parents had wished for a boy. Meanwhile M had taken a job with which she felt satisfied, but she relinquished it after the birth of her second child. M did not say so herself, but both the father (F) and P herself knew that P's birth had been a very unpleasant event for M. She had often felt very sick during the pregnancy—"very ill", as she later used to tell P—and felt bitterness towards F. After P's birth she remained at home. She says that from that time on she had sacrificed herself to her family. She had taken care of the children all alone and had also sewn their clothes. Her conversation revealed resentment against this role, which, however, she assumed with a martyr-like eagerness; it appeared as if M would be repeating masochistically the situation after her father's death, when she had also "had to sacrifice herself". There was, for instance, something quite typical in that M related, with great self-pity, how her sisters had wondered and felt pity for the fact that her hands, which had been admired as beautiful, were spoiled by constant laundering. ... M's attitude towards P has always been covertly hostile, with an admixture of contempt, and M's attitude towards P's illness was surprisingly cold.

I had read in the psychoanalytic literature—for example in Otto Fenichel's *The Psychoanalytic Theory of Neurosis* (1945), that schizophrenic symptoms can be divided into two categories, the first pertaining to the breakdown and regression of the patient's normal psychic functions (regressive symptoms) and the second to the effort to regain the equilibrium that had been lost, but within the illness and in a pathologic manner (restitutional symptoms). Sarah's Guide was a most illuminating example of the latter category: it was her supporter and guide, and simultaneously a kind of ideal ego, which also helped Sarah to express her emotions better than she would otherwise have been able to do—though in a way that was separate from her own personality. In retrospect, I also would stress the significance of the Guide in serving Sarah's symbiotic needs: this hallucinatory figure followed her like a helping parent.

My research on the mothers convinced me that disorders in the intra-familial relationships were significant for the pathogenesis of schizophrenia, but it also made me realize that neither the mothers nor the fathers should be blamed for their child's illness; rather, they needed to be understood. We are actually dealing with the—mostly unconscious—consequences of the parents' problems that they have been helpless to face, problems that have been inherited by them from their own homes and have usually been aggravated by their marital relationship. I found it easy to agree with Sarah's Guide, who criticized her mother for suppressing her normal feelings of anger ("Mrs. K thinks a good child is a child whose behaviour is three times more controlled than that of an adult"), but I could also visualize this mother as a young girl who had herself been forced to support the mother she secretly hated after her father's suicide.

After her discharge, Sarah continued in psychotherapy with me for more than a year. Her condition seemed to develop favourably. But there came a setback: the examinations and teachers continued to seem as frightening as before, her anxiety increased, she did not sleep well, she was unable to concentrate, and the accusing and frightening elements began to dominate her hallucinations. I soon concluded that a rehospitalization was approaching.

Then, in his perplexity, the young and inexperienced psychiatrist-to-be made an inappropriate move. During one session, Sarah leaned her head against the table in desperation. Feeling sympathy, I began softly to stroke her hair. I had not permitted myself to approach her thus before. The outcome was astonishing. Sarah lifted up her head and said she now heard my voice in herself: "Yrjö Alanen is speaking, he has become my Guide."

Transference psychosis, with which I was now faced, was a new and embarrassing experience for me. I denied talking to Sarah in any way other than I had been talking to her previously—that is, through our conversation. This was confusing to Sarah, because she kept hearing my voice in her head instead of her previous Guide. Sudden as the shift was, I realized that there had been predictive signs of it: the Guide had already acquired features reminiscent of me prior to this occasion, which was shown by, for example, its increasing medical knowledge.

The inclusion of the therapist as part of the patient's psychotic world—whether in a good or a bad sense—is relatively common in the psychotherapy of schizophrenia, and I have subsequently had several experiences of it, though not as dramatic as in Sarah's case. Several therapists—for example, Searles (1965) and Benedetti (1975)—consider transference psychosis a regular and even a necessary part of the course of psychosis therapy.

I have subsequently considered it a mistake that I denied Sarah's delusion pertaining to myself. It would not have been necessary for me to confirm this internalization verbally; it would have been enough not to contradict it, but to understand it as one stage of the therapeutic process. I also consider it a mistake—due to my own insufficiently controlled countertransference feelings—that I stroked Sarah's hair, and ever since that time I have avoided an approach of this kind. Frieda Fromm-Reichmann (1952) has written that the therapist should try to maintain his or her empathically listening attitude unchanged in different situations, and this seems to me optimally to guarantee the therapeutic relationship and the continuity of the therapeutic process. The interaction between Sarah and myself might have developed more peacefully and in better accord with our internal resources if I had abstained from showing her my empathy in the form of physical contact.

Sarah's fate was ultimately sad. After the transference psychosis, she became increasingly restless and was rehospitalized, which would probably have been unavoidable anyway. I continued to meet her there, but our therapeutic relationship was never again the same as it had been originally. She continued to hear my voice inside her head, and this "Yrjö Alanen" probably grew more and more different from the one who came to see her on the ward. Another psychiatrist even applied electroshock treatment to try to remove him from Sarah's head.

Having been discharged from hospital, Sarah continued psychotherapy with another therapist, who was as inexperienced as I was—there were hardly any others available in Finland at that time. A few years later she was hospitalized as a chronic patient. I tried to contact her while I was writing the manuscript for this book, but I was told that she had died of cancer, having been in the hospital almost without interruption for more than 20 years. She had been living in her own world, her personality seriously disintegrated, talking to her hallucinations. The Guide and the psychiatrists had been replaced by a number of good and bad spirits, including Jesus Christ, Gautama Buddha, and Lucifer.

Eric, significance of individual psychotherapy

Over the following few years I had several psychotherapeutic patients suffering from psychoses classifiable as schizophrenic. I met most of them first in the Lapinlahti Hospital, as I did Sarah, but some consulted me privately. These therapies were supportive in that I intended to help the patients face their actual problems, but I also used the psychoanalytic approach to help them to have better insight into the background of their difficulties and to grow as human personalities. Such a combination of approaches is common in the psychotherapy of psychotic disorders.

My personal psychoanalysis, which I started in 1955, was of crucial significance for my development as a psychotherapist. It helped me to clear up a great many of my own problems and made it possible for me to approach the problems of my patients in an empathic way, yet retaining sufficient internal distance and not allowing my own anxiety to interfere with the development of the interactive process. Although the personality of the therapist is more important in the psychotherapy of psychotic patients than in the more technical therapy of neuroses, I agree with Vamik Volkan (1987) and others, who have emphasized the importance of the therapist's own psychoanalytic treatment as a prerequisite for successful long-term therapy of psychotic patients. There are some exceptions to this rule, some rare natural talents who are better able than most of us to understand the problems of psychotic patients, mostly through personal experience. One of these talents in Finland was Allan Johansson, who, in the 1980s, compiled his lifetime experience in a book (Johansson, 1985) illustrated with cases of catamnestic periods of up to 30 years. He, too, considered psychoanalytic training and the associated personal therapy important, although he had been able to carry out exceptionally successful therapeutic relationships even before such training.

In 1962 I published a description of my own experiences in *Nordisk Psykiatrisk Tidskrift* (Alanen, 1962). I also included an informal follow-up account of 26 of my patients. I excluded the sudden, clearly reactive cases and only included patients with more persistent symptoms— a few of them, however, could best be described as "borderline schizophrenics", and some were still in therapy. I considered the findings encouraging: 17 of the 26 patients were in good condition. Not all were completely free from psychotic symptoms, but in their normal environment they were able to cope in a satisfactory manner corresponding to their previous social level.

Discussing the prognosis, I emphasized the importance of the patient's contact ability. Some patients were dominated by autistic isolatory features, including a fear even of the interactional relationship with the therapist and a desire to withdraw from it, while some others were more trustful, transferring needs for support and dependence to their therapist even at early stages of our relationships. Therapy was considerably more successful in the latter group than in the former. The duration of psychotherapy was also clearly significant: a therapeutic contact that was possibly less intensive, but of long duration, resulted in better outcomes than did intensive short therapy.

Eric was one of the patients who responded most favourably to therapy. He consulted me, at first three times and then twice a week, for 18 months. When I left to study in the United States, he took up therapy with another psychiatrist, but he returned to me when this colleague left for further education. My work with Eric lasted for several more years.

When I first met Eric, he was just over 30 years old, and his personality was quite different from the rigid stereotype generally presented in textbooks of schizophrenic patients. He was exceptionally flexible—in a compliant way—and had good contact ability, in addition to which he was also one of the most talented of my patients. These factors were certainly part of a personality structure favouring good prognosis. Although Eric's disorder clearly included schizophrenic features, they did not—probably because of his skilful adjustment and our therapeutic cooperation—result in serious disintegration. He never needed to be hospitalized. Neuroleptic drugs were prescribed for him, in small dosages and for a shorter time, beginning with the nursing-home period described later. I am not convinced that they were necessary even then.

During his first session, Eric sat in his chair, pensive and hesitant, with an occasional friendly but slightly mechanical smile, telling me of his life situation generally, yet keeping back his most personal thoughts. During the second session he began to speak more openly of his experiences and beliefs. He told me that his previous superior at work had become "schizophrenic" three years previously: "I received messages through ambiguous speech." Eric's wife also "became schizophrenic"; she began to enjoy confessing infidelities in a similar "second-degree language", thus causing pain to her husband. The psychiatrist whom Eric had consulted one year previously on the advice of a friend had behaved similarly: 75% of his speech had been "sheer nonsense", and

Eric had not been able to say much himself, as he was immediately silenced with coughs and mutterings. Some kind of "therapy" had, however, been going on ever since he stopped those visits. Eric was "fed" experiences, and his "internal pressure" was regulated; there were possibly also hearing devices that his wife could control and turn on at will. Eric felt himself to be a "robot" whose life was being controlled by others. He asked whether I had now been appointed in charge of this "therapy", whose strings, he thought, were being held by an American.

I told Eric that I was now his therapist, and that we should together find out what this was all about.

Eric's psychotic experiences had begun when he projectively placed the onset of "schizophrenia" in his boss. This man had criticized Eric for negligence in his job, apparently without any reason. Eric had liked this boss, but felt he was becoming increasingly hostile towards him. This was shown by the boss's expressions and behaviour and gradually by this "second-degree" speech, which Eric felt to cause unbearable "pressure variations" in himself. There was either excess pressure or a "hole" through which all pressure was depleted, leaving him quite weak and his will controlled by others.

Using classical psychiatric terminology, we might say that Eric had begun to live increasingly in a world of delusions of reference. By "second-degree language" he meant meanings pertaining to himself that were implicit in the speech of significant others. The others did not themselves recognize these meanings—but they may often have been close to subconscious attitudes expressed by them unintentionally. For example, a man in the company had looked out of a window and said, "It's getting overcast", which was considered by Eric to express his increasing hostility towards himself. The "second-degree language" thus came about in Eric's own mind, and he used its expressions also to concretize the anxiety he felt to be overpowering.

Delusions of reference were also associated with physical delusions of influence. Eric believed, for example, that his wife was able to use certain digital movements connected with her needlework to give—often at a certain time—her husband a "sleeping shock", which gave Eric "a cap on his head".

Despite his delusions, Eric continued to cope astonishingly well in his social environment. He had got a new job, but he told me during the therapeutic sessions that even there he had almost daily experiences of "pressure regulation" by fellow workers. He did not tell them about his experiences, but he confided in a superior he felt to be protective. The latter cautioned Eric to keep such things strictly secret, mentioning three members of the working community who would certainly not understand him. They were precisely the "hole-makers", said Eric. I considered this a good example of the "double book-keeping" already described by Eugen Bleuler (1911), which is frequently encountered especially in mild forms of schizophrenia: although the patient feels his delusions to be real, he simultaneously has a latent feeling of illness, which makes him hide his symptoms from non-understanding neighbours.

Many of Eric's psychotic delusions could be understood symbolically, but he experienced them at the concrete level. It was not always clear to what extent he understood the symbolic nature of his experiences and expressions. At one time, for example, he described himself as a "car", meaning that other people were able to control him as they were able to steer a car. He once asked me to steer him. I said I would rather be a driving instructor, who would teach him to steer himself. I assumed Eric could understand this symbolism, and he certainly did. Nevertheless, he called me in an extremely worried state one morning, saying that he had received a wrong-number telephone call asking whether he had a car to sell.

Problems of self-esteem both in the working community and especially in relation to his wife were clearly at the core of the difficulties that had resulted in Eric's illness. This was reflected in his psychotic fantasies of his wife's infidelity with more and more men. Eric's jealousy of her affection towards their two small children may also have influenced these dynamics. The quarrels over these imaginary incidents ultimately led to a situation where divorce began to seem inevitable. At that point Eric came to spend a summer in the countryside in a nursing home where I was working as a psychiatrist. That summer was very important for the development of our therapeutic relationship. Eric felt the atmosphere of the nursing home to be extremely beneficial, helping to balance his condition. While in the nursing home, he developed a new term, "tent", to describe a satisfactory condition of interpersonal solidarity, where a pressure balance prevailed, because people freely provided each other with pressure whenever necessary. "Couldn't we set up a tent", Eric occasionally said to me even later, when he felt that our mutual pressure variations threatened his own well-being.

Empathic understanding of the concrete language of psychotic experiences—of which the Finnish psychoanalyst Eero Rechardt (1971) has written an illuminating article—is one of the things I learnt while being Eric's therapist. In the nursing home, our mutual interaction developed to a stage that has been called "complete symbiosis" by Harold F. Searles (1961). During the sessions we had at that time I occasionally found myself using psychotic expressions I had borrowed from Eric. If an outsider had been present to listen to our discussions, he would probably have been quite baffled by what he heard. But I naturally also realized that the therapist's task is not merely to understand such expressions, but also to reveal their symbolic nature and thereby endeavour to increase the patient's sense of reality.

This may be called "interpretation upwards" (Rechardt), and it cannot succeed without mutual understanding of the patient's problems even more widely than is suggested by his figures of speech. "Interpretations downwards", to probe and disclose the unconscious, which are frequently used in the psychotherapy of neurotic disorders, may often be unnecessary or even harmful in the therapy of schizophrenics. I once went so far as to suggest to Eric that in his fantasies of his wife's escapades he seemed to imagine himself in her position: was he possibly able to imagine in his wife the feelings he himself had towards these men? Eric burst out laughing heartily, whereby he—to the benefit of our therapeutic process—seemed to discard for good this misjudged, or at least badly timed, attempt at interpretation. Even the interpretation of his aggressive feelings, evidently influencing his projective delusions, did not have much effect early in the therapy.

Understanding Eric's problems, which we achieved by analysing together his family and developmental background during the course of the therapy, was of crucial significance, however. His mother appeared to have been an exceptionally quick-tempered and domineering person—which characteristics Eric at first depicted with almost tearful idealism. Later on he described his childhood as hell: he had, for instance, been forced to kneel down before his mother to apologize for his small tricks, while the mother pulled at his hair so hard that tufts of hair tore out. Eric had felt his younger brother to be his mother's favourite, who was fed and pampered differently from himself; this gave us access to the foundations of his jealousy. He spoke less about his father, who seems to have been the more passive of the parents, subordinate to his wife. It was no wonder, therefore, that Eric found himself struggling with similar problems in adult life, and that new father figures, such as superiors in work and the therapist, were important for him.

Eric's therapy thus gradually concentrated on pointing out and interpreting the connections between his childhood family background and his current problems. We discussed, for example, his childhood experience of love requiring submission, which left no space for one's own will. We also realized that the mother who demanded submission was thereby "relieving her pressure". The "sleeping shocks" found their counterpart in the necessity to go to bed at a certain regular time in childhood. Eric soon developed an ability to perceive such connections himself. "If you are just told to obey throughout your childhood, it's no wonder you grow up a robot." As we proceeded in our exploration of the influences of childhood, the questions of sexuality and the problems of closeness and distance in human relations became increasingly important. These questions also became topical when Eric found a new female friend after his subsequent divorce.

There is no need to describe in detail the later course of Eric's therapy after my return from the United States. He had practically no psychotic delusions, though they sometimes still peeped out as "white rabbits". This term, which Eric himself used humorously, aware of its symbolic significance, was derived from an American film *Harvey*, in which James Stewart, in the role of the main character, sometimes sees in company a friendly creature of this kind, which is invisible to the others. Eric realized that he was having similar experiences—milder forms of recurrent "second-degree" ideas—especially when he was unable to understand the aggression of other people and the reactions they caused in him. If one was rationally aware of them, one did not need "white rabbits". He was also sometimes helped in anxiety-provoking situations by his speculation of how the therapist would cope—this was called "permissible projection" by Eric.

It was not, however, easy to give up the "white rabbits" completely. "It's sort of nostalgic to leave them and be always healthy", Eric once said, showing increasing insight into himself. Nevertheless, the "rabbits" gradually left the stage for good.

I often marvelled at the insight Eric developed upon growing out of his psychotic experiences as to the unconscious motives of both himself and other people—a feature not altogether rare in patients of this kind. Thus Eric wondered, when his boss occasionally gave "military" commands, whether he should "oppose him for his own good—but, then, I'm not his nursemaid". This also implied the psychotic theme of "exchanging pressure", but now at a non-psychotic level. And when we once, later on, mentioned the "sleeping shocks" given by his first wife, he pointed out: "It was just a need for contact." This obvious interpretation had not occurred to me, while I was trying to understand the dynamics of the mutual aggressive feelings between the spouses.

Eric had remarried while undergoing therapy with my colleague, and his new marriage turned out moderately happy, as far as I could judge. After the termination of our therapy he published a doctoral dissertation and worked in an intellectually demanding office for more than 20 years. I met him again recently, asking for his permission to publish my experiences of his therapy. He gave me permission, hoping that this book might increase the understanding of interpersonal problems and modify attitudes in, for example, working communities. He was in good condition both physically and psychically, and he had not been in need of psychiatric help or medication since his therapy.

The experience with Eric and other patients led me to believe that at least part of psychoses of the schizophrenia group are understandable psychologically, and that the patients suffering from such psychoses can recover their mental integrity through psychotherapy. The recovery is part of a process of personality development, which, as it advances, makes psychotic symptom solutions unnecessary. It is also true that setbacks occur, but—if the continuity of the therapy is guaranteed—the recurring psychotic stages or the aggravation of the symptoms of patients undergoing psychotherapy are milder than previous episodes, unlike in patients who have not had a psychotherapeutic relationship.

As far as I can see, there is hardly any consistent difference observable in the course and outcome of the psychotherapy of schizophrenic patients with a good prognosis and that of long-term neurotic patients. In both cases the symptoms usually subside gradually, and not always completely: even after successful psychotherapeutic treatment, the tendency to symptoms may persist (indicating the express of unresolved areas of conflict) and be manifested in problematic situations, though they are less conspicuous and under better control than before therapy. Because psychotic symptoms involve a more profound disturbance of the sense of reality, with much greater social handicaps—including the reactions of the people close to the patient—this analogy between them and neurotic symptoms is often ignored.

However, I also treated psychotic patients whose therapy was not successful.

Paula and family therapy

The research on families, which I continued to pursue, increased my understanding of schizophrenia. It also showed me the need to give increased attention to matters pertaining to the family environment in my therapies. It took long, however, before I began to practise family therapy along with individual therapy. This form of therapy was unknown in Finland at that time, and remained so for some time after the year (1959–1960) I spent in the United States, where the pioneers of family therapy had begun their work. The Department of Psychiatry at Yale University, where I spent a useful year as a member of Theodore Lidz' team, was not the best possible place with respect to integrating family and individual therapy—although the team was considered, with reason, the central pioneer in schizophrenia-oriented family research. They were using family therapy at Yale, but the therapeutic focus was on individual therapies and community therapies, which were supplemented by separate meetings with the patients' parents to study the family dynamics and support the patients' therapy.

However, I was able to observe, behind the one-way mirror, conjoint family therapy conducted by Stephen Fleck, where I thought the therapist indicated by his own behaviour to the patient how the latter could get along with his father. When I visited the National Institute of Mental Health, I saw a family therapy session conducted jointly by Lyman C. Wynne and Harold F. Searles, which impressed me considerably. It seemed to me that the therapists had divided up their roles: Searles acted as "stimulator", who asked quite bold questions or interpretations, while Wynne remained a safe father figure, who held the reins and helped to perceive the situation in an integrated manner.

I have subsequently realized that there also were some more personal matters, which were part of my own family background and which I only later became aware of, that caused me to resist becoming a family therapist. These included a fear of emerging anxiety and aggression towards the patients' parents, which was due to my empathic understanding of the patient and consequent projective identification. On the other hand, I was not sure whether I could remain sufficiently loyal to the patient in a situation where we would be attacked by his or her domineering parents. I started family therapies at a stage where my own anxieties had been alleviated enough by my psychoanalysis and I was better able, in a therapy situation, to conceive of myself as a therapist of both the patient's parents (or spouse) and the patient.

As these personal feelings of mine illustrated, family therapy is more diversified and more difficult to control than individual therapy. This is one reason why family therapy is currently considered a task of a therapeutic team or at least of two therapists, not one therapist working alone.

In the mid-1960s, when I started family therapy of schizophrenic patients in the Lapinlahti Hospital, which had become the Clinic of Psychiatry of the University Central Hospital of Helsinki, I met the families alone. I found support in a family therapy seminar I had started at the same time, where we listened to the audiotaped family therapy sessions and discussed them with my colleagues. My initial experiences of this new mode of treatment were mainly favourable and soon convinced me that family therapy may be significantly helpful in the therapy of many schizophrenic patients.

One of my first family therapy patients was Paula, a 24-year-old female student. She had been hospitalized four times over the preceding couple of years. Her psychotic state, which was dominated by restlessness, disorganization, occasional thought disorders, and delusions, was always alleviated in the hospital, but soon deteriorated when she was discharged, necessitating rehospitalization.

As I became acquainted with Paula's family environment, I found the parental relationship to be strained and conflict-ridden. Her father was a rigid man with obsessive and distrustful features, who tended to dominate his family. The therapy also revealed his strong feelings of inferiority and fear of being ignored. The mother was outwardly calmer, but she was frustrated and tended to cling to her children, trying to isolate the father from the rest of the family—as she had felt that he isolated her from the outer world. Their three daughters were "divided" between the parents, as is typical of schismatic families (Lidz, Cornelison, Fleck, & Terry, 1957b). Paula was considered the most submissive of the children, and she was attached to her mother.

When Paula was in the hospital for the third time, one of my colleagues made a serious attempt at individual therapy with her, while I met her parents. This arrangement, however, aroused strong suspicions in Paula. Even her individual therapy had to be discontinued when her condition at home again deteriorated and she gave up her visits to the therapist.

When Paula was admitted for the fourth time, I began joint sessions with her, her parents, and the sister who lived at home. I had hesitated to undertake this task, because I had been afraid that Paula would be crushed under the continuous, often quite serious quarrelling between her parents. It did not occur to me at the time that Paula was quite used to it. Although she sometimes drew her head back during the stormiest altercations and retreated into her own world, she generally coped quite well, beginning, when supported by the therapist, to express her own views. She was well motivated to family therapy for the very reason that she considered her illness to be originally due to family conflicts.

One of the most favourable effects of this family therapy was that Paula's aggressiveness, which had at first found expression, in an uncontrolled and incoherent manner, during the psychosis, gradually began to acquire more organized and balanced forms, becoming integrated into her personality. A parallel development took place in the whole family, supporting Paula's integration: the atmosphere of the therapy sessions, which was initially dominated by chaotic quarrelling, soon became more peaceful, and the family began, stimulated by Paula's statements, to discuss seriously the problems of their mutual relationships.

I illustrate this with the following audiotaped extracts. At this point the joint sessions had been going on weekly for three months.

The first extract begins with the family discussing whether Mary, Paula's younger sister, should continue to be present at the therapy sessions. Mary had been attending up to that time but was absent from this session.

THERAPIST: What do you think, would it be good if she continued to attend? She came because she lives in the family, is a member of the family, and it seems that it would be especially important for Paula that Mary would also attend, as there has been a kind of tens...

MOTHER: Yes . . .

THERAPIST: ...ion between them, too.

MOTHER: It would certainly be good, and I would say that Mary could continue to come.

FATHER: Let's try to make her come. [*Emphatically*] We can make Mary come even if she doesn't want to. [*Laughing*] She doesn't suffer if I say: You come now, girl . . .

MOTHER: It would certainly be good if Mary also came here, that she wouldn't be left out altogether.

THERAPIST: What do you think about this, Paula?

PAULA: Well, I don't really . . . [*pauses*]

THERAPIST: You don't really . . .

PAULA [*stammering*]: Well, I've had a different . . . like I've . . . ever since the beginning I've had a different position in our family from Mary, I mean in the sense that . . . er . . . I mean Mary has always had a different position from me in our family . . . I mean . . . er . . . it's like . . . like, I mean it, doesn't really make any difference. She could be here, all right, but then again I don't really know, but is it sort of late now . . . I mean, to put right the relationships, but . . .

THERAPIST: Do you still feel that this different position has some effect on you?

PAULA: It doesn't affect me in any way any longer.

[*Pause*]

FATHER: What do you mean by this different position?

PAULA: Well, you know . . . you should know it, more or less, what kind of position Mary has in our family. Mary is a very domineering personality and . . . I mean . . . er . . . very domineering personality . . . and [*speaking in a louder voice*] I'm sure you know what I'm trying to say, what the difference is between Mary and me in our family, and you must know it!

MOTHER: Paula probably means that Mary always gets what she wants, and Paula doesn't—is that what you mean?

PAULA: That's about it . . . I mean like when Mary . . .

MOTHER: If there's something she doesn't want to do, she doesn't do it, and if there's something she wants, so it's done as she wants it. I think this is what you mean?

PAULA: Yes, something like that.

FATHER [*sighs*]

MOTHER: So . . .

FATHER: I was just . . .

MOTHER: But Mary is a bit like, I mean she wants to . . .

FATHER: What I would say is that it may be some . . . but has it occurred to you, Paula, that it's your reaction to Mary?

PAULA: It isn't ... it isn't originally, it came when I ... it isn't ... I mean it doesn't depend on that, but I sort of know it, because I get along just fine with Mary, much better than Cathy does, for instance. [*Cathy is the eldest sister, who has moved away from home.*] Mary and Cathy don't get along at all.

MOTHER: They certainly don't.

PAULA: I get along with Mary just fine, but there're the conditions ... er ... [*stammering*] ... the conditions ... the conditions I sort of have in our family.

FATHER: What are these conditions?

PAULA: I mean, I always have to admit everything, and Mary just never gives in in anything, I mean in anything ... like there's still ...

FATHER: So you and Mary ...

PAULA: Yes.

FATHER: ... I mean the relationship between you two.

PAULA: Yes, it reflects our relationships from the point of view of the whole family.

[*Pause. Father sighs.*]

MOTHER: I see quite well what Paula means, I see it quite well now.

FATHER: Yes, well, I ...

MOTHER: I would like to give one example, can I?

FATHER: Yes, sure.

THERAPIST: Yes.

MOTHER: I just give this one example. We were saying at one time that Paula would get this room that Mary has. This is a bigger room, and as it would sort of be for Paula, who's ill, like it used to be ... I mean she was sort of used to it and always went to bed there when she was not well. And now we were saying that Paula would get that room ... and it was decided that Paula would have it, but when we began to talk to Mary about it, what we should do about it, so it turned out in the end that Paula did not get that room, but had to take the other one, and

Mary had that room. This shows what kind of position . . . that it's like this. Wasn't this so?

PAULA: I mean if you think that . . . I mean I'm the one who's ill in the family, and you would've thought that the one who's ill would've got the better room and the one who's healthy would've moved out. If you think that the illness has really sort of developed inside the family, that it's not my private property, this illness of mine, but that it's really something that comes out of the family. So you could've expected me to get that room.

MOTHER [*sighing*]: Yes.

PAULA: I mean I sort of gave in just like that . . .

MOTHER: Yes.

PAULA: I knew it for sure that Mary will get the better room, that she can keep it , so I didn't even try to make any claims on it. I just accepted the other room, and I also lived in that other room.

FATHER: Well now, about this room still . . . er . . . I mean I've got the impression from what Mum has said that Paula is really satisfied, and that's precisely because there's that curtain and you always see the movement there and you . . .

PAULA: I've never . . .

FATHER: . . . you've . . . you have yourself . . .

MOTHER: At first she . . .

FATHER: You have even said so yourself, that and . . . er . . . wouldn't it be so, Paula, that you could feel some satisfaction that you've been able . . . er . . . and that you have a good room, too . . . that you've been able in this way to build harmony in the family, that it doesn't matter if you have that room. Mary, maybe . . .

PAULA [*angry*]: What do you mean when you say that I don't matter, when I'm at home. Do you mean that . . .

FATHER: No . . . I don't, but what I mean is that it hasn't been in any way inconvenient for you to live in that room. You've been quite happy about it. Haven't you?

PAULA: Well, yes, but I would be even happier if . . . I mean, I was happy not to have to share a room with Mary, but [*louder*] I would've been even happier if I had had the better room, but I'm perfectly happy about that (current) room, too, perfectly happy.

Paula, who is supported by her mother—in opposition to the father—brings forth her views with increasing force, though using her illness as a weapon. The father's remark on how Paula has been able to bring about harmony in the family through her submissiveness is a good example of a desire to maintain the kind of family homeostasis described by Don D. Jackson (1957), a state of equilibrium that is often quite difficult to change in these families, and which is regulated by unwritten rules based on the mutual emotional and power relationships between the family members.

Paula was not content with the assumption that her bitterness was essentially due to her necessity to submit. As the session continued, she pointed out that she was actually referring to intrafamilial relationships wherein she was not—unlike her sister Mary—"accepted just as I am". With regard to school performance, for example, she was set greater demands than were her sisters.

Paula's appeals touched especially the father, who was actually also Paula's main target. The father was, at that time, making an attempt to make contact with Paula, asking about her condition and personal matters too frequently and in a way that Paula found irritating. During one of the following therapy sessions the father described with obvious pertinence the way in which his relationship with Paula had been less adequate from the beginning than his relationships with the other daughters:

FATHER: This is now, I guess, the matter . . . and the reasons lie deeper, and . . . and . . . you cannot in this way . . . well, it is obviously impossible to rectify them. I only remember that last time Paula revealed that she hasn't received recognition, and this point has preoccupied me a lot, and I guess that it was also meant for the father. Well, now, the mother has perhaps been close . . . very close to Paula, and even as a big girl . . . a year ago, and even this year, when I am away from home, Paula comes to sleep with the mother, and [coughs], well . . .

MOTHER: No, not any longer, of course . . .

PAULA [simultaneously]: It was when I . . . when I was ill . . .

FATHER: No . . . also while she's well . . .

[*All of them speak excitedly and simultaneously*]

PAULA: I'll tell you, I preferred to sleep in that bed because it was so cool there as there was that window . . .

FATHER: Well, yes. Let it be so . . . but . . . but, well . . . I guess that it's so that you have once longed for your father and your father hasn't understood you and has warded you off, or has not . . . . that is to say, hasn't come to meet you somehow, and you again are so sensitive and shy that you haven't been able to come, even though your father would have been . . . would have been able to receive you then . . . that this has now happened with you, whereas it isn't so with your sisters, who have been more active, they themselves have made the initiative, and so forth, that there is such a reason deeper here, somehow and, well . . . I believe that you also understand it yourself now, and that after this conversation perhaps . . . it will begin to clear up better, you'll understand your father too . . . we must all understand, all of us . . . [*entreatingly*] also you have to understand me, that is to say you have . . .

PAULA: I tell you frankly I cannot stand your asking . . . [*general laughter*] . . . I tell you frankly that I don't stand . . .

Paula was naturally unable to comply with her father's attempt to alter their relationship so rapidly, because this inevitably also involved anxiety-provoking elements. During the following session she and her mother attacked the father, taking their turn in defending the previous psychological homeostasis of the family. Over the next few weeks the therapist also got the impression that Paula wanted revenge for her father's rejection which she had experienced, by now rejecting him herself. Even so, their dialogue also suggested obvious mutual satisfaction, and Paula gradually grew closer to her father.

The weekly family therapy sessions were continued altogether for 18 months, during which period the family atmosphere and the intrafamilial relationships clearly developed favourably. Paula showed, probably because of her father's new understanding of her, alleviation of her previous pent-up bitterness and appeared to be liberated from the bonds it had caused. The mutual relationship between the parents also improved, which had a further liberating effect on Paula. She partly got rid of her symbiotic reliance on her mother. She took a job and was finally also able to resume her studies. She continued to have some paranoid–psychotic features, though clearly less obvious than before.

This family therapy was, however, discontinued too soon, as the therapist moved to another locality. The family were not motivated to see another therapist, nor was I able to persuade Paula to return to individual therapy, which seemed to me the optimal solution in that situation. Paula continued to develop favourably for some time after the discontinuation of family therapy. She even completed her studies and was married. But these life changes also brought with them new problems, which resulted in setbacks and even occasional aggravation of the paranoid symptoms. However, Paula has managed to avoid new cycles of hospital treatment.

Apart from the family therapy of patients, often seriously ill, who lived with their parents, I also had some experience with couple therapy of schizophrenic patients and their spouses. Problems of the marital relationships often featured quite notably in these cases, and the outcome of therapy varied a great deal, depending, for example, on the attitudes of the spouses.

As I reviewed our experiences with family therapy (Alanen, 1976; Alanen & Kinnunen, 1975), I perceived—as in the case of individual therapies—the importance of the duration of the therapy for the development of changes that take place in intrafamilial relationships. My orientation as a family therapist was psychodynamic, being based on the psychoanalytic frame of reference that was familiar to me, though it had naturally been complemented and widened by family-dynamic findings. The motivation of the different family members—including the patient—to discuss shared problems proved an important prognostic factor. In optimal cases the families themselves contained wholesome resources for change and for an alliance with the therapist. In some other cases, however, my efforts met with resistance, which often caused the therapy to be discontinued at an early stage.

The main problem in the further development of the psychotherapeutic treatment of schizophrenia appeared to be the question of indications: when was it useful to choose individual therapy, when family therapy, and when were the two to be combined? As far as I could see, these two modes of therapy were not mutually exclusive but, rather, complementary methods, and the choice between them was best made independently in each case.

In 1968 I was nominated Professor of Psychiatry at the University of Turku and Medical Director of the psychiatric university hospital that had been founded the previous year as part of the public health care system of the City of Turku. In the Turku Clinic of Psychiatry I met with a stimulating and constantly renewed group of colleagues and students. Research on the development of the treatment of schizophrenia became one of the main goals we shared.

CHAPTER TWO

General notes
on schizophrenia

S chizophrenia is a serious mental illness that usually becomes
manifest in adolescence or in early adulthood. It is characterized by partial disorganization of personality functions, developmental regression, and a tendency to withdraw from interpersonal contacts into a subjective internal world of ideas, often coloured
by hallucinations or delusions. The illness may begin suddenly or
gradually, and its symptoms either improve or become chronic to
different degrees. Many patients have better periods with only minor
symptoms and worse periods when the symptoms are re-aggravated.
Schizophrenia differs from the mental illnesses of definite organic
origin in that it does not involve dementia or disorders of memory,
orientation, or intelligence comparable to the latter.

Symptoms

One central aspect of the disorganization of personality is the *loss of
reality testing*, which is usually considered a symptom pathognomic
of all psychotic disorders. It means that the ability to differentiate
unambiguously between internal experiences and sensations (per-

ceptions) of the external world has been lost, which results in the emergence of hallucinations. Auditory hallucinations are particularly common in schizophrenia, although all the sensory functions may be involved. The loss of reality testing, in a milder form, is also typical of delusions, which are due to subjective misinterpretation of observations of the surrounding world.

It is further typical that the *psychological boundary* separating the self from others tends to be blurred in schizophrenia. The patient may, for example, feel himself to be simultaneously himself and an actor he has seen on television, or he may interpret the sensations he feels in his lower abdomen to be the sensations of someone else. To an even greater extent, this problem affects the patient's ability to draw a line between internal ideas of oneself and of others (self- and object-representations).

Using psychoanalytic language, we might therefore say that the *disintegration of personality functions* in schizophrenia pertains primarily to the ego—that is, the part of psychic functions responsible for their logical integration, the control of the internal balance, and the adjustment to the external world.

Eugen Bleuler (1911), father of the term "schizophrenia", considered it particularly typical of this illness that the patient suffers disorders, gaps, and shifts of associations, which impair his train of thought, interfering with the maintenance of intention or attention. David Shakow (1962), an experimental psychologist, has stated that schizophrenic patients find it difficult, in their thinking and other functions, to follow the holistic major sets, but cling to minor or segmented sets. In other words, they do not see the forest for the trees.

A closer look at these thought disorders may reveal their connections to the patient's personal associations: unlike healthy people, the schizophrenic patient is at the mercy of these associations, which tend to interfere with his thinking. Many schizophrenics have also described experiences of having had thoughts extracted from their brain or alien ideas forced into their mind.

Regression of ego functions refers to deterioration of the modes of thought and conception governed by organized and realistic-level logic, and their consequent substitution by a more archaic logical system compatible with the ideational modes of the "primary process" of dreams and the unconscious. This process has been described in different ways, emphasizing different aspects. E. von Domarus (1944) and Silvano Arieti (1955) spoke of "paleologic thinking", while Norman Cameron (1938) preferred the term "overinclusion", implying that a given shared feature may lead to different but inclusive associations. For example, a patient calls herself "Virgin Mary" because she is a virgin and Mary was also a virgin (Arieti, 1955). I would especially like to emphasize, following K. Goldstein (1948), *concretization*—a pointedly concrete interpretation of symbolic expressions. We are able to interpret the symbols as symbols, but our patients interpret them as part of the reality they take to be concrete. Good examples of this were given by Eric, as described in chapter one.

Concreteness of this kind is also apparent in physical delusions: the psychological influence of another person may be experienced as a concrete-level touch induced by him or her from a distance. In auditory hallucinations, the concretization may appear as blame directed at the patient, who deals with his or her inner thoughts as if they were fact; the patient is blamed for being a whore if she has sexual thoughts in her mind. Also, characteristically, regression in schizophrenics' ego relates external events to one's self. One female patient, for instance, took a worn-out car tyre in the yard to be a malicious hint at her "worn" sex organ. In its most extreme form, such egocentricity develops into omnipotent thinking. But even a meaning interpreted as global reveals and reflects the personal meaning underlying it.

One of the patients in our hospital claimed that wars and unemployment would have been eliminated from the world if his relationship with his former female friend had continued. If this had been so, it might have prevented the onset of his illness—at least temporarily—and his later violent tendencies and unemployment. We can thus see that even this ostensibly senseless association has a kind of sense in it, when we recognize the regression of the patient's experiential world to an omnipotent level.

The verbal expressions of deeply regressed schizophrenic patients are frequently very scant and blocked, or so full of extremely subjective phrases and neologisms, or at least semantically idiosyncratic words, that they are difficult or almost impossible to understand. In some cases, however, the patient's life course and developmental history may provide unexpected illumination on his/her cryptic speech, as shown by the following examples.

I interviewed for educational purposes an extremely lonely young man. As I inquired about the onset of his illness, he told me that he had lost part of his bones. When I further asked what he thought the possible cause of this to be, he replied: "Probably dying." The patient also said that he had been living in the sea mud under the water, and that it had been difficult to move "in any sector" because the "meridians" were so narrow that they hardly allowed him to turn around. When asked about hearing voices, he at first denied this, but he then said that he heard telephone conversations at a distance of 50 metres even when he was indoors.

We can well understand what the patient means by his "dying": he describes an experience of psychological death. This became apparent in a rather upsetting way when the patient later said to me: "I would like to be a human being again someday—now I am not a human being any more." The meridians turned out to be air spaces in which the patient could move, routes that he found safe and was able to use; when outside them, he felt a disturbing popping in his head.

The patient's claim to be living under the surface of the sea might also be understood symbolically. A member of the ward staff present at the interview was, however, able to provide some illuminating information: after the divorce of his mother and stepfather, the patient had been living in a small hut whose floor, at least according to his own report, was below sea level, which is why it was always flooded in the spring. At a distance of 50 metres from his hut there was a telephone booth, which used to be the main location of his auditory hallucinations.

Another patient said he was suffering from diabetes, which was not true. The significance of this delusion became comprehensible, however, when the patient told his therapist that when he had temper tantrums as a child, his parents often said: "Now your liver is secreting too much sugar in your blood."

Similar disintegration as in thought functions also takes place in *affective expressions*. Many psychoanalytic researchers, especially, tend to consider affective disorders of even greater importance in schizophrenia than are thought disorders. Particularly acute manifestations of schizophrenia are often dominated by panicky anxiety and/or agitation. This reflects the horror brought about by the fatal change in the experiential world (*disintegration anxiety*) and is generally also related to the hallucinations or delusions penetrating into consciousness. This may later result in a sense of losing one's own personality or a death of all feeling. The young male patient in the above example described such experiences in a startling manner. "Affective extinction" of this kind is particularly common in the hebephrenic forms of schizophrenia.

But milder forms of affective torpor can also be regarded as a consequence of autistic development, a tendency to withdraw into oneself, which is often—though not always—associated with schizophrenia. This tendency frequently also involves a loss of energy and a passive indifference both towards the outer world and towards one's own condition.

Varying opinions have been expressed concerning the nature of autistic and affective symptoms, such as isolation and passivity. Biologically oriented researchers often differentiate between productive or *positive symptoms*—anxiety, thought disorders, delusions, and hallucinations—and *negative symptoms* such as passivity, isolation tendencies, and impoverishment of speech (Andreasen & Olsen, 1982). An important criterion for this differentiation is that neuroleptic drugs predominantly affect the positive symptoms. Many of these researchers assume that negative symptoms are due to an organic disease process (Barnes, 1989).

From the viewpoint of a psychotherapist or ward community, autism often turns out to be a secondary or relative phenomenon: an empathic approach may help the patient to give up his/her autism quite quickly. Donald L. Burnham and his co-workers (Burnham, Gladstone, & Gibson, 1969) described the basic problem of the schizophrenic patient as a "need–fear dilemma": on the one hand, the patient feels the need to have more contact with people, while on the other hand he/she is afraid of such contact for fear of being misunderstood or rejected, or being "swallowed by the other" and thereby deprived of his/her own personality. Therefore the patient withdraws.

Affective disorders also include *weakening of impulse control*, which is seen both in acute schizophrenia and in chronic patients. It may result in poorly controlled violent outbursts of rage or—especially in the case of chronic patients—be combined with regressive behaviour indifferent to the moral principles and reactions of the environment, such as masturbation in public.

Despite this, the homicide rate of schizophrenics is only slightly higher than the population average, although the crimes that they do commit tend to attract much publicity. Homicidal acts occur generally in a paranoid panic state. Suicides are more common: 3–13% of the schizophrenic patients commit suicide, usually during the first two years of their illness (Caldwell & Gottesman, 1990; Miles, 1977).

The predisposition to schizophrenia does not correlate with intelligence, but in many cases it is related to a sensitivity towards other people. It may also stimulate artistic talents. Most schizophrenic artists, however, have lost their creative power after the manifestation of their illness (e.g. the poets Friedrich Hölderlin and J. J. Wecksell, who lived the final decades of their lives as mentally extinguished hospital tients), or else their symptoms have made their art more difficul outsiders to appreciate (e.g. the painters C. F. Hill and Ernst Josephson). But there have also been different courses of development: August Strindberg, having recovered from his inferno phase, was able to utilize his psychotic "dive" to the psychic level governed by the primary process to heighten his artistically expressive talent (e.g. "The Road to Damascus" and "The Dream Play").

Subgroups

Schizophrenia is not a single unified illness. Eugen Bleuler (1911) had already spoken of "nuclear and marginal groups", which differed notably from each other both in the intensity of symptoms and the prognosis, and the same dichotomy, though differently formulated, has persisted until the present time.

The nuclear group of schizophrenia is considered to consist of three essential subcategories: *hebephrenic, catatonic,* and *paranoid.* Disorganization and regression of the ego are most profound in hebephrenic (or, according to the DSM system, disorganized) schizophrenia, which also has the earliest onset, being usually manifested before the age of 25 and often gradually. Auditory hallucinations are particularly dominant in this type of schizophrenia (though they are also found in milder disorders, sometimes even as the only psychotic symptom). Catatonic schizophrenia, which usually has an acute onset, also includes psychomotor disturbances in addition to the other symptoms; these take the form of either stuporous standstill or panicky, sometimes violent agitation. Paranoid schizophrenia is dominated by delusions and associated hallucinations; apart from auditory hallucinations, somatic sensations of being influenced by others are especially common, while disintegration of ego functions is less conspicuous.

In the ___ of chronic patients it is more difficult to discriminate ___ bcategories. Many of them tend to show the conse-___ ionalization, such as apathetic hopelessness, adapta-___ tivity and loss of everyday social contacts and skills. ___ stablished by the American Psychiatric Association ___ 4–IV: American Psychiatric Association, 1994), the ___ *hizophrenia* is used of patients showing features ___ e subtype.

Apart from these nuclear forms, there are *schizophreniform psychoses*, which are less serious and often precipitated by current conflict situations.

The use of this name, originally introduced by Langfeldt (1939), has varied. In the Scandinavian countries, it has meant acute psychoses with confusion or perplexity at the height of the psychotic episode, absence of symptoms typical of severe schizophrenia (including negative symptoms), good premorbid functioning, and, almost invariably, a good prognosis. In the DSM system, it is used of psychoses in which the symptomatological criteria of schizophrenia are met but the length of them (including prodromal, active, and residual phases) is restricted. In DSM–IV, the length of a psychotic episode is defined to be at least one month but less than six months, and a further specifier is used to indicate the presence or absence of features that may be associated with a better prognosis (see above). If the length of the psychotic episode is less than one month, the diagnostic category of *brief psychotic disorder* is used (American Psychiatric Association, 1994).

More prolonged and/or recurrent milder psychotic disorders have also been called *borderline schizophrenias.*

The symptoms of schizophrenia and bipolar affective psychosis may occasionally be combined in such a way that the patient shows, simultaneously, both schizophreniform symptoms and a typical manic or depressive change of mood. These psychoses are called *schizoaffective psychoses* (originally named by Kasanin, 1933), and their prognosis tends to be better than that of typical schizophrenia, even if often characterized by recurrent episodes.

The boundary between schizophrenia and psychoses due to alcohol and/or drug abuse may occasionally also be obscure. In the Oslo subproject of the Scandinavian Multicentre Psychotherapy Project dealing with first-admitted patients (Alanen, Ugelstad, Armelius, Lehtinen, Rosenbaum, & Sjöström, 1994), for example, there was a notable group of young patients with a dual diagnosis of drug abuse and a psychosis of the schizophrenia group (Hjort & Ugelstad, 1994). Such patients are probably increasing in number in metropolitan environments (Allebeck, Adamsson, Engström, & Rydberg, 1993; Linszen, Dingemans, & Lenior, 1994.)

The age limits for the risk of developing schizophrenia are usually set at 15 and 45 years. Cases of childhood schizophrenia are also seen, though rarely, and they are not to be confused with early infantile autism (even if the separating line may be difficult to draw) . There are also patients aged over 45 who become ill with psychoses whose symptoms are similar to those of paranoid schizophrenia.

Paranoid psychoses with delusions limited systematically to a certain problem area, but without other disorders of ego functions or hallucinations, are not classified as schizophrenias. Even this diagnostic boundary may be difficult to define exactly.

Although the clinical characteristics of typical schizophrenia are generally easy for psychiatrists to recognize, we may conclude that patients included in marginal or atypical psychoses of the schizophrenia group are not distinctly different from patients with other psychotic disorders, such as affective, paranoid, and reactive psychoses. It is for this reason that the theory of general psychosis—an umbrella term for all psychotic disorders—still has its proponents (see, for example, Einar Kringlen's 1994 paper dealing with this topic).

On DSM diagnostics

Even if other diagnostic systems are also used, especially by researchers, the currently official system of diagnosing schizophrenia is largely parallel to the latest version (DSM–IV) of the *Diagnostic and Statistical Manual of Mental Disorders*, published by the American Psychiatric Association (1994).

This classification illustrates the contractual nature of the diagnostic boundaries defined for schizophrenia. As referred to above, "schizophrenic disorders" are separated from "schizophreniform disorders" mainly on the basis that certain distinct psychotic symptoms, together with separately defined preliminary or residual symptoms, have persisted for a minimum of six months in the former category and for more than one month, but less than six months, in the latter. In the earlier DSM–III version, the lower boundary line was defined as two weeks. It is further proposed that there is some deterioration of social functioning present in the schizophrenic disorder.

A generally applicable diagnostic system is important for comparative epidemiological research, as well as otherwise facilitating communication about schizophrenia. One of the motivating factors behind the development of the DSM classification—published as DSM–III (American Psychiatric Association, 1980)—was the observation made in a

British–American collaborative research project (Cooper et al., 1972): it turned out that schizophrenia in London was something quite different from schizophrenia in New York, where the diagnostic boundaries were set wider and included some cases now called "schizotypal" or "border-line" personality disorder.

From the epidemiological viewpoint, it is also advantageous that the diagnostic labels of the DSM classification are not related to aetiologic concepts, as was often the case with earlier diagnostic systems, but are based on symptomatic definitions (in accordance with the old Kraepelin-ian principles). This minimizes the effects that conceptual differences among psychiatrists and schools of psychiatry may have on comparative findings. From the viewpoint of developing psychiatric treatment, how-ever, the classification involves the great risk of concentrating on symptoms and their categorization at the cost of understanding patients and their life situations.

One should realize that the planning of treatment has not been the basis for developing DSM classification. The treatment of patients also requires other approaches: an effort to understand how the illness is related to the patient's personality development, his/her life course, and his/her interpersonal relationships.

There is the further risk that the DSM criteria for discriminating between schizophrenic and schizophreniform disorders are ascribed a significance that is used to predict the patient's prognosis to too great an extent and often also influences it—a phenomenon that certainly does not lack historical precedent.

Schizophrenia
from a public health perspective

The difficulty of defining the limits of schizophrenia is also reflected in the incidence and prevalence rates reported in the literature. If the relatively comprehensive set of criteria first suggested by Eugen Bleuler (1911) is applied, it turns out that 0.7–1% of the population reaching the age of 45 has suffered from schizophrenic psychosis. The "point prevalence"—that is, the proportion of adult population with schizophrenic syndromes at a given time—is lower than this, being 0.1–0.8% (Eaton, 1985). However, in an American multicentre study (ECA) the six-month period prevalence of schizophrenic/

schizophreniform disorders was found to be 0.6–1.2% (Myers et al., 1984), even according to DSM–III criteria, whereas the lifetime prevalence was 1.1–2.0% (Robins et al., 1984).

If the diagnosis is delimited strictly, as was done in two British investigations (Shepherd, Watt, Falloon, & Smeeton, 1989; Wing & Fryers, 1976), the annual incidence—that is, the number of new schizophrenic patients admitted into psychiatric treatment units each year—appears to be only 7–14 cases per 100,000 inhabitants. A survey carried out in six different areas in Finland in the 1980s revealed an average of 11–14 new DSM–III-diagnosed "schizophrenic disorders" per 100,000 inhabitants; when the "schizophreniform disorders" were included, the incidence went up to 16–20 (Salokangas et al., 1987). In the other Nordic countries the incidence figures tend to be somewhat lower (see Alanen et al., 1994).

It was interesting to note that although there were no significant differences in the annual incidence between the districts located in different parts of Finland, the number of schizophrenic inpatients was three- or even fourfold in some areas (mainly in eastern Finland), compared with the "best districts" (the southwestern and southern parts of the country). The project team of the national programme for developing the treatment and rehabilitation of schizophrenia, who carried out these comparative surveys, postulated the difference to be mainly due to the social conditions, including the effects of migration, on the one hand, and on the other to the fact that a hospital-centred orientation tended to increase along with the increasing number of hospital beds available in the district (Alanen, Salokangas, Ojanen, Räkköläinen, & Pylkkänen, 1990b; State Medical Board in Finland, 1988). A similar difference in the prevalence of schizophrenia between the different parts of Finland was also seen in the psychiatric part of the Mini-Finland Project supervised by Ville Lehtinen, where the estimates were made on a large population sample aged over 30 years. In this study, the prevalence of schizophrenia varied from 0.9–2.1% (Lehtinen & Joukamaa, 1987).

According to epidemiological data, schizophrenia morbidity is roughly the same throughout the world, although there are numerous regions for which there are no reliable data available. Higher-than-average morbidity rates have been reported, for example, for Ireland (Torrey et al., 1984), for the Catholic population of Canada, for northern Croatia, and for the Tamil population of southern India and Sri Lanka (Murphy, 1973). Referring to findings presented above, eastern Finland may be added to the list. There are also interesting observations recently reported in some industrialized countries which suggest that there has been a minor decline in the incidence of schizophrenia in the past few decades (Der, Gupta, & Murray, 1990; Munk-Jorgensen & Mortensen, 1992). These observations have not been sufficiently corroborated so far.

The International Pilot Study conducted by the WHO in the late 1960s and the early 1970s also showed that the forms of schizophrenia are, in principle, similar on the different continents and in different cultures (World Health Organization, 1979). The findings obtained by Lambo (1955) in Nigeria as early as the 1950s suggested, however, that the members of the Yoruba tribe living in their traditional village culture generally had psychoses that consisted of twilight and confusion states, while the tribesmen who had moved to towns often suffered from paranoid states reminiscent of the psychoses of the white population. In a report recently published by the WHO on ten countries (Jablensky et al., 1992), broadly defined schizophrenia was shown to be more common in developing countries, whereas narrowly defined schizophrenia was equally common in both industrialized and developing countries.

From the viewpoint of both national economy and public health, schizophrenia is the greatest psychiatric problem, although many other psychiatric disorders, particularly the neuroses, are more common. Epidemiological studies carried out in Finland have shown the overall incidence of notable psychiatric problems to affect about 20% of the population. Approximately 400 people per 100,000 population annually make their first contact with units providing psychiatric health care services, but only one out of every 20 such people has a psychosis of the schizophrenia group. Despite this low figure, at the end of the 1980s 10% of *all* the disability pensions granted on the basis of various illnesses were for schizophrenia; in the 16–45-year age group the proportion of schizophrenics on pension was more than 20%, according to the National Pensions Institute in 1989. In Norway and Sweden, the proportion of schizophrenia is lower, probably partly depending on the use of more restrictive diagnostic criteria.

These figures reflect the relative severity of schizophrenia, its early onset, and the consequent long duration of the illness. They also underline the need to invest the resources allotted to the treatment of schizophrenia as effectively as possible at the early stages of the illness, when the chances of ensuring a favourable outcome are the best.

Prognosis

Despite the arbitrary nature of diagnostic boundaries, the findings on the long-term prognosis of schizophrenia have shown relatively good agreement.

One of the most widely known follow-up studies was Manfred Bleuler's in 1972. His series consisted of 208 patients admitted successively during the years 1942–1943. Of these patients, 152 had reached a stable state lasting five years or more prior to their death or the follow-up examination carried out 23 years later. Of the patients, 20% had recovered completely, 33% were slightly ill, 24% moderately ill, and another 24% seriously ill; when only the first admissions were considered, the corresponding percentages were 23, 43, 19 and 15%. Bleuler noticed that the psychological status of a schizophrenic patient does not, on average, deteriorate once five years have elapsed since the outbreak of the psychosis; more often there is a tendency towards further improvement (Bleuler, 1972).

The Swiss series of Ciompi and Müller (1976), the West German series of Huber, Gross, Schüttler, & Linz (1980), and the series collected in America by Tsuang and his co-workers from Iowa (Tsuang, Woolson, & Fleming, 1979), similarly showed about half of the patients to be in a relatively good condition after a long follow-up period, while the other half were in poor condition. All of these findings were based on very long follow-up periods, and most of the patients had been admitted before the beginning of the neuroleptic era. A five-year follow-up study by Harris, Linker, and Norris (1956) in Britain following insulin shock treatment showed that 45% of patients had recovered socially. In a follow-up study of similar duration ten years later, the team of G. Brown and J. K. Wing (Brown, Bone, Dalison, & Wing, 1966) obtained a corresponding recovery percentage of 56% in a group treated with neuroleptics; in addition to this, 34% of the patients lived in their communities as "social invalids". Harris had reported 21% for "social invalidity". The improvement of the prognosis was probably due both to the introduction of neuroleptic drugs and to the progress made in outpatient care. In a series collected more recently by Shepherd et al. (1989) comprising only first-admission schizophrenic patients, the prognosis was good—with "no or only slight deterioration"—in 58% of the cases, and the same result was obtained by Bland, Parker, and Orn (1976) in Canada in a ten-year follow-up of new schizophrenic patients.

Exceptionally good prognostic findings were reported by Harding et al. (1987), who analysed the 20- to 25-year outcome of patients who had participated in an extensive rehabilitation programme in Vermont, in the 1950s. Of the schizophrenic patients, most of whom had been in hospital for long periods—and who were retrospectively found to meet the DSM–III diagnostic criteria—68% had no psychotic symptoms at the time of the follow-up (some of these were supported by neuroleptic medication), and most were coping moderately well psychosocially.

In a recent meta-analysis of the twentieth-century outcome literature, Hegarty et al. (1994) considered 40% of schizophrenic patients to have improved after follow-ups averaging 5.6 years. The proportion of patients who improved increased significantly after mid-century (for 1956–1985 vs. 1895–1955, 48.5% vs. 35.4%). However, during the past decade the average rate of favourable outcome had declined to 36.4%, which, according to the authors, reflected the re-emergence of narrow diagnostic concepts. One may ask whether this was the only reason for the decline.

In the WHO investigations mentioned above, the prognostic findings were both interesting and unexpected. Both the clinical and the social prognosis of schizophrenics was better in the developing countries than in the industrialized parts of the world. In the first investigation, the best two of the five prognostic groups included 34–48% of the patients in the United States, Great Britain, Denmark, Czechoslovakia, and the Soviet Union, whereas the corresponding figures for developing countries were 86% in Ibadan, Nigeria, 66% in Agra, India, and 53% in Cali, Colombia (WHO, 1979). A parallel finding was also made in the subsequent investigation carried out in 10 different countries (Jablensky et al., 1992). There has been disagreement as to the reasons for these findings. The most plausible assumption may be that proposed by Mosher and Keith (1979)—namely, that the main reason for the differences in prognosis is influence of the social environment. The extensive family and village networks of the more primitive communities support the sick individuals better than do Western people, who tend to isolate themselves in their own living units (see, for example, the descriptions of Tanzania by the Finnish child psychiatrist Forssen, 1979). It is also easier to resume work and other activities in less differentiated societies. The relatively milder forms of the disease in the developing countries probably also influence this finding, but the causal relation may work both ways.

Some other studies (Hsia & Chang, 1978; Raman & Murphy, 1972; Waxler, 1979), as well as the review by Lin and Kleinman (1988), have confirmed the preliminary findings of the relatively good prognosis of schizophrenia in less developed areas. Waxler (1979), who worked in Sri Lanka, especially emphasized the significance of cultural beliefs and less labelling.

The effect of employment conditions on the social prognosis of schizophrenia is obvious in the series of prognostic studies carried out by K. A. Achté, J. Lönnqvist, O. Piirtola, and P. Niskanen (1979) in Helsinki. Of the 100 schizophrenia-group patients first admitted into hospital in 1950, 59% were socially recovered—that is, able to work despite their possible symptoms—after five years; the corresponding percentage was 68% for the 1960 admissions and 54% for the 1970 admissions. The authors postulated that the introduction of neuroleptics had a beneficial effect on the prognosis from the 1950s to the 1960s, but the poorer employment situation worsened the social prognosis in the 1970s. The latter postulation was confirmed by a report published by K. Kuusi (1986) on patients admitted into hospital in Helsinki in 1975: only 38% of them met the criteria of social recovery five years after their admission. In Kuusi's series the diagnostic criteria for inclusion were stricter than they had been previously. Still, 58% of the patients—which is more than in the older series—were without obvious psychotic symptoms.

I return to follow-up data of the psychotherapeutically oriented Turku series and the Finnish Multicentre Study (NSP Project) in chapter five.

It has been observed in various studies that the factors predictive of a good outcome include a lack of nuclear symptoms or their short duration, an acute onset as compared with a gradual onset, manifestation of schizophrenia at an older age, a lesser tendency to isolation, presence of affective expressions, a heterosexual couple relationship established before the onset of the illness, and the "normality" of interpersonal relationships in general, as well as a job and a satisfactory financial position prior to the illness (e.g. Gelder, Gath, & Mayou, 1984; Simon & Wirt, 1961).

In the Finnish NSP Project, described in chapter five, the psychosocial factors were more significant prognostically than was clinical symptomatology. One important factor predictive of the patient's subsequent development turned out to be the prognostic variable developed by us in Finland: maintenance or loss of the "grip on life"

(Salokangas, Räkköläinen, & Alanen, 1989)—that is, whether the patient had, by the time of the admission, maintained or abandoned his/her aspirations towards age-appropriate goals pertaining to other people and social life.

Men and women do not differ as to their schizophrenic morbidity, but nearly all recent prognostic surveys (see, for example, Goldstein & Tsuang, 1990; Salokangas, 1983;) have shown that the average long-term prognosis is better for females than for males. The reason for the sex-bound differences can be assumed to consist of either biological factors or differences in the psychosocial roles. The former might include the effect of progesterone, which possibly affords a relative protection from the psychosis and comes to an end at the menopause (Häfner et al., 1994).

But we must bear in mind that all that I have said above about the factors influencing the prognosis is based on average findings; there are exceptions in individual cases due to early and active treatment as well as to environmental factors. In a follow-up study made in Turku, the influence of such factors came out significantly even in the statistical analysis (Alanen, Räkköläinen, Laakso, Rasimus, & Kaljonen, 1986). Luc Ciompi writes:

> For everyone who does not link the concept of schizophrenia itself to an obligatory bad outcome, the enormous variety of possible evolutions show that *there is no such thing as a specific course of schizophrenia.* [Ciompi, 1980, p. 420]

Illness models

The premises of researchers concerning the origins and nature of schizophrenia continue to be highly contradictory. They are often also extremely one-sided: the relatively narrow field of study adopted in one's own work is regarded as the only correct approach, and one's view is restricted by blinkers that effectively shield one from seeing any other field.

The polarization of clinical practice may have diminished somewhat during the past few years. But it continues to exist and notably hamper the development of the treatment of our patients. After all, therapeutic approaches are determined by our theories of the nature of the illness.

In Exhibit 2.1, I have compiled the most important contemporary approaches to the causes and the nature of schizophrenia—the "illness models of schizophrenia". The central claim of each approach has been expressed as a—perhaps slightly exaggerated—catchphrase, and the most important modes of therapy according to the principles of each approach have been presented.

The names and catchphrases of the approaches reflect one central cause for the divergence of the concepts: their scientific backgrounds, research methods, and frames of reference for the findings differ notably from each other. Any investigator willing to cast off his blinkers and acquaint himself with another research approach must really enter a different world and abandon for a moment his or her criteria for scientific research.

The *biomedical model* is deeply embedded in the natural–scientific research culture and the medical tradition founded upon it. It has therefore always been given a prominent position by investigators of schizophrenia with medical training. Surveying recent schizophrenia research, it is easy to see that the projects and publications with a biomedical orientation dominate quantitatively.

Methods similar to the biomedical ones—empirical experimentation and measurement, statistical analysis of results—are also applied in some psychologically and sociologically oriented psychiatric research. The psychological models in Exhibit 2.1 are, however, based on a different approach to case-specific understanding. The *individual psychological and interactional models* are close to each other in this respect, although they are separated by some radical differences that have also been a source of dispute among different schools. Both differ from the biomedical model in that their findings are difficult to verify with methods acceptable in the natural sciences, such as experimentation. The reproducibility of the therapeutic results is also less convincing, because they are always dependent on the development of the interactional relationship between therapist and patient. As early as the 1950s, Whitehorn and Betz (1960) noted the considerable influence of the therapist's own personality on the therapist–patient relationship.

Despite all this, the research that applies psychological models is empirical and experiential, and observations based on profound case-specific knowledge, whenever they reveal a recurring pattern, can also be generalized as common knowledge. Using the terminology of the German philosopher Jürgen Habermas (1968), we might say that

---

EXHIBIT 2.1
Illness models of schizophrenia
and treatment modes related to them

---

1. BIOMEDICAL
   "The illness is based on an organic brain process"
   - psychopharmacological treatment
   - other somatically oriented treatments

2. INDIVIDUAL PSYCHOLOGICAL
   *"The illness is based on a deep-rooted disorder
   of the personality development"*
   - individual psychotherapy
   - application of individual psychological principles
     in other modes of treatment (e.g. group therapy,
     family therapy, art therapy)

3. INTERACTIONAL
   *"The illness is part of a disordered interactional network
   and/or manifested as problems of interactional adaptation"*
   - systemic family therapy
   - dynamically oriented group therapy
   - therapeutic communities

4. SOCIAL AND ECOLOGICAL
   "The patients should have support as members of community"
   - environment-centred mental health activities
   - rehabilitation

5. INTEGRATED
   *"All the approaches presented above are justified.
   Their significance as well as their mutual relation are
   weighed differently in different cases"*
   - treatment should be carried out comprehensively
     and according to case-specific needs

---

these approaches differ from biomedical research in that their interest of knowledge is hermeneutic–emancipatory (not natural–scientific or technical), aiming at a liberating developmental process made possible by an understanding of the phenomena at hand. In individual therapy, this process takes place through a dyadic relationship between patient and therapist, who tries, using this relationship, to discover the distortions in the patient's previous development and to promote new personality growth. In the interactional model, the individual's symptoms are seen as an indication of the interactional network or system, generally the family, of which the patient is a member, and efforts are made to alter its interactions.

The fourth—*social and ecological*—approach is not based on the kind of aetiologic theory formation underlying the other approaches. I have therefore formulated a more pragmatic catchphrase for it. Despite a lack of aetiologic focus, the methods of this approach—that is, milieu-oriented mental health work and rehabilitation—are just as important as the other methods. Mental health work supports the healthy development of individuals and communities and thus helps to prevent psychiatric illnesses. Rehabilitation helps especially chronic patients to cope more satisfactorily in society. Rehabilitative work, which is extremely important for schizophrenic patients, can easily be combined with any aetiologic approach. Rehabilitation is accepted generally and does not evoke resistance among biomedically oriented researchers in the way that psychological methods more strictly committed to aetiologic premises often do.

It may be asked whether we should also talk about an "antipsychiatric" model. The representatives of this orientation—such as Szasz (1961) and Goffman (1961)—gave a beneficial airing to the excessive hospital orientation of psychiatric work and its implicit violence and violation of human rights. I do not consider their ideas to be as important aetiologically as they are sociologically. It is true that labelling, which they considered particularly detrimental, may have a notably unfavourable influence on the patient's prognosis, especially his/her possibilities of coping in his/her social environment. It should be realized, however, that labelling is almost always a secondary phenomenon due to the individual's role as a patient, which comes about at or after the onset of the illness.

Schizophrenia has also been described as a way of maintaining one's individuality, a refusal to adjust to the conventional ways of life. It is quite true that in a psychotic condition, particularly a prolonged one, it is possible to recognize desperate and distorted attempts at protecting "one's self" in an anxiety-provoking human environment that seems to be destroying individuality. Theodore Lidz, my American teacher, once said that unless schizophrenia existed, someone would soon invent it. What would be more natural—he meant—than that an individual who has experienced contacts with fellow human beings to be overwhelmingly frightening should isolate himself and begin to live in a fantasy world of his own. This is not, however, a matter of voluntary choice, but something due to an inner impulse.

It is my opinion, that the first four separate models described in Exhibit 2.1 have their own research-based justification and therapeutic significance. At the same time, each of them also has its limitations. We should therefore try to create an *integrated model of schizophrenia*, which I have also included in Exhibit 2.1. In this model, the biomedical factors, the aspects of individual development, and the factors implicit in the patient's closest interactional network as well as his psychosocial situation are all considered. The same applies to the treatment, which should utilize all the modes of therapy included in the different models. The selection of the modes of treatment should not, however, be done in a vaguely "eclectic" manner, but on the basis of a case-specific evaluation of the therapeutic needs.

CHAPTER THREE

The origins of schizophrenia: an attempt at synthesis

Starting-point:
necessity of an integrative approach

S chizophrenia studies based on biomedical, genetic, individual psychological, interactional psychological, and social approaches have all provided findings that should be taken into account when trying to analyse the pathogenesis and nature of schizophrenia. The need for comprehensive thinking seems obvious.

I do not agree with theories according to which schizophrenia is regarded as a clearly organic disorder, with no relation to psychosocial environmental factors. Interactional relationships with other people are part of human biology. They play a crucial role in human psychosocial development and the underlying cerebral functions. My experiences as a psychotherapist and family researcher convinced me that individuals fallen ill with schizophrenia should not be placed outside this general rule, which is the basis of all integrated psychobiological psychiatry.

The most dramatic evidence for the fundamental significance of interactional relations for human personality development comes from the observations on children who have grown up wild, without any human contact, surviving under animal care in a warm climate. It is not easy to find reliable information on the development of these so-called wolf children, but it appears that they do not learn to speak, their facial expressions are undeveloped, and even their drive functions remain rudimentary (Malson, 1972; Rang, 1987). Interactional relationships with other people thus prove a necessary prerequisite for human development.

The developmental significance of interaction is not restricted to man, as demonstrated by Harry F. and Margaret Harlow (1966), who experimented with rhesus monkeys. Baby monkeys separated from their mothers grew up seriously disturbed both socially and sexually compared with infants brought up by their biological mothers. Auditory and visual contact with other monkeys did not help if the babies were deprived of physical contact, and mother surrogates made of metal wire or furry material were also useless. For human development, the effects of interactional relations are even more significant than they are for animals, whose behaviour is based more on instincts. Human beings therefore need a longer time to grow from infancy to adult maturity. The stages of cerebral development are also longer in man, and development is most massive in early infancy. Still, the developmental growth of the human cortex (especially the frontal lobes) continues past the age of 20, which is unparalleled in other primates. The increasing dominance of the newer centres (neocortex) in man is also noticeable in the development of transmitter activities, such as in the form of a "developmental lag" of dopaminergic activities (M. and A. Carlsson, 1990); apes have a denser pattern of dopamine receptors in their cortex than do adult humans.

The key to species-specific development is to be found in the genetic make-up of man. On the other hand, the genetically determined long period of development shows that the interactional experiences and the chances for identification and learning related to them are increasingly significant for the development of the human personality, compared with other species. As Lidz (1964) has emphasized, human beings have two endowments, one based on our genes and a second sociocultural one, based on the effects of our developmental environment.

If schizophrenia is related to disturbances of human personality development, as is suggested by psychologically oriented research, it is only natural to postulate that interactional relationships contribute to this pathogenesis, not only on the psychological but also on the biological level.

Studies on predisposition to schizophrenia: the role of biological factors

The factors involved in the pathogenesis of schizophrenia have been shown to be both multilevel and complex. I discriminate here between factors associated with vulnerability to schizophrenia and factors related to its onset, though the two are closely connected.

During recent decades, biologically oriented schizophrenia research has become quite extensive and versatile (for reviews, see, for example, Sedvall & Farde, 1995; Syvälahti, 1994; Weinberger, 1995). It would be overwhelmingly difficult to give a comprehensive review of this field of research. I shall concentrate on a short description and discussion of findings that now seem to be most significant aetiologically. I thus put aside, for example, neurophysiological and biochemical studies, apart from a short reference to the effects of and links to transmitter substances in schizophrenia, a topic about which new and more conclusive findings will probably be made in the future.

We can now discriminate between two groups of biological factors obviously predisposing to schizophrenia: *minor structural abnormalities of the brain* on the one hand, and the effect of *hereditary factors* on the other. Both factors clearly increase the vulnerability for becoming schizophrenic but are, at least in the light of contemporary research findings, not clearly specific to schizophrenia or influential in all of the patients.

Structural abnormalities of the brain

This is especially obvious for the abnormalities of the brain, suggested as early as the 1960s by pneumoencephalographic studies (Haug, 1962; Huber, 1961), first demonstrated with computer tomography (CT) by Johnstone et al. (1976) and soon confirmed by other investigators (e.g. Andreasen et al., 1990; Nasrallah, McCalley-Whitters, & Jacoby, 1982; Nybäck, Wiesel, Berggren, & Hindmarsh, 1982; Suddath et al., 1989; Weinberger, Torrey, Neophytides, & Wyatt, 1979) using CT or magnetic resonance imaging (MRI). The prevalence of these abnormalities—an enlarged ventricle/brain ratio, a smaller volume of certain structures, especially of those in the medial temporal lobes, and of the thalamus—has ranged between 6 and 40% of schizophrenic patients (for reviews, see Cleghorn, Zipurski, & List, 1991; Lewis,

1990; Syvälahti, 1994). According to studies of monozygotic twins discordant for schizophrenia, even affected twins—including those whose ventricles were small—tend to have larger ventricles than their healthy twins (Reveley, Reveley, Clifford, & Murray, 1982; Suddath, Christison, & Torrey, 1990). However, findings similar to those made in schizophrenia have also been obtained in other conditions. Rieder et al. (1983), in a CT study, found brain abnormalities in schizoaffective psychoses and in bipolar affective illness almost as often as in schizophrenia; with regard to manic psychoses, this was shown by Nasrallah et al. (1982). Hauser et al. (1989) made a MRI study of patients with primary affective illness, with the same result.

The structural abnormalities are not directly related to either the onset of the illness or its subsequent course: these findings remain unchanged during follow-up (Nasrallah et al., 1986; Illowsky, Juliano, Bigelow, & Weinberger, 1988). This is quite contrary to typical organic brain disorders, such as Alzheimer's disease, in which the deterioration of the psychic condition is related to the progress of a massive illness process in brain tissue. Nor can the findings be explained away as consequences of treatment—they are also detected in recently diagnosed unmedicated patients, particularly young men.

The origins of these structural abnormalities are unknown. They may be heterogeneous in nature. There are several aetiological possibilities. Weinberger (1987) enumerates the following: a hereditary encephalopathy or a predisposition to environmental injury, an infectious or postinfectious state, an immunological disorder, toxic or metabolic disorders, perinatal trauma, or some other early factors affecting the development of the nervous system. He adds two factors that he considers "highly unlikely" but remotely possible: early psychosocial (e.g. interpersonal) factors might produce a structural brain lesion in plastic neural systems, or schizophrenia might not be a discrete event or illness process at all, but, rather, one end of the developmental spectrum that, for genetic and/or other reasons, would occur in about 0.5% of the population.

The theory that structural disorders result from early damages caused by physical environmental factors has been supported by many. However, the assumptions of the role of obstetric complications, originally based on risk surveys of the children of psychotic mothers (Cannon et al., 1993; Mednick, Parnas, & Schulsinger, 1987), have not been confirmed in some extensive studies of unselected schizophrenic populations (Davis, Breier, Buchanan, & Holstein, 1991; Done,

Johnstone, & Frith, 1991). They are still included as a possible aetiological factor in a number of cases (McNeil et al., 1994). The role of maternal influenza during the second trimester of pregnancy, on the other hand, seems more plausible in the light of recent investigations (Mednick, Machon, Huttunen, & Bonett, 1988; Huttunen, Machon, & Mednick, 1994). This is also supported by the nature of brain findings: lesions originating from a later period of time should have left traces in the glial tissue of the brain, and no such traces have been found (Roberts, 1990). However, in a large British survey (Sham et al., 1992), the role of maternal influenza seemed relevant in only a small fraction of the patients, and other criticisms have also been expressed (e.g. Crow, 1994).

A recent MRI study (Bremner et al., 1995) indicated that the volume of the right hippocampus was statistically significantly smaller in those suffering from combat-related posttraumatic stress disorder (PTSD) than in carefully matched controls; no such difference was found in the volume of other brain regions. The investigators present several potential explanations for their findings, which resemble hippocampal findings in patients with schizophrenia, including glucocorticoid-mediated damage to the hippocampus associated with stress. On the other hand, alterations in hippocampal morphology may have preceded PTSD, presenting a premorbid risk factor for its development.

Still, I also find it difficult to believe that early interpersonal influences—or later stress related with panic anxiety—could bring about clear morphological changes in the brain. It is more probable that somatogenic effects are more primary than are psychogenic ones, but, when present, could induce a restricting effect on the range of developmental possibilities in psychological functions and their integration.

The aetiological interpretations of the relationship between these findings and schizophrenia are not unanimous among the leading investigators. Weinberger and his co-workers (Weinberger, 1987; Weinberger, Berman, Suddath, & Torrey, 1992) have repeatedly postulated that their significance may be understood through the rich interconnected network between different brain regions, whose overall functioning may be affected by local abnormalities. On the other hand, Andreasen et al. (1994), while presenting an image of an "average schizophrenic brain", proposed that the diverse symptoms of schizophrenia "could all result from a defect in filtering or gating sensory input, which is one of the primary functions of the thalamus in the human brain". However, it should not be forgotten that the findings, as revealed by currently available imaging methods, cannot be regarded as specific to schizophrenia.

They most probably constitute risk factors for this disorder, and possibly also for other conditions.

Hereditary factors

The role of predisposing hereditary factors in the aetiology of schizophrenia has been clearly verified by research, but it has proved to be relative.

In most series of schizophrenic patients, the parents turn out to have schizophrenia in 4–6% of the cases, the siblings in 8–12%, and the children in 10–15%. Compared with these figures, those presented by early twin researchers for the morbidity of identical twins spoke strongly in favour of the importance of hereditary factors, particularly as the morbidity of non-identical twins with schizophrenia did not differ notably from the corresponding value of ordinary siblings.

Table 3.1 shows the results of *twin studies* of schizophrenia. They indicate that the findings published since 1960 differ from the older findings in that the co-morbidity rates of identical twins are clearly lower in the more recent studies—30 to 50% at the most—and even then a rather wide scope of diagnostics is needed. Nevertheless, even the recent studies show that the co-morbidity of identical twins is consistently higher than that of non-identical twins.

The authors of the early twin studies collected their material from hospitals on the basis of clinical records and personal inquiries, while most of the subsequent investigations are based on either census registers of twins (the Northern European studies) or at least successive hospital admissions. Identity diagnoses of identical twins are now confirmed with serological tests. Furthermore, many of the earlier investigators, for example Kallmann (1946), reached their conclusions by following a proband-wise (not pair-wise) calculation, in which every concordant twin pair was counted twice. When Kallmann further applied a "shorter" method designed to take into account the relation of the subject's age to the risk of morbidity, he was able calculate an 86% schizophrenia risk for an identical twin whose twin partner had become schizophrenic.

Studies of discordant monozygotic co-twins of schizophrenic patients and of the children of two schizophrenic parents have yielded particularly conclusive evidence to contradict the monogenetic theories of schizophrenia. Both groups display a widely variable spectrum of

TABLE 3.1

Pairwise concordance for schizophrenia in twins according to different twin studies

Author	Year	Country	Monozygotic twins		Dizygotic twins	
			N	Concordance %	N	Concordance %
Kallman	1946	USA	174	59–69	517	9–10
Slater	1953	England	37	65	112	9
Inoye	1961	Japan	55	36–60	17	6–12
Tienari	1963	Finland	16	0–19	21	5–14
Gottesman & Shields	1966	England	24	42	33	9
Kringlen	1967	Norway	55	25–38	172	8–12
Pollin et al.	1969	USA	80	14–27	146	4–8
Fischer	1973	Denmark	21	24–48	41	10–20
Tienari	1975	Finland	20	15	24	7.5
Kendler & Robinette	1983	USA	164	18	268	3.5
Onstad et al.	1991	Norway	24	33	28	4

Note: Concordance rates have always been calculated pairwise and without using any shortening methods, which, in some of the studies, leads to somewhat lower figures than those reported by the authors. Where there are two figures given, the lower one indicates the concordance for schizophrenia, and the higher one also includes borderline schizophrenia, schizophreniform psychosis, and/or suspected schizophrenia.

disorders, in addition to which a great many co-twins as well as children of psychotic couples grow up psychically quite normal (Kringlen, 1967, 1978; Onstad, Skre, Torgersen, & Kringlen, 1991). These findings seem to disprove theories of a specific schizophrenic genotype, which, apart from the cases developing into a schizophrenic phenotype, should be manifested as schizophrenia-spectrum personality disorders.

We might here also refer to the fact underlined already by many early schizophrenia researchers: that since the fertility of schizophrenic subjects is lower by about 50% than that of the normal population, the incidence of schizophrenia—if it were an exclusively monogenous hereditary disease—should decrease markedly from generation to generation through "natural selection". No such decrease has occurred, however. This fact seems to contradict both dominant and recessive modes of heredity.

The significance of non-manifested genotypes can be approached also by analysing the incidence of schizophrenia among the off-spring of identical twins discordant for schizophrenia. Two such surveys have been published. The first was that of Gottesman and Bertelsen (1989), who made a follow-up study until 1985 of the offspring of the twin series gathered by Fischer (1973). The second was conducted by Kringlen and Cramer (1989), who followed the series collected by Kringlen (1967) in the same way. Gottesman and Bertelsen reported practically no difference in the incidence of schizophrenia and related disorders between the children of schizophrenic and their non-concordant identical twins: 16.8% of the children of schizophrenic co-twins and 17.4% of the healthy co-twins showed disorders. Kringlen and Cramer, in turn, found a clear (though not statistically significant) difference, 17.9% and 4.4%. Gottesman and Bertelsen regard their finding as a definite indication of the significance of genetic factors, whereas Kringlen and Cramer emphasize the importance of environmental factors. This contradiction between the two reports is a further example of the problems inherent in this field of research.

Identical twins have not only the same genes but almost invariably also the same growing environment. It was hoped that *studies of adoptive children* would differentiate better than twin studies the hereditary pathogenetic factors from those originating in the environment.

The best-known of the adoption studies dealing with schizophrenia is the series of studies designed by two American researchers, S. S. Kety and David Rosenthal, the central part of which was conducted on Danish populations. The results of this Danish–American adoption study demonstrated: (1) that children born to psychotic mothers and placed in adoptive families had a greater disposition to schizophrenia or disorders close to it than did adoptive children whose biological parents had not suffered from psychoses (Rosenthal et al., 1968, 1971); (2) that the biological relatives of adopted children who had become schizophrenic often had more serious mental disorders than their "adoptive relatives" (Kety et al., 1968, 1994); and (3) that, according to a rank ordering, a group of adoptive parents of adopted children who had become schizophrenic were less disturbed than a group of biological parents of the schizophrenic children reared in their homes (Wender, Rosenthal, & Kety, 1968). During the course of these investigations, Rosenthal and Kety developed the concept of the *schizophrenia spectrum*, by which they meant that the schizophrenia group also includes genetically a number of less severe disorders (especially non-affective functional psychoses and schizoid and paranoid character disorders), these disorders being notably more numerous than actual schizophrenias.

The results of these studies have been interpreted as speaking strongly in favour of genetic factors associated with schizophrenia and against the effect of environmental factors. However, their methodology and the interpretation of their results has also been strongly criticized, especially by psychodynamically oriented family investigators (Lidz & Blatt, 1983; Wynne, Singer, & Toohey, 1976).

The extensive Finnish adoptive family study conducted by Pekka Tienari and his co-workers (Tienari, 1992; Tienari et al., 1987, 1993, 1994) is less well known but is, in my opinion, the most important study clarifying the roles of hereditary and environmental factors in schizophrenia. It is based on almost 200 children given up for adoption by women who had been inpatients in Finnish mental hospitals from 1960–1979, because of psychoses of the schizophrenia group, and is compared with matched controls. The investigation also included the assessment of the global mental health of the rearing environment, based on interviews as well as on a battery of psychological tests. The Tienari study is the only adoptive study planned and carried out with a combined genetic and psychodynamic expertise.

The main findings of this study are presented in Tables 3.2 and 3.3. Even though still considered preliminary by the team, the results can be regarded as conclusive. They confirm clearly the importance of both genetic and psychological environmental factors for the vulnerability for schizophrenia as well as the interaction between them and genetic factors. Of the adopted-out children of psychotic mothers 14 (9%) have

TABLE 3.2

Outcome diagnoses of index and control adoptees

Adoptee diagnoses (and six-level mental health ratings)	Index adoptees			Control adoptees
	A (n = 136)	B (n = 19)	Total (n = 155)	Total (n = 185)
(1, 2) No diagnosis	67	7	74 (47.8%)	97 (52.4 %)
(3) Neuroses and mild personality disorder	29	5	34 (21.9%)	59 (31.9 %)
(4, 5) "Soft-spectrum" non-psychotic personality disorders	27	4	31 (20.0%)	27 (14.6 %)
(6) Functional psychoses	13	3	16 (10.3%)	2 (1.1 %)
"Spectrum psychoses"				
(6a) DSM–III–R schizophrenia	(7)		(9) (5.8%)	(2) (1.1%)
(6b) Schizophreniform	(2)	(1)	(3) (1.9%)	(0) (0%)
(6c) Delusional disorder	(2)	(0)	(2) (1.3%)	(0)
— Bipolar psychoses ("non-spectrum")	(2)	(0)	(2) (1.3%)	(0)

Source: Tienari et al., 1993.

A = Confirmed RDC/DSM–III–R diagnoses of schizophrenia in biological mothers.

B = Other "spectrum psychoses", including schizoaffective, schizophreniform, atypical, and delusional psychoses, but not bipolar or alcoholic psychoses, in biological mothers.

Significance of index versus control adoptee differences: Total "soft spectrum" (4, 5, 6a–c) vs. non-spectrum (1–3, plus bipolar psychoses), $\chi^2 = 8.0691$, $p = 0.0045$; "spectrum psychoses" (6a–c) vs. all other diagnoses, $\chi^2 = 10.183$, $p = 0.0014$; schizophrenia (6a, b) vs. others $p = 0.0206$ (Fischer's Exact Test); "soft-spectrum" non-psychotic personality disorders vs. non-spectrum (psychotic adoptees excluded), $\chi^2 = 2.558$, $p = 0.1097$.

TABLE 3.3

Outcome diagnoses of the adoptees in relation to global mental health ratings of the adoptive families

	Adoptee rating	Adoptive Family Ratings			
		1–2 healthy	3 "neurotic"	4–5 severely disturbed	Total
Index	1–2 healthy	47	17	5	69
	3 "neurotic"	9	11	13	33
	4–5 personality disorders	2	7	20	29
	6 functional psychoses	0	4	9	13
	total	58	39	47	114
Control	1–2 healthy	51	27	12	90
	3 "neurotic"	20	22	17	59
	4–5 personality disorders	3	9	13	25
	6 functional psychoses	0	0	2	2
	total	74	58	44	176

Source: Tienari, 1992.

become ill with schizophrenia or a closely related psychosis, while the corresponding number among the matched control group was 2 (1.1%). However, it was also found that the disorders of the adopted children clustered strongly in the rearing environments whose global mental health was assessed as disturbed. This was true of both index and control adoptees. A logistic regression analysis, which included the genetic difference between the series, showed that the most powerful factor preceding mental disorder in the adoptee was disturbed intrafamilial communication. After exclusion of this variable came conflicts between parents and children, combined with the genetic variable, and as a third factor lack of empathy, also combined with the genetic variable. Especially noteworthy is the conclusion that a wholesome family environment seems to protect from disturbance even those children whose biological mothers have been ill with schizophrenia.

In the late 1980s, *molecular genetic studies* based on the possibility of locating genetic markers in chromosome charting studies became possible. Since then, there has been very intensive study to find the evidence that would connect schizophrenia to a specific gene. However, thus far the results of these linkage studies have yielded almost exclusively negative and/or contradictory results (e.g. Barr et al., 1994; Coon et al., 1994; for a critical review, see Portin & Alanen, 1997). The postulates of specific genetic factors located in different genes in different cases still seem possible, and the same can be said of the hypothesis according to which two or three genes together could lead to a predisposition for schizophrenia. Results of a large international (families from eight countries) two-stage genome-wide search for schizophrenia susceptibility genes (Moises et al., 1995) suggested that a more complex oligogenic or polygenic model is most likely to be correct. In this study, based on families from eight countries and a narrow diagnosis of schizophrenia, five different loci, in chromosomes 6p, 8p, 9, 20, and 22, were found, which, acting in concert, could cause susceptibility for this disease. In another recent international multicentre study, Williams et al. (1996) found that a polymorphism of the 5-HT 2-A receptor gene, located in the long arm of chromosome 13, was 1.3 times more general in schizophrenia than in the general population ($p = 0.003$).

Both the overall quality of the variably based genetic and family-dynamic findings and the postulated clinical continuum of schizophrenia and the personality disorders within and outside the schizophrenia spectrum rather suggest a collective effect of several genes acting less specifically but in interaction with causative factors of another kind. It is most probable that the genetic predisposition to schizophrenia is polygenic, and the effects are dependent on interaction with physical and psychosocial environmental factors. Even the possibility that the genetic susceptibility to schizophrenic psychoses generally represents one extreme of normal human genetic variation cannot be excluded. In that case, an individual's genetic vulnerability to schizophrenia could be characterized as merely one extreme of normal human genetic variability (Portin & Alanen, 1997).

Some researchers have postulated that a part of schizophrenia would be caused by genetic factors, and another group would be related to brain damage. Efforts to confirm this have, however, led to contradictory findings, giving only limited support to this hypothesis.

This kind of theory has been presented by Reveley et al. (1982) as well as by Suddath et al. (1990), based on their findings of enlarged cerebral ventricles in discordant identical twins. Because the schizophrenic twins regularly had larger ventricles than their healthier co-twins, the brain abnormalities appeared to be independent of genetic factors. Reveley, Reveley, and Murray (1984) supported their findings by pointing out that in their series there was a "family taint" only among patients with no enlargement of the cerebral ventricles. However, DeLisi et al. (1986), while studying the ventricle/brain ratio of schizophrenic patients who came from sibships more than one member of which had schizophrenia, found that the ventricular enlargement was not likely to be restricted to those without the "taint". Furthermore, according to other studies (Cannon et al., 1993; Torrey et al., 1994), a positive correlation between ventricular enlargement and genetic risk for schizophrenia was found.

Other attempts to discover a difference between hereditary and "sporadic" schizophrenia—the latter group of patients having no schizophrenia in their families—have not yielded conclusive findings. Sedvall and Wode-Helgodt (1980), for example, noted differences in the metabolic products of spinal fluid transmitter substances between two patient groups, one with other cases of schizophrenia in the family, the other with none. O'Callaghan et al. (1991) found evidence for the occurrence in connection with winter births—with a possible connection with increased maternal influenza—to be confined to patients without a family history of mental disorders. These findings have remained disputable and/or not sufficiently confirmed.

The influence of the two groups of biological predisposing factors on the prognosis of the patients seems to differ. Structural brain abnormalities do have some correlations with outcome—chronic patients and those with negative symptoms exhibit such changes more often than do patients with a better outcome—even if there is no obvious connection with the different subtypes of schizophrenia. The genetic factors, on the other hand—as defined by the appearance of other cases of schizophrenia in the family history—do not have a similar correlation with outcome (Ciompi, 1980).

Studies on predisposition to schizophrenia: the role of psychosocial factors

In Exhibit 2.1, I separated the psychodynamically oriented studies of the nature and causative factors of schizophrenia into two sections. The aim of the individual–psychological approach, represented by psychoanalytically oriented studies, is to discover, in a dyadic relationship with the patient, how the illness is linked to the internal growth of the personality, shaped by constitutional factors and early interactional relationships. The interactional approach, in turn, focuses on the study of interpersonal relationships and networks—mostly families—wherein the individual's development and life events take place. In both cases, psychotherapeutic treatment is closely connected with research.

Psychoanalytic research and family-dynamic research, while close to each other, approach schizophrenia from mutually complementary viewpoints. The differences in their basic premises result in a different weighing of pathogenic factors. I shall briefly review the development of both approaches.

Psychoanalytic studies

Sigmund Freud's experience with psychotic patients—who are not very suitable for treatment by the classical psychoanalytic method he invented—was not extensive. Even so, he promoted a highly significantly psychological understanding of schizophrenia, both theoretically and through the famous analysis of the autobiographical memoirs of Dr. Daniel Paul Schreber, a lawyer who suffered from paranoid schizophrenia (Freud, 1911c). Freud postulated that schizophrenic psychosis involved a conversion of libido (i.e. pleasure-seeking drives) away from external objects and directed towards oneself. The psychodynamics of psychosis consisted of two stages: the first stage of the abandonment of object relations was of basic significance and was often followed by symptom formation that could be interpreted as an effort to revive the lost object relations, yet in a manner that was egocentric and megalomanic and isolated from real objects.

In a paper on narcissism published three years later, Freud (1914c) further specified his views on the early development of the libido and its relation to schizophrenia. The first postnatal stage is objectless, characterized by "pure autoeroticism". This is followed by primary narcissism, where the object of libido is oneself. It is only after this that the libido begins to be directed increasingly towards other people, while the "ego libido" is retained at the same time, and constant partial and reciprocal shifts take place between it and the "object libido". Schizophrenic psychosis involves a return to the stage of primary narcissism and at the same time—as was particularly underlined by Abraham (1916)—a psychological regression to the early levels of the first year of life. This meant that the early mother relationship and frustrations connected with it became of central importance in psychoanalytic theories of schizophrenia. However, Freud and his co-workers also considered hereditary–structural factors significant in the origins of traumatic fixations of libidinal development.

The theory of primary narcissism was connected with a therapeutic pessimism. In his essay "The Unconscious", Freud (1915e) emphasizes the therapeutic inaccessibility of schizophrenic patients, as opposed to "transference neuroses", resulting from the abandonment of libidinal object cathexes, preventing the transference necessary for any therapeutic relationship.

In a couple of later papers, published in 1924 after the creation of his theory of the structure of psychological functions (id, ego, superego), Freud (1924b, 1924e) proposed a definition of the difference in development between neurosis and psychosis in a more parallel way: neurosis is a consequence of conflicts between ego and id, while psychosis is an analogous outcome of conflicts between ego and outer world. In neurosis, the ego represses the anxiety-provoking drives, whereas in psychosis the ego is overrun by the id and loses its commitment to external realities.

However, the views expressed by Freud about the therapeutic inaccessibility of schizophrenic patients overshadowed these later papers and were weighty enough to keep the interest of most psychoanalysts to these patients largely theoretical. A notable exception to this rule was Freud's faithful pupil and fellow worker Paul Federn, who successfully treated schizophrenic patients with psychoanalytically oriented psychotherapy (including supportive parameters) in Vienna, beginning as early as 1906. However, he only published the major reports of his abundant experience with psychotic patients during the 1940s, having moved to the United States (Federn, 1943, 1952).

In America, Adolf Meyer (1906, 1910), at the beginning of the century, presented psychodynamic views on the causes and nature of schizophrenia, based on a pragmatic psychobiological approach. Psychotherapy with these patients became more common than in Europe and was greatly influenced by the pioneering work of *Harry Stack Sullivan* (see Sullivan, 1962). Keeping a certain distance from Freud's theories, Sullivan regarded schizophrenia as the result of a process that proceeded through several stages. He especially emphasized the significance of the disorders of self-esteem as well as that of an overpowering, "uncanny" anxiety about the development that ultimately resulted in schizophrenia. The individuals susceptible to schizophrenia are those with many dissociated—in psychoanalytic terms, repressed—life fields, drives, and other emotional needs of this kind. However, the dynamics of the personality may also undergo changes that affect the dissociated experiences both favourably and unfavourably, especially during school-age and early adolescence. Schizophrenia may become manifest at that time, but the personality may also be reinforced.

The therapists of the *"Washington School"*—including Frieda Fromm-Reichmann (1950, 1952) , Otto A. Will, Jr. (1961), and Harold Searles (1965)—further developed the psychotherapy of schizophrenic patients, combining psychoanalytic starting-points with those derived from Sullivan's views. Searles especially published illuminating descriptions of the intensive but ambivalent symbiotic needs for dependence typical of schizophrenic patients that undermine their psychic stability. These are needs that "he cannot allow to recognize in himself, or if recognized in him he dare not express to anyone, or which are expressed by him in a fashion that, more often than not, brings an uncomprehending or relatively rejecting response from the other person" (Searles, 1961). However, it became clear that Freud's view of the therapeutic inaccessibility of schizophrenic patients was not correct, even if the establishment of therapeutic relationships, especially with chronic patients, was an arduous and time-consuming task.

A significant step towards understanding the psychology of schizophrenia and other serious disorders derived from the theories presented by the psychoanalysts of the *British Object Relations School*, especially *Melanie Klein* (1946, 1975; see also Segal, 1973). According to Klein, infants have primitive object relationships from birth, initially with "part objects", the most significant of them being the mother's breast. In order to be able to understand Klein, one has to realize that a majority of the infantile psychic functions consist of unconscious fantasies, which, however, are in constant interplay with the way the infant experiences reality. A central part of these fantasies pertains to satisfactory, "good", or frustrating, "bad", experiences of one's own and of the world. If an infant who is hungry, and who has an omnipotent hallucinatory idea of a good and nourishing breast (as is shown by the movements of its mouth and fingers), is promptly nourished even in reality, it feels its own goodness and the goodness of its objects to be powerful and reliable. If not nourished, the infant develops an idea of the badness and persecutory character of the object, and the ensuing hatred becomes more powerful than his/her love.

The early, primitive defence mechanisms of the infant are denial, splitting, projection, and introjection. Klein (1946) introduced *projective identification* as a new and important defence mechanism: it is based on an omnipotent phantasy that it is possible to split parts of the self and the internalized objects away from the self and place them in an external object, where they are preserved and controlled, while it simultaneously is possible to continue to identify with them. Projective identification is mostly applied to parts of self that are felt to be dangerous or that—at later stages—cannot be accepted as part of one's ego image. Projective identification is also a useful concept in understanding family psychology, and I shall return to it later.

According to Klein, the first year of the infant's life already involves two developmental stages or positions, which are of fundamental significance for the subsequent development of personality. The first of them, the paranoid–schizoid position, is dominated by splitting and projective and introjective processes, which are used to defend against threatening "bad" objects as well as a hateful ego and the persecutory anxiety aroused by these mental images. Fixation to this stage confers a vulnerability to subsequent regression into a paranoid or schizophrenic state. With regard to schizophrenia vulnerability, constitutional factors—for example, the strength of the death instinct (assumed by Freud in the 1920s to be the reverse of life-sustaining libido)—are crucially important. The second stage, the depressive position, beginning soon after the age of six months, coincides with the development whereby the baby is able to perceive the mother as a whole object and begins to realize that good and bad experiences can be associated with one object and one ego, instead of there being separate "good" and "bad" part-object representations. The infant also recognizes its helplessness and dependence on its mother as well as its jealousy towards other people. This recognition mobilizes concern for the object (mother) who has previously been attacked when bad (frustrating), and a desire to make good the damage felt to have been done. These "reparative" feelings, based on concern for the other (the object), form the basis for normal healthy guilt and morality later in life and a decreased susceptibility to subsequent psychosis. The depressive states in later life are due to internalization of the feelings of anger towards the object and their application to one's own ego, as Freud (1917e) originally described.

W. R. Bion, a psychoanalyst of the Kleinian school, postulated that the fear felt by the psychotic patient, which reaches back to the paranoid–psychotic position, results in projective identification characterized by an attempt to destroy all observations and intrapsychic representations of one's self and the object—an attempt, as it were, to obliterate completely the psychic world filled with representations that provoke anxiety (Bion, 1967). This would result in serious distortion in early ego development. This is frequently observable as a prepsychotic deficiency in ego functions in an individual who later becomes schizophrenic as well as a disorganization of thought functions upon the onset of psychosis. There is a simultaneous attempt to break the links between the objects and the self as well as between different objects. Bion also postulated that early processes of this kind may, through internal splitting, result in a situation where a separate "schizophrenic" core of personality is established, which is excluded from consciousness and is not integrated in the partly hollow growth and development of the rest of personality, but may emerge during subsequent regression triggered by anxiety. This could explain why certain individuals tend to regress to the schizophrenic level rather than the neurotic one.

The American psychoanalyst *Otto F. Kernberg* (1975, 1984) demonstrated that the primitive defence mechanisms—splitting, early forms of projection including projective identification, denial, omnipotence, primitive idealization and its counter-pole, devaluation—are of central importance in the psychic function of the borderline personalities in particular. Kernberg regarded the "borderline personality organization" as a relatively stable structure. However, there are also psychosis-prone patients with various defensive mechanisms. Thus, in a Finnish study of first-admitted schizophrenics, a group of regressed patients with underlying borderline personality was found (Räkköläinen et al., 1994). Kernberg criticized the more speculative parts of Kleinian theories and especially her timing of the early developmental phases: whereas Klein placed even the oedipal stage in the first year life immediately after the depressive position, Kernberg locates even the early positions defined by Klein at later stages. Together with his followers—one of them being Vamik D. Volkan, known for his contribution to psychotherapy of psychotic or nearly psychotic patients (1987, 1990, 1995)—Kernberg created a theoretical frame of reference capable of combining the propositions of Klein and the child psychoanalyst and investigator Margaret S. Mahler (1968; Mahler, Pine, & Bergman, 1975)—positions that were originally quite far apart. Figure 3.1 shows the early phases of personality development, as depicted in a paper by Volkan (1981).

J. S. Grotstein (1977) also combined the ideas of the American and British psychoanalytic schools. The development begins with an autistic phase, which, according to him, involves a preliminary orientation towards objects through "adhesive identification". This is followed by a symbiotic phase, which is parallel to Klein's paranoid–schizoid position. After this, more developed defence mechanisms are gradually adopted. Unlike Kernberg, Grotstein presents differentiation and integration as temporally parallel phenomena; they make up a dual track along which personality development proceeds towards more holistic experiences.

The effects of constitutional factors and early interactional relationships are intermingled in many ways, and they cannot be discriminated by means of psychoanalytic research. It is also disputable how much the kind of development that predisposes to schizophrenia should be ascribed to primary deficiencies of personality formation, and how much to internal personality conflicts. Federn (1952), emphasizing deficient ego boundaries, supported the former alternative, the *deficiency theory*. Other proponents of it include, for example, Hartmann (1953)— who pointed to the inability of the schizophrenic ego to neutralize aggressions—London (1973), and Salonen (1979), whereas Kleinian postulates on the early conflicts and defence mechanisms can be classified as *conflict theory*. It was also supported by Arlow and Brenner (1969), starting from different premises. Grotstein (1977) and Pao (1979)—who categorized the schizophrenic illness in different subtypes based on a combined psychodynamic and family dynamic assessment of the grade of the patient's disturbance—assume an intermediary position at this point, which also seems justifiable to me.

The influence of recent advances in neurobiological research on psychoanalytic theory has not been rapid. However, some efforts towards the integration of these two disciplines have been published. Most noteworthy is Michael Robbins' book *Experiences of Schizophrenia: An Integration of the Personal, Scientific, and Therapeutic* (1993), based on long-term psychotherapeutic work with these patients. For Robbins, it

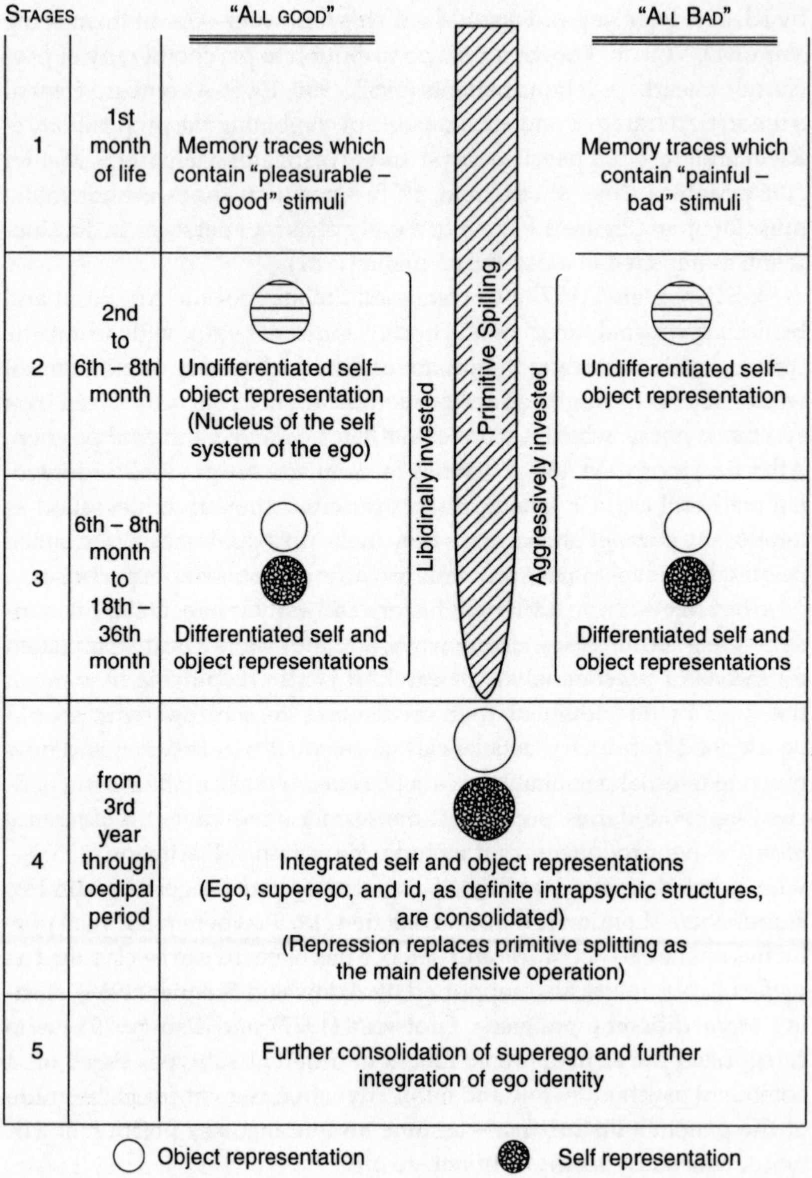

STAGES		"ALL GOOD"	Primitive Spilling	"ALL BAD"
1	1st month of life	Memory traces which contain "pleasurable – good" stimuli		Memory traces which contain "painful – bad" stimuli
2	2nd to 6th – 8th month	Undifferentiated self–object representation (Nucleus of the self system of the ego)	Libidinally invested — Aggressively invested	Undifferentiated self–object representation
3	6th – 8th month to 18th – 36th month	Differentiated self and object representations		Differentiated self and object representations
4	from 3rd year through oedipal period	Integrated self and object representations (Ego, superego, and id, as definite intrapsychic structures, are consolidated) (Repression replaces primitive splitting as the main defensive operation)		
5		Further consolidation of superego and further integration of ego identity		

○ Object representation   ● Self representation

FIGURE 3.1. The development of internalized object relations (Volkan, 1981).

seems likely that schizophrenia "is the expression of a cerebral variant, a differently functioning brain than a normal one with some discrete defect". A constitutional vulnerability and deficits and abnormalities of primary parenting have, from the beginning, a combined effect on the development of a person predisposed to schizophrenia.

According to Robbins, there are two main areas of primary disorders. The first of these is a vulnerability in the area of organization and affinity, manifested as the schizophrenic's aversion to contact with other human beings and—related to this—a deficiency in psychological differentiation and integration. The second handicap is formed by problems with intensity and regulation of stimulation, both external and internal, especially marked with regard to rage and its management. Because of this, and referring to his own experiences, Robbins emphasizes that the schizophrenic's early development, including the symbiotic situation, is not comparable to the normal development of the symbiotic phase as described by Mahler and her co-workers (1975) and also reflected in Searles' (1955, 1965) writings. Robbins calls the symbiotic situation of a schizophrenic "prototypic", characterized by a passive, global, and indiscriminate adaptation to others. In psychotherapy with schizophrenics, the goal of the therapist is—after the initial phase of engagement in the pathologic, prototypic symbiosis—to stimulate development towards a more normal, growth-promoting symbiosis and in this way to adequate psychological differentiation and integration. Despite his consideration of the constitutional handicaps, Robbins views' of the possibilities of psychotherapy in schizophrenia are relatively optimistic.

Heinz Kohut, the developer of *self psychology* (1971, 1977), did not focus on schizophrenia. However, his theories, which form an antithesis to the drive-based psychoanalytic theories, are interesting from the viewpoint of schizophrenia research. According to Kohut, the representational developments pertaining to the self on the one hand and objects on the other—which correspond to Freud's division into narcissistic and object-oriented libido—can be examined as parallel but separate phenomena not bound to each other in the way suggested by Freud. Nevertheless, Kohut considers some of the most intensive narcissistic experiences to be related to object representations. Kohut calls these narcissistically cathected objects *self-objects*. For the children, parents are always both objects of an emotional relationship and self-objects, which are used in the service of the growth of self and in the maintenance of its investments.

According to Kohut, the sensations and experiences associated with drive gratification in infantile development are consistently subordinated to the child's experience of the relation between the self and self-objects. The mother and the other adult caregivers are at first self-objects for the infant, and the infant's view of itself and others—that is, its personality—grows primarily from this foundation through identifying interaction. Kohut points out that this is of crucial importance on two counts, and he continues:

> It changes our evaluation of the significance of the libido theory on all levels of psychological development in childhood; and, consequently, it changes our evaluation of some forms of psychopathology which classical theory viewed as being caused by the personality's fixation or regression to this or that stage of instinct development. [Kohut, 1977, p. 80]

Kohut's views of aggression are typical. Aggression is, admittedly, part of the individual's personality, and it has its biological foundation. Nevertheless, Kohut postulates that destructive aggression (so important in the schizophrenic psychodynamics!) originally comes about because of the inability of the infant's early self-object environment—that is, primarily its mother—to respond to the infant's needs with optimal—not maximal—empathy. It is not primarily drive-based but, rather, a result of developmental disintegration, which is due, above all, to narcissistic fury aroused by damaged self-esteem (Kohut, 1977).

I shall later on examine the usefulness of the self-object concept for both the theory and treatment of schizophrenia.

Psychodynamic family studies

The first systematic investigation of the family background of schizophrenia was published by Kasanin, Knight, and Sage in 1934, who noted that 60% of the parents of 45 schizophrenic patients showed the characteristic feature of over-protection, while only a few of the parent–child relationships could be described as rejecting—certainly a finding that was not in very good accordance with prevailing psychoanalytic theories. The end of the 1950s and the early 1960s became the groundbreaking period of psychodynamic family studies. The simultaneous but largely independent works of some American teams were of central significance.

Theodore Lidz and Ruth W. Lidz published in 1949 a study of the childhood family environments of 50 schizophrenic patients, noting that 90% of the childhood homes of these patients were seriously disturbed (Lidz & Lidz, 1949). Working with his team at Yale University—with Stephen Fleck and Alice R. Cornelison as his closest co-workers—Lidz then specified his findings by analysing in close detail the families of 17 schizophrenic patients. The findings were published in several papers after the mid-1950s and were later compiled in a book, *Schizophrenia and the Family* (Lidz, Fleck, & Cornelison, 1965). The main findings can be divided as follows:

1. In 60% of the cases, one or both parents had serious personality disorders; three of the parents showed clearly psychotic features. Fathers were as badly disturbed as mothers (Lidz, Cornelison, Fleck, & Terry, 1957a). The team speaks of a *transmission of irrationality* in this context, by which they mean that from their parents children learn disturbed ways of thinking, which are thus transmitted from one generation to another (Lidz, Cornelison, Fleck, & Terry, 1958).

2. Two types of disturbed parental marriages were differentiated: *schismatic*, where the relationship between the spouses was characterized by persistent, continuous, hostile discord, leading to chronic "undercutting" of the worth of one partner to the children by the other; and *skewed*, where the family atmosphere was dictated by a disturbed dominant parent, the spouse being, in most cases, more healthy in his or her thinking but dependent, if not submissive, on the other and thus unable to counteract the dominant parent's pathogenic influence (Lidz et al., 1957b).

3. Owing to their mutual dissatisfaction, the parents made emotional demands of their children which should have been satisfied by their mutual relationship. This "violation of the generation boundaries", reflected by the emotional symbiosis between a parent and a child, often arouses panicky anxiety, being coloured by incestual and/or homosexual proclivities, which cause notable problems in the developing sexual identity of the children.

4. The fathers of psychotic male patients are often passive, offering a poor model of masculinity for sons to identify with, while the mothers are dominant and dependent upon their sons for their own emotional satisfaction and completion. The group of female

patients, on the other hand, included many fathers who turned to their daughters in a seductive manner and emotionally cold mothers with poorly developed femininity.

In the concluding part of their book (Lidz et al., 1965) Lidz and Fleck consider that schizophrenia is a kind of emotional and cognitive deficiency disease, involving serious defects or distortion of the parental nurturance and guidance as well as of the transmission of adaptive abilities in these families to their children. Lidz and his team founded their theory firmly on the psychoanalytic theory of personality development, but the findings also suggested new theories of the pathogenesis of schizophrenia that were notably more comprehensive and covered a longer developmental span than the earlier views.

Another pioneering group for family research worked at Palo Alto, California, around the well-known anthropologist *Gregory Bateson*. His starting-points lay in cybernetics and communications theory. Based on family therapy and other encounters with family members, Bateson, together with Don D. Jackson, Jay Haley, and John Weakland, developed the concept of the of the *double bind* (Bateson et al., 1965), which became widely known and referred to the phenomenon that they assumed to be the essential cause of the communication disorders resulting in schizophrenia.

The starting-point for the double bind is a situation where one individual (e.g. a parent) sends another individual (e.g. a child) messages at two different levels that are mutually incompatible. The incompatibility usually prevails between the verbal and the non-verbal, emotional communication. As an example, we can take a mother who calls the child to hug her, but as the child approaches, stiffens with an unresponsive expression, causing the child to stop, whereupon the mother says: "Well, why didn't you come?" The double bind further implies that the "victim" is unable to escape the situation, as he is dependent on the individual who makes the double bind. This is the situation between a small child and his or her parent.

The communications involving a double bind are quite confusing to the child, for whom it becomes impossible to respond to them in a satisfactory manner. As a consequence, he learns contradictory and obscure forms of communication (which may be adequate from his viewpoint in his relationship with the parent), and, even more significantly, he learns to avoid interpersonal situations because of the anxiety that they arouse and develops a tendency to withdraw into his own world. The concept of double bind also has psychodynamic dimensions and is easy to apply to relations between three individuals—such as the father, the mother, and the child in schismatic families.

In schizophrenia research, this concept has been criticized by demonstrating that the phenomena implied by it are by no means restricted to the families of schizophrenic patients. However, what may matter is the extent to which behaviour of the double-bind type dominates the growing-up atmosphere or whether it occurs as a marginal feature. Bateson himself later endeavoured to separate this concept from its original aetiological emphasis. He also pointed out that communicative conflict situations of this kind may—in addition to their negative effects—also stimulate individual creativity (Bateson, 1973).

Two teams working at the NIMH near Washington also based their work on conjoint family therapy with schizophrenic patients. Bowen (1960; Bowen, Dysinger, Brodey, & Basamania, 1961) defined the formation of an undifferentiated ego mass as being characteristic of these families. Any efforts at differentiation aroused exceptionally intense anxiety in these families. Bowen and co-workers also became known for their three-generation hypothesis, which suggested that the schizophrenic disorder develops as a consequence of progressive psychic immaturity. The team lead by *Lyman C. Wynne* developed the concepts of "pseudo-mutuality" (Wynne, Ryckoff, Day, & Hirsch, 1958) and "pseudo-hostility", describing family atmospheres that completely deny and isolate certain emotions (dissociation in Sullivan's sense). In pseudo-mutual families the parents tend to show both each other and their children a pretence of an eternally harmonious family; the expression of hostility is not accepted, and the children therefore feel an immense fear of hostile emotions arising in themselves and tend to repress and deny them. In pseudohostile families constant bickering holds the family enmeshed while emotions of endearment and affection have to be repressed or suppressed.

In collaboration with the psychologist *Margaret T. Singer*, Wynne analysed *communication deviances* (CDs) of the parents of schizophrenics. Great attention was aroused by these studies, where Singer, working on large patient population, was able to pick out with 90% accuracy the Rorschach test protocols of parents who had a schizophrenic child and those whose children were less seriously disturbed (Singer & Wynne, 1963, 1965; Wynne & Singer, 1963). The findings were based on family communication patterns, later codified into 33 or 41 categories of CDs in the parents. The findings were largely confirmed by the team's later work (Singer, Wynne, & Toohey, 1978); however, they could not be considered fully specific for schizophrenia. Along the axis of schizo-phrenia–borderline–neurosis–normal a certain continuum of communi-cation disorders for all groups of family members was found. In 1978 Wynne defined the communication studies as a research strategy ori-ented to one dimension of the interpersonal relationships—communica-tion skills being a prerequisite for enduring relatedness—that could be described as an intermediate variable between genetic endowment and the eventual symptomatic breakdown in adolescence and adulthood, "perhaps formative and contributory to acquired vulnerability", rather than a separate aetiological factor. He also emphasized that the CD scores were not directly related to the degree of clinical disturbance—for instance, they proved higher among the parents of schizophrenic patients than among their clearly psychotic children (Wynne et al., 1977). Nor did Wynne agree with the suggestions of some authors attributing the disorders of intrafamilial communication as secondary to the child's illness and his influence on the family (Wynne, 1978). Several authors (see Doane, 1978; Rund, 1986) at least partly confirmed the CD findings, a notable exception being the work published by S. R. Hirsch and Julian Leff (1971) in London.

More or less similar findings on the disturbances of the parents of schizophrenics and their growing atmosphere were also made in some European studies (Alanen, 1958; Alanen, Rekola, Stewen, Takala, & Tuovinen, 1966; Delay, Deniker, & Green, 1957, 1962; Ernst, 1956; Laing & Esterson, 1964; McGhie, 1961). The investigations we made in Finland were complementary to the American studies (esp. those of Lidz et al., 1965) in that series were larger and control groups were also studied. The atmosphere in the families could be divided into two groups: "chaotic" and "rigid". The chaotic families included parents suffering from psychosis or borderline disorders and were characterized by non-predictability of communication. The rigid families showed extremely formal and confining attitudes; the children were tightly bound by hopes and fears transmitted to them by their parents. Symbiotic relations were common, especially between schizophrenic sons and their mothers. The families of typical neurotic patients, serving as a control material, showed clearly less serious disturbances; some families with rigid fea-tures were seen, but these features were generally less serious and less dominated by parental projective identifications (Alanen et al., 1966).

The starting-points of family researchers led them to view the family situations holistically, as a *system*, rather than analysing separately the relations between certain family members. This was especially true of Bateson's team as well as of Wynne and Bowen, with their interest in communication theories and family therapy. The influence of children on their parents was also taken into account. Wynne, for example, approaches the schizophrenic child as both a disturbed and a disturbing family member. The originator of systems theory and its relevance to biological and psychological processes was von Bertalanffy (1956).

As the forms of family research and family therapy have become more advanced, the system-oriented approach has gained more and more prominence. It sees the family as a psychological whole, where all the members are continually influencing each other. Like other functional systems, the family is an open system, whose members are also in contact with the extrafamilial environment, in jobs, schools, friendship circles, and so on. An important family dynamic perception was reported by D. Jackson (1957), who realized that a certain overall psychological equilibrium prevailed in families, which was determined by the mutual psychological needs of the family members and their mutual power relations, and which also tended to resist change. He called this phenomenon *family homeostasis*. Family studies have regularly revealed an exceptionally rigid homeostasis in a notable portion of families of schizophrenic patients—although there also are forces aiming at change, which should be stimulated during the family therapy.

The works of many psychodynamically and systemically oriented family researchers and family therapists—for example, of Helm Stierlin (1972, 1974, 1976, 1983; Stierlin, Rücker-Embden, Wetzel, & Wirsching, 1977), Ivan Boszormenyi-Nagy and J. L. Framo (1965), R. D. Scott and his co-workers (Scott & Alwyn, 1978; Scott & Ashworth, 1967, 1969), as well as Mara Selvini Palazzoli with her Milan group (Selvini Palazzoli, Boscolo, Cecchin, & Prata, 1978, 1980)—have been important with regard both to the theory and to the treatment of schizophrenia, and I return to some of their findings later.

Many psychodynamic family studies have been criticized because of their methodological or conceptual weaknesses (e.g. Hirsch & Leff, 1975; Jacob, 1975; Riskin & Faunce, 1972). The question touches on the theory of science: what value should be attributed to hermeneutic research based on clinical and understanding observation as compared with the scientific–behaviouristic approach? In my opinion, case-specific psychodynamic family studies (no more than individual psychological studies) cannot be disregarded. The EE (expressed emotion) measurements—based on the number of critical comments and of signs of emotional involvement noted during the parent's interview (Brown, Birley, & Wing, 1972; Vaughn and Leff, 1976; and see the reviews by Kavanagh, 1992, and Jenkins & Karno, 1992)—tell us something of the climate in the families, but not what underlies the remarks made by patients' parents nor the psychological history of these remarks.

Some interesting empirically oriented family studies, in addition to those of Wynne and Singer, were also made. David Reiss (1971) gave complicated tasks requiring mutual communication to the families. He demonstrated that the work of "schizophrenic families" was characterized by particular sensitivity to intrafamilial consensus (consensus sensitivity), while behaviour of an opposite kind was typical of the group with character disorders (distance sensitivity).

At the University of California in Los Angeles (UCLA), Michael Goldstein and Jerry Doane conducted a study including 65 families, each with a child aged 14–15 years, who sought outpatient therapy for non-psychotic disorders (Doane, Goldstein, Miklowitz, & Falloon, 1986; Goldstein, 1985, 1987). The methods used were CD, EE, and AS ("affective style" based on the remarks made by the parent to the patient during a conjoint meeting). Fifteen-year follow-up of the youths was feasible in 45 cases. Four of the subjects were diagnosed with schizophrenia during this follow-up. All of them came from families where both parents showed "high" baseline EE and negative interactive behaviour (AS). If the families had a better-than-average initial AS-profile as well as low CD, the offspring developed no schizophrenia-spectrum disorders. The results thus indicate that families with AS and EE disorders have a greater risk of having an offspring with schizophrenia-spectrum disorders than do other families, and that the disordered intrafamilial patterns of behaviour antedates the onset of the disorder and is not a reaction to the psychotic behaviour of a schizophrenic child.

Attitudes towards psychodynamic family studies of schizophrenia have been influenced by their interpretation—even by some professionals, such as Torrey (1983)—as an accusation aimed at the parents for causing their children's illnesses. Such an interpretation of the findings of family studies is a misunderstanding. It is not implied by these studies that a parent with a distorted attitude towards his or her child is consciously causing him harm. Rather, the parents are seen as victims of their own problems, which they have been powerless to face. We can understand them just as well as their children and also find the roots of their problems in *their* own childhoods and later life. The mother of Sarah, whom I described in chapter one, is an example of this.

as of the current intrafamilial relationships, even in situations dominated by schizophrenic patients' developmental needs. The parents'
style of responding to them provides important insight, thus comple-
menting psychoanalytic research by shedding light on the reciprocal
nature of family factors influencing both normal and dysfunctional
personality development. It furnishes a wider perspective on the opportunities extant in the patient's family environment for identifications
that may promote or hinder personality development and change.

From the psychological view, schizophrenia is essentially a disorder
of ego functions. Research on the interactional family dynamics of
schizophrenics has contributed to our knowledge of the preconditions
for ego development and its disorders but has not yet been adequately
integrated with psychoanalytic theories of schizophrenia. Another important domain of knowledge that has not been adequately applied to
the psychodynamics of schizophrenia is the self psychology developed
by Kohut, which touches upon family-dynamic research in several
respects.

Five psychodynamic propositions

On this basis, I formulated five integrative propositions (Alanen,
1994):

1. Psychodynamic factors related to vulnerability to schizophrenia
    are not restricted to the early mother–child relationship; family
    research emphasizes the continuity of intrafamilial disturbances.

2. Parental personalities and their effects on parent–child relation-
    ships are critically important.

3. Primitive psychological defence mechanisms—particularly pro-
    jective identification—occur commonly in the psychodynamics
    of these family networks and tend to hinder individual develop-
    ment.

4. The persistence of symbiotic needs is typical of schizophrenia
    vulnerability. These needs are also characteristic of their transfer-
    ence relationships; self psychological viewpoints may assist un-
    derstanding what they are like: delayed needs to retain primitive
    self-object relationships but also ambivalent needs to obtain new
    self-objects that would make further personality development
    possible.

5. The overall pattern of intrafamilial relations—including the influ-
    ences of the children, with their different innate inclinations, on
    their parents—is crucially important.

Early frustrations alone are not crucial

According to the libido theory proposed by Freud and Abraham, the
core of the schizophrenic disorder consists of an abandonment of
object relations and a regression to primary narcissism—a psychological state where interpersonal relations do not yet exist. The causes
of schizophrenia should therefore also be found at this stage of development, mainly in the frustrations that have caused libidinal
development to be arrested at a stage where the libido was primarily
directed towards one's self.

As already pointed out, this notion caused the widespread therapeutic pessimism of psychoanalysts towards schizophrenia. The very
possibility of establishing a therapeutic relationship with such severely
regressed patients has been doubted, or it has been postulated that it is
possible to approach such a regressed patient only by providing non-
verbal experiences of gratification, in indirect or symbolic forms (e.g.
Tähkä, 1984). Psychotherapeutic experiences, however, have shown that
such pessimism was exaggerated, while empirical studies of small
babies (Stern, 1985) have revealed the infant's primary object orientation
and thereby disproved the idea of a primary lack of objects.

The significance of indirect oral drive gratification was obvious for
Sechehaye (1955), whose classic work, *Symbolic Realization*, promoted
significantly the bloom of psychosis therapy that began in Central
Europe in the mid-twentieth century. She offered to Renée—a seriously
regressed schizophrenic patient, who subsequently wrote about her recovery—a slice of apple across her breast, saying: " 'It's time to drink the
good milk from the apples of maman. Maman (the name used by the
patient of her therapist) will give it to you.' . . . Renée then leant herself
against my shoulder, put the apple on my breast and ate it with her
eyes shut, solemnly and full of immeasurable bliss" (p. 43). But should
we not, in this event described by Sechehaye, emphasize the patient's
experience of being understood holistically and empathically by the
therapist rather than the oral gratification in itself? My own therapeutic
experience seems to speak in favour of this interpretation.

According to psychodynamic family research (Alanen, 1958; Alanen et al., 1966; Bowen, 1960; Bowen et al., 1960, 1961; Lidz et al., 1965; Scott & Alwyn, 1978; Scott & Ashworth, 1969; Stierlin, 1972, 1976; Wynne et al., 1958), one of the most frequent findings in the families of schizophrenic patients was the presence of excessively binding or over-involved parental attitudes towards children, rather than rejection or indifference. It was also revealed that the disordered interactional relationships were continuous, as they were still apparent when the grown-up child came to treatment.

When investigating the mother–child relationships of schizophrenics in the 1950s (Alanen, 1958), I frequently encountered signs that the mutual relationship had had a poor beginning. It often happened that a mother spontaneously began to vent her bitterness, telling me that she had been anxious or depressed at that time, due to marital difficulties or other serious problems. The most extreme subgroup consisted of psychotically disturbed or emotionally inhibited mothers whose manifest disturbance had probably made it very problematic for their infants to establish their first relationship. But I also met several mothers who said that caring for the baby had been a particularly gratifying experience for them right from the beginning. It was easy to believe them, because even at the time of the study these mothers tended to have a conspicuously possessive relationship towards their now fully-grown child. The mother–child relationship thus involved psychological features that were probably related to the child's disturbed development, but in a way that the influence became obvious only when the child grew out of infancy to the phase in which he/she should have become more independent. It thus appeared that both maternal attitudes and other characteristics of family dynamics were long-acting factors that affected the patient throughout the most important years of his or her development.

It is also appropriate here to note that studies of external, measurable criteria have repeatedly revealed that children who have spent their infancy in conditions that appear particularly inadequate—not only socially, but also as regards the continuity of interpersonal relations—do not usually develop schizophrenia or other psychoses (though they may occur more commonly than normal) but develop asocial or sociopathic disorders involving lack of object constancy and inability to adjust to the surrounding community and its rules. Findings of this kind have been obtained from both adult-age follow-ups of children who have spent their infancy in such inadequate conditions (e.g. Beres & Obers, 1950;

Heston, 1966) and comparative retrospective surveys of the early environments of adults or children suffering from psychoses, neuroses and personality disorders (Malmivaara, Keinänen, & Saarelma, 1975; Stabenau, Tupin, Werner, & Pollin, 1965).

My observations of the "faithfulness" of many schizophrenic patients to their therapist (in contrast to sociopathic patients) demonstrates their ability to establish a long-term object relationship. It may have to begin at a symbiotic level, but it reflects the satisfactory aspects of the early mother–child relationship, which were also stressed by Searles (1958). Robbins (1993) also refers to an initially unintegrated part of the patient's personality, "based on loving and caring", which emerges during the psychotherapeutic process and provides fuel for his/her development.

Lidz and his co-workers (Lidz, 1992; Lidz et al., 1965) especially have criticized the schizophrenia theory of Freud and Abraham, who postulated that the level of regression categorically indicated the origin of the disorder. According to developmental psychological research also, the continuity of the environment generally seems to be more predictive for behavioural outcome than is any particular form of early infant experience (Emde, 1988).

Significance of the quality of parental personality

Although transference in individual therapy informs the therapist about patients' early relationships with parents and other significant people, the effect of these relationships on the patient's development is always reflected in the mirror of his or her own psychic processes. It has not been possible to study the other parties of the early interactional processes or the interactional system as a whole until the more recent family research.

The pioneers of ego-psychological psychoanalytic research, Hartmann, Kris, and Loewenstein, were well aware of their limited viewpoint, when, at the end of the first part of a series of papers on the formation of psychic structures, they said: "The systematic study of large numbers of life histories from birth on, based on an integration of many skills of observation, permits the greatest chance for verification or falsification of hypotheses" (1946). Hartmann (1958), when discussing his theories of early psychic development, also made it clear that his theories are applicable to the growth of an infant in an "average expectable environment". According to family studies, a child prone to schizophrenia has not grown up in such an environment.

Though psychotic or near-psychotic disorders were only diagnosed in about 10% of the parents of schizophrenic patients, personality disorders graver than neurosis are much more common among them. In a population collected by our team in Helsinki in the 1960s and analysed with both psychiatric and psychological methods, disorders that had an obvious adverse effect on ego functioning were seen in almost two thirds of the parents of typical schizophrenics—equally frequently in mothers and in fathers—whereas the corresponding figure for the parents of typically neurotic patients was about 20% (Alanen et al., 1966). In two subsequent studies conducted at Turku, which covered a more extensive and unselected population of patients first diagnosed for schizophrenia-group psychosis, similar disorders were seen in about half of the parents (Alanen et al., 1986; Räkköläinen, 1977). In the psychoanalytic frame of reference, most of these parental disorders correspond to narcissistic and borderline-level personality disorders. A certain relationship between narcissistic personalities and disposition to psychoses was also found in Mattila's (1984) study, in which these kinds of personalities were found to be more common among those who fell ill with psychoses in inter-middle age.

Serious parental personality disorders were also found in the empirical communication deviance studies by Wynne and Singer (Singer et al., 1978; Wynne & Singer, 1963; Wynne, Singer, Bartko, & Toohey, 1977). Apart from genetic factors, these disorders are significant in both the children's object relation development and in their identification processes. Concerning the latter, the effects of the distorted sense of reality of many of these parents should be emphasized. They may not be psychotic but show paranoid or other weird ways of thinking, which interfere with the development of the sense of reality in the children, who identify with them and become predisposed to thought disorders ("transmission of irrationality": Lidz et al., 1958).

Especially illuminating examples of partial or occasional "contagion" with parental psychotic delusions were shown in Anthony's (1968, 1969) field-work. He and his co-workers found out that many of the children in the families of schizophrenic parents believed in their parent's psychotic ideas occasionally, or they may have believed in them while they were at home, but not outside the home. Some school-age children were found to have personal delusional reactions, which resembled those of their parents. The disorders were communicated most effectively when the parent had paranoid psychosis or "reactive" psychosis, frequently dominated by chaotic affective attitudes. The children of autistic parents with catatonic or hebephrenic psychosis, in turn, made a more definite distinction between themselves and their psychotic parents—but often lacked adequate care. It is obvious that the transmission of disturbed modes of thinking from one generation to the next is the more effective, the fewer opportunities the children have for establishing significant interpersonal relationships outside the home.

Involvement of ego defences with interactional relations

Apart from the problems of identification, the qualitative personality disorders of the parents have other, possibly even more primary effects on the children. These arise from the fact that the psychological boundary between one's self and others—here the children—is often blurred in disorders involving ego pathology. Although few of these parents are among the seriously disturbed borderline patients we often encounter in our clinical practice—and many of them regard their disordered features as ego-syntonic—that is, they approve of them and do not regard them as signs of disturbance—they often display the kind of primitive defence mechanisms described as typical of borderline and narcissistic personalities (Kernberg, 1975). It is characteristic for many of these parents that the defectiveness of ego boundaries drives them to dominant and exploitative attitudes towards their children.

As has been emphasized by Viljo Räkköläinen and myself (Alanen, 1980; Räkköläinen & Alanen, 1982), these "lower-level" psychological defence mechanisms, though intrapsychic, also function interpersonally and influence object relations. I called this part of their defensive functions transactional defence mechanisms (Alanen, 1980). By relying on other people or fantasies about them, these defensive functions serve to protect the person from anxiety caused by internal or external threats—most typically, separation anxiety. Warding off anxiety successfully depends on whether the other person behaves in the manner expected of him or her, or whether such fantasies can be sustained. In such a dyadic relationship defensive mechanisms easily become complementary, arresting the processes of development and growth. Such parental defence mechanisms often contribute significantly to the disturbance of the child's separation–individuation development, both in early childhood and during adolescence (Räkköläinen & Alanen, 1982).

Projective identification (described above in discussing Melanie Klein's school) occupies a central position in these transactional defence mechanisms. It externalizes and transfers unconsciously both self-representations and object representations into another person, with whom one has a close relationship, and re-lives these representations through the other. Of the terms coined in family-dynamic research, projective identification is closely associated to delegating, as defined by Stierlin (1972, 1974), though delegating may take place on a more conscious level.

As emphasized by Ogden (1979), the interactional relationships characterized by projective identification are often connected with direct pressure put on the "recipient" that he or she should behave in a manner congruent with the projection.

I treated in family therapy a young man who developed a schizo-affective psychosis while in the armed service. Ever since his son's infancy, this man's father had entertained an image of him as weak and delicate and needing special protection in order to get along in life. The father himself—a highly narcissistic person—had been successful, but had had to fight continually, particularly in his youth, against his own hidden "weakness", which he did not accept and which he also associated with his image of his own father. When the son went into the army, the father kept warning him that he might become a target of ridicule from other youths: "I did not, I managed to get along well, but what about you, as you are so unable to defend yourself?" he asked. Another feature of the dynamic picture of the family was that the mother's attitude towards the son was one of close and anxious attachment. This aroused envy and aggressiveness in the father, for which his projective defence mechanism provided an unconscious outlet.

Anneli Larmo (1992), a psychoanalyst and family therapist, studied the impact of parental psychosis on the family and the children and concluded that the processes based on projective identification are crucial in the dynamics of interactional relations transmitted from generation to generation in these families—both with regard to the parents' relationships with their own parents, their spousal relationships, and their relationships with their children.

Similar interactional dynamics can be observed in other borderline-level defences. Splitting frequently serves projective identification and other projective processes. The use of omnipotence and idealization or devaluation as defences also requires the presence of another person. It is often a matter of extending oneself narcissistically at the expense of others, or of achieving the same goal by identifying with the idealized person and attributing omnipotence to him or her.

These defences engender the binding and possessive interactional relationships that have been described in the families of schizophrenic patients by Lidz and co-workers, the present writer, Stierlin, and others. They also explain the tenacity with which many parents of schizophrenic patients stick to the gratifications and notions they have developed during earlier developmental stages of their children. The parents are not conscious of the narcissistic quality of these attributes and expectations and of their importance for their own mental balance.

Transactional defence mechanisms often serve to maintain resistance in the family against the patient's development towards individuation. It would, however, be an error to view these primitive defence mechanisms in an exclusively negative light. In an empathic family therapeutic relationship they may transform into positive resources in support of the patient's development.

As has been pointed out by Volkan (1987), recent psychoanalytic literature has increasingly implied that Freud's structural theory, which focuses on the intrapsychic conflicts among ego, superego, and id, though useful for the understanding of neurotic disorders, is insufficient in the domain of serious disorders deriving from preoedipal problems—or, to use Mahler's (1968) terms, symbiotic problems or problems dating back to the separation–individuation stage. A psychoanalytic approach to the study of internalized and externalized object relations has crucially enhanced our understanding of borderline personalities and, according to Volkan, is necessary for the understanding and treatment of schizophrenia. It is also important to realize that preoedipal psychopathology is not restricted to the schizophrenic patient, but operates in other family members as well.

The need for self-objects
as the basis of symbiotic dependency

Psychotherapeutic experiences have demonstrated that the tendency towards symbiotic dependency is a characteristic feature of schizophrenic patients. It evolves even in autistically withdrawn patients as soon as contact with them has been successfully established. During the psychotherapeutic process, it is easy to observe that the symbiotic needs have their origin in these patients' prepsychotic personality development. However, opinions of the nature of these needs are not unanimous among psychoanalysts.

The term *symbiosis*, in the sense used by Mahler (1968; Mahler et al., 1975), has recently been challenged by developmental psychologists and some psychoanalytic theorists. Tähkä, among others, questions the concept, stating that "only by assuming the presence of a primary self in the baby's world of experience will it be possible to think that somebody has a delusion of his oneness with the mother" (Tähkä, 1993). It is more probable, however, that there may be a desire for a fully gratifying object—a "perfect" mother. Although the elementary foundation of the infant's self begins earlier than it had been assumed (Stern, 1985), I tend to agree with Tähkä. The goal of the transference relationship we have called symbiotic is to acquire an idealized and understanding mother (or parental) figure rather than desiring to merge with the mother and lose one's own personality (which is a significant fear among our autistic schizophrenic patients, hampering them in relating to their therapists).

In *The Analysis of the Self*, Kohut defined *self-objects* as "objects . . . which are either used in the service of the self and of the maintenance of its instinctual investments, or objects which are themselves experienced as part of the self" (Kohut, 1971, p. xiv). It follows from this definition that the relations of children to their parents are, to a significant degree, self-object relations. This is especially true of the processes whereby children build up their personalities both through the love their parents show towards them and through identification with them. The need for self-objects is not restricted to childhood, however. The mother as a self-object is followed by the father and parental substitutes (grandparents, teachers, etc.), during adolescence by peer groups and later by spouse, friends, and—when it comes to therapeutic relationships—by the therapist. "We never outgrow our need for confirmation, support, idealization and the experience of kinship, without them we wither" (Pines, 1992).

In the family, it is not only the children who use their parents as self objects. The parents also feel their children to be both individuals separate from themselves and complements to themselves, perpetuators of their lives. In this way, children are self-objects to them. It is the pathogenic intensity of this phenomenon that earmarks many families of schizophrenic patients. What we observe is an exaggerated form of normal interpersonal relationships. The narcissistic aspect of the parent–child relationship becomes pathological only if it remains disproportionately strong, foreclosing a more mature and age-appropriate relation-ship appreciating the child as a personality separate from oneself. This may be the core of the tragedy experienced by many parents of schizo-phrenic children: they typically show a tendency to live too much through their children, or an excessive need to keep the relationship unchanged, due to unconscious difficulty giving up the gratifications that children as self-objects have given them.

This emerges most cogently in many mothers of schizophrenics who have felt the early infancy of their children to be "the happiest time of their lives". Motherhood has evoked in them—as in other mothers—a new attitude towards life, and their empathic attempt to understand the representational world of a baby brings about a strongly interactional regression into a world of infantile, orally and symbiotically coloured gratifications. For the mother, satisfaction of her own frustrated needs for empathic love and care can be achieved through projective identifica-tion with the child she is caring for. But problems arise when it becomes necessary to give up these regressive gratifications and return to those more appropriate to the life of adult human beings. This had been dif-ficult for many possessive mothers of schizophrenic patients I have met. Mourning of the loss of loved object, which would have been a pre-requisite for a mature development, had been made difficult by earlier traumatic relationships and—often quite pointedly—the unsatisfactory nature of the marital relationship.

Over time, these narcissistically coloured interactional relationships become laden with increasing ambivalence attributable both to the mother's previous development and to her contemporary life situation. For example, if the marital relationship has not been satisfactory, she may have felt reluctant about having the baby in the first place. The desire to possess and control the child may thus gradually develop in a critical direction, even devaluing characteristics of the growing child. According to my studies, a dominance of this side of the ambivalence is more usual in the family background of female schizophrenic patients (Alanen, 1958).

This defective development and its causative factors are not con-scious and are not under the mother's control. These problems are traceable to the mother's own childhood. In the background of a domi-nating mother we may find a frustrated little girl seeking empathy and understanding. And quite soon there enters the father, who has also been and continues to be frustrated emotionally and has his own self-object needs directed to his wife and child.

The ambivalent quality of the relationship is even more obvious if we consider it from the child's viewpoint. It involves an increasing lack of parental empathy towards the child's own aspirations, whenever they are not accordant with the narcissistically based needs of the parent. Schizophrenic patients often tell their therapists of their parents' lack of understanding. But at the same time they also feel that they have been significant for their parents, and that the parents love them in their own way. These feelings often result in anxiety-provoking conflicts between the child's attempts at separation and independence on the one hand and the archaic feelings of love and demands for intrafamilial loyalty on the other.

Like many other pathogenic factors, the psychodynamic picture I have outlined here cannot be considered specific for schizophrenia. Similar relational configurations based on unconscious parental self-object needs are also seen in the background of less seriously disturbed patients, though generally in a less exaggerated form. And it should be emphasized that we also encounter patients whose developmental environment has been characterized by a lack of people affording sufficient self-object relationships.

As early as the 1960s, I used the term "dependency needs of the ego" (Alanen, 1968; Alanen et al., 1966) to describe an important part of the symbiotic needs directed by schizophrenic patients to their therapist. These needs could not be interpreted exclusively on the basis of Freud's libido theory. One essential component is the need of the patient's ego to find new opportunities for identification within a permanent and under-standing therapeutic relationship, which would help him or her to control better the anxieties previously felt to be intolerable. Kohut's analytic account of the quality of the self and self-objects seems to provide a solution to these problems: we are dealing with a need for an empathic self-object and a holistic—if often ambivalent—need to interact with this self-object in a way that helps the disintegrated personality to generate again its incomplete growth process through transmuting internalization. This provision should not be confused with uncritical indulgence.

Significance of the overall system of intrafamilial relations

In contemporary family research and theory, attention is focused on systemic networks of interpersonal relationships in which the individual members are constantly influencing each other. This insight was significantly pioneered by studies dealing with the intrafamilial environments of schizophrenic patients. There emerged a wide unanimity among the researchers that the psychological factors associated with the pathogenesis of schizophrenia extend far beyond the mother–child dyad. This dyad is—despite its importance for the origins of individual development—not a closed system, but inseparable from a more extensive network of psychological relations. The labelling term "schizophrenogenic mother" is, for this reason alone, inappropriate.

The different dimensions of the overall family findings include the schismatic and skewed marital relationships described by Lidz et al. (1957b), the atmosphere of "pseudo-mutuality" described by Wynne et al. (1958), and the "chaotic" and "rigid" families defined by us (Alanen et al., 1966). The significance of the family system as a whole for the vulnerability of children to psychotic disorders has also been confirmed by empirical studies. According to analysis of covariance executed by Wynne et al. (1977), the communication deviance scores, for the parents as a couple and for the mothers and fathers separately, all continued to discriminate the severity of disorder in index offspring even when the effects of major demographic variables and the parents' own severity of disorder were taken into account. However, the discriminations were most striking for the parents as pairs. Similarly, according to Tienari et al. (1994), the risk of an adopted child becoming psychotic or developing other disorders graver than neurosis showed a higher correlation with the overall rating of the family's mental health status than with separate ratings of each of the adoptive parents.

With family research, the significance of the father in the pathogenetic study of schizophrenia became apparent, in contrast to the earlier psychoanalytic conceptions. Families were found in which the core of the difficulties seemed to lie in the personality of the father: both the family study carried out by our team (Alanen et al., 1966) as well as that by Scott and Alwyn (1978) also included a noticeable number of symbiotically binding fathers. As a matter of fact, a classic example of a pathogenic father was already available from the family environment of Daniel Paul Schreber, the subject of Freud's (1911c) classical treatise on paranoid schizophrenia (see Niederland, 1984).

On deeper levels, we regularly also find disturbances in the parents' own family backgrounds, most notably in prolonged dependent relations. In some cases this is directly observable in the contemporary configuration—the parents continue to maintain pathological interdependent relationships with their own parents—often revealed by psychological fixation to frustrations they have experienced in their childhood homes. The observations on the families of patients who developed schizophrenia while married similarly demonstrate the significance of the mental health status of the whole family system (Alanen & Kinnunen, 1975). Even in these cases, predisposition to schizophrenia is usually associated with the persistence of strong symbiotic needs for dependence—now generally transferred towards the spouse.

However, psychodynamic comprehension remains very defective if it only proceeds backwards in a linear way and fails to take into account the child's innate characteristics and his or her own role in the development of intrafamilial psychodynamic patterns. Children are an inseparable part of the systemic whole. Because of the linear individual–psychological tradition, these patterns have not been considered sufficiently in the psychoanalytically oriented investigation of schizophrenia.

Theoretically, the role of the innate characteristics of children and their vulnerability have been emphasized by many psychoanalysts, for example, by Freud and Hartmann. Margaret Mahler and her co-workers (1975) illuminated this point by commenting on the differences between children in their ability to "utilize the mothering object" during their early development. This ability is influenced both by biological factors controlling the development of each child and by the evolving patterns in the interpersonal environments. However, clinically oriented investigations of the connections between these factors have remained sparse.

Robbins (1993) emphasized this topic from the standpoint of a schizophrenia psychotherapist also familiar with the findings of recent biopsychiatric research. As mentioned earlier, he describes two basic vulnerability areas: those of "organization-affinity" leading to aversion of contact with other human beings and passivity; and of problems with intensity and regulation of stimulation. These vulnerabilities are constitutional. Together with environmental influences, they lead early in life to pathological symbiotic development. Greenspan (1989) referred, on the basis of his studies of infants, to specific constitutional auditory–verbal–affective vulnerabilities that would be associated with disordered thought patterns, especially when coupled with environments that tend to confuse affective meanings at behavioural–gestural and symbolic levels.

From an integrative point of view, these ideas are very interesting, requiring further investigation. According to my experiences, however,

Robbins overemphasizes the passivity of schizophrenic patients: it fits some patients but not others. Many schizophrenic patients appear, when their therapy is progressing, to be quite active in many areas, such as studying, writing, or painting; that is, in developing their personalities outside the therapy. This points to the restricting effects of the early interpersonal environment. Other schizophrenic patients find such activities more difficult, if not impossible. Are these the patients who would, in biopsychiatric investigations, reveal deficiencies in the structure of their brains?

It is highly probable that children with structural brain abnormalities are handicapped in developing their integrative ego functions. I have suggested that they most probably also have greater than normal problems in establishing relationships with the people who act as their early self-objects (Alanen, 1994, 1997). Such a hypothesis corresponds to the viewpoint presented by Robbins (1993) with regard to the primary disturbances of "organization-affinity" of schizophrenic patients, leading to an aversion to contact with other human beings. Such infants may also tend—as soon as they have managed to set up an interactional relationship—to become intensely attached to their self-objects, rendering their development at the separation–individuation phase more problematic than usual.

The formation of early self-object relationships is an interactional process that depends on both participants. Thus the people acting as self-objects (mainly the mother) are affected by the interaction and may tend to maintain or continue a symbiotic relationship with children who seem to demand or seek it. From a systemic point of view, it is an interactional phenomenon that is influenced by *both* the qualities of the infant *and* the tendency of the mother—or of other self-objects—to develop symbiotic relationships.

Findings of larger cerebral ventricles of the schizophrenic co-twins among monozygotic twin pairs discordant for schizophrenia (Reveley et al., 1982; Suddath et al., 1990) may be related to the prolonged symbiotic needs of children. Tienari (1963), when studying discordant identical male twins, found an increased predisposition to schizophrenia among those who were more passive than their brothers and had therefore remained more dependent on their mothers. Onstad, Skre, Torgersen, and Kringlen (1994) found that schizophrenic probands were more overprotected by parents (especially fathers) than were their discordant monozygotic or same-sexed dizygotic co-twins. Are such findings related?

In the majority of schizophrenics with no known structural brain abnormalities, the disturbed development seems to be rooted in the interpersonal realm, though the predisposing role of the children's genetic factors should not be overlooked. We should once again remember the systemic cycle: not only do the parents affect their children, but the children also influence their parents, and adult schizophrenics impose serious stress on relatives as well as the reverse.

Prepsychotic personality development

Descriptions of the prepsychotic personality

Findings on the prepsychotic personalities of schizophrenic individuals have revealed two opposite poles: a tendency to withdraw from contacts, which is often called schizoid, and a symbiotic need for reliance. Most patients fit somewhere on the continuum between these two extremes. The schizoid tendency to avoid contacts and to turn inward into one's own mental life is particularly notable in the most typical forms of schizophrenia. For example, 61% of the 142 schizophrenic patients examined by Dein (1964) in Denmark had this kind of personality.

In the family study conducted by our team, which covered both the patients and their parents and siblings (Alanen et al., 1966), 20 of the 30 typical schizophrenic patients had shown autistic, withdrawing tendencies prior to the psychosis. Only 12 of them had clearly shown such tendencies before school age, while the remaining 8 became more clearly withdrawn at puberty. We also noted that the patients, even prepsychotically, were regularly more markedly dependent on their parents than were their healthier siblings.

Such findings are quite understandable in the light of the need–fear dilemma proposed by Burnham et al. (1969). The autistic–schizoid tendency may hence be seen as a consequence of the increasing anxiety felt in relation to other people, especially at puberty, and an attempt to solve the need–fear dilemma by avoiding social relationships. Underneath this tendency may hide an ability to establish symbiotic relationships.

According to Mednick and Schulsinger (1968), hypersensitive prepsychotic personalities, who are apt to withdraw from interpersonal relationships into their inner psychological world, were typical particularly of patients with milder schizophrenic disorders. They emphasized that weak impulse control, impaired ability to concentrate, and incipient thought disorders were typical prepsychotic features in those who later developed serious schizophrenic psychoses.

An especially interesting report of the personalities of later schizophrenics is the follow-up based on the prospective U.K. national birth cohort comprised of a random sample of 5,362 births in England, Scotland, and Wales during the week of March 3–9, 1946 (Jones, Rodgers, Murray, & Marmot 1994); 43 years later, 30 cases of schizophrenia were found, corresponding to a risk of 0.63%. The statistically significant prepsychotic predictors of schizophrenia included later development of walking and more speech problems than controls, and the continuity of an aloof, solitary habit, avoiding social interaction. However, there was no grossly abnormal speech or motor behaviour in adolescence. At 15 years, teachers rated these youngsters as being more anxious than the others in social situations ($p = 0.003$), unrelated to intelligence quotient. On the other hand, there was no evidence of increased antisocial or aggressive behaviour, nor of conspicuous differences between girls and boys. No significant sociodemographic predictors were found, but health visitors' ratings indicated that more mothers of the future schizophrenics showed worse than average general understanding and management of their children when the child was 4 years old ($p = 0.02$). The British study thus confirms the theories of adult schizophrenia as a developmental disorder, the origins of which may be found in early life. The schizoid avoidance of social contacts dominates the picture of the prepsychotic personality.

However, the presence of schizoid gestures does not mean that the person in question should necessary become schizophrenic. According to a recent study (McGorry et al., 1995) so-called prodromal features of schizophrenia (much the same as the features typical of schizotypal personality according to DSM–IV) are "extremely prevalent" among older adolescents and unlikely to be specific for subsequent schizophrenia.

Early self-object relationships in schizophrenia

The experiences connected with early self-objects crucially programme the development of our psychological functions. This process is not restricted within the psychological sphere, but also involves the biological level, influencing the functional development and integration of neural networks.

In early infancy, the need for self-objects (mother or her substitutes) is absolute, biologically and socially. But these needs are not restricted to infancy: the self-object relationships continue throughout the developmental cycle. Children build their personalities both through empathic approval that parents provide for their emotions and actions, and identification with parents.

In the development of a schizophrenia-prone individual, these processes have remained deficient. The disorders of self-object relationships that contribute to the vulnerability to schizophrenia seem to have dissimilar mutual weighting in different cases. On one end of a continuum are those patients who suffered from a poor beginning of their early self-object relationships; on the other end are those patients with a confusingly binding propensity of these relationships. The common denominator is the lack of self-objects' sufficiently empathic responses to support individual development.

It is of vital importance to understand that most of those falling ill with schizophrenia have not been rejected children, even if we do find such persons occasionally. Many have been too important for their parents as self-objects. This is felt by the child as a demand for compelling—though ambivalent—internal loyalty, which makes him comply to the parents' needs, even when his/her own developmental challenges would require psychological separation from them. Conflicts in which they are caught when the problems become critical may be very anxiety- and guilt-laden and have a direct connection with the onset of psychosis. In this respect, the situation of directly rejected children is often less deleterious because it is possible for them to vent their anger on parental figures more directly, with fewer guilt feelings.

The following example is an extreme one, but it serves to illustrate the pattern of mutually disordered self-object relations between a mother and a child.

The patient, a 17-year-old schoolboy, who was admitted with symptoms of severe hebephrenic schizophrenia, was the only child in his family. His appearance and behaviour were characterized by helplessness, disorganization, and child-like regression on the one hand, and extremely intense anxiety with catatonic, stereotypic praying and sudden outbursts of aggression on the other.

The family situation was skewed. The patient's father was a hardworking and relatively successful man, who was, however, passively dependent on his wife. A few years before the onset of the son's illness, the father had had a somatic attack of illness, which had impaired both his health and his family-dynamic role. The patient's mother was an extremely possessive person, who viewed things strictly in terms of black or white. Her overriding ideal was goodness and compliance; she praised both of her "boys" (her husband and son) for being good. Expressions of anger were almost completely prohibited in the family, and an atmosphere of pseudomutuality prevailed. The patient had submitted to the mother's expectations: he had been a good boy and had avoided everything evil. At school he had been considered a well-behaved boy who was more childlike than his age-mates. During the year preceding his illness, he had become "absent-minded" and reserved, and his school performance had fallen off. He was hospitalized because of increasing anxiety, which had resulted in bouts of violence completely unexpected by the family.

The patient was admitted at a time when the family-oriented approach was not yet a regular part of our therapeutic practice. The possessive attitude shown by the mother during her visits on the ward, however, led to an attempt at family therapy. The need for a family approach was also apparent in the light of the patient's problems during leaves, where his behaviour was unpredictably aggressive. He even attacked his mother physically. In the joint family sessions the mother's attitude was reserved; for her, the most important thing was to make the son understand that he must not be angry. The father's attitude during the therapy sessions was passive and compliant with his wife, while the patient remained quiet.

The mother had been 5 years old when her father died, and she had then been reared by her maternal aunt. She praised her foster-mother as having been an "extremely good" and excellent person, denying all of her possible disappointments and frustrations. Religious ideals had been important in her upbringing, and she still held to them. She indulged her son like a little baby and expected him to be unquestioningly obedient to her own ideals. The idealization of her foster-mother presumably helped the patient's mother to deny her disappointment and resentment at being abandoned. Her possessive attitude reflected both the lack of boundaries between her and the other family members and, quite probably, her extreme need to rely on them and keep them close to herself. She felt as if her son—and actually even her husband—were part of herself, and the son's aggressive behaviour therefore aroused both fear and intense internal anxiety in her. The son's aggression towards his mother only became manifest during the psychosis, simultaneously raising intense feelings of guilt in him.

In the therapy of a family of this kind, the most important thing is to listen to and understand the mother. This is even more urgent than supporting the son's attempt at separation—which can be postponed. The therapist and his supervisor (myself) did not realize this well enough at the time, and the therapy was terminated quite early, as the mother claimed a need to go into the countryside to take care of her foster mother.

Searles (1961) emphasized that the symbiotic relation between the mother and the child persists when the mother (or other self-object) is unable to recognize *consciously* her need to use the child as a complement to herself and is therefore incapable of giving him up. She remains incapable of mourning the abandonment she suffered and her early frustrations reinvoked by giving up the care of the child, when the child begins to show needs for individuation.

Importance of the period of adolescence

Despite the crucial significance of the early development, the process of individuation must be seen as a long-term developmental process that continues throughout childhood and adolescence, culminating in adulthood. Successful growth into adulthood requires that the self-object relationships are gradually—never completely—replaced by more mature object relationships. It is characteristic of such relationships that one experiences others as individuals separate from oneself, with goals of their own—that is, there are clearly differentiated internal self- and object-representations. Furthermore, the relationship with others is based on equality—at least in a relative sense—and concern for each other's needs, and not on self-centredness, which is inherently typical of the needs applied to self-objects seeking support for one's own actions and emotional balance.

The problems often culminate when the individual approaches the developmental challenges of adolescence. These include control of awakened sexuality and finding a sexual partner, gaining independence from one's parents, and finding one's place in the community through occupational competence. All this is difficult for an individual whose personality is inadequately organized, who is excessively (and often mutually) dependent on his/her parents, and who finds it difficult to establish relationships with age-mates because of delayed psychological development and consequent liability to disappointments.

The need for self-objects outside the home involving objects of identification and sources of approval is great at this stage, and the more acute the need is, the weaker the existing basis for adult growth. A successful, or unsuccessful, course of adolescent development is often crucially significant for the individual's ability to avoid—or not avoid—the risk of schizophrenic psychosis. As Sullivan (1956) pointed out, issues of self-esteem are extremely significant during this developmental process. Successful extrafamilial interpersonal experiences in adolescence may lead to a more balanced development and a diminished risk of psychosis. On the other hand, the development takes a more negative turn when frustrations in interpersonal relationships lead to passivity and withdrawal and the traumas to self-esteem are counteracted by internal narcissistic fantasies.

Problems dating back to the oedipal situation often add to the prepsychotic conflicts of schizophrenic patients, sometimes quite concretely. Lidz and his co-workers (1965) emphasized that the parent–child relationships in these families—apart from the children being easily drawn into the contradictory, often double-bind-like relationship between their parents—frequently also show incestuous tendencies and/or tensions, which are enhanced by the unsatisfactory quality of the parental marital relationship. They may be either hetero- or homosexual, and they often remain latent and unconscious. Even so, they give rise to intense anxiety at puberty, interfering with normal age-appropriate development.

The difficulties of establishing heterosexual relationships with age-mates are thus often aggravated by both the double binds with the parents and—partly as a consequence—the adolescent's or young adult's underdeveloped personality and the anxiety aroused by the recognition of sexual drives.

One female patient included in my family study was said to have been attached to her father in her childhood, often sitting willingly in his lap, being, however, afraid of his hot temper. When she was 14, she began to develop a powerful dislike for the father. The repulsion was associated with the fear that the father would be looking at her with erotic interest. It was difficult for her to be in the same room with him. Gradually she became more and more reclusive also in her social relations. In fact, there must have been something exceptional in the father's attitude, of which the following event is an indication. Once, when the patient was 16, she had been berrying in the forest. The father heard voices of drunken men from the forest and was out of his senses for fear that his daughter would be raped, and, when she came home, he gave her a beating with a cane, even though the patient had not even seen the men.

The marital relationship of the parents seemed to be quite unhappy, which had increased the problems of both spouses. The father was morbidly jealous, scolding his wife, for example, for "excessive cheerfulness" in social situations. The mother was agonized and insecure and felt guilt, trying hard to repress her aggressive feelings towards the father. Sex life was repulsive for her.

The onset of the psychosis, at the age of 25, was sudden, accompanied by strong "hypnotic" ideas of influence, which were associated with a man who had been sitting next to her at concerts (both had season tickets). The patient was beset by strong fears, had "surprising experiences of close ideational communications", and felt that the man took sexual control of her through them. The acute phase was followed by a strongly autistic, disintegrated, outwardly inhibited psychotic state, behind which there was hiding a strong, painful, psychotic ideational world, dominated by "approaching" men and women, including the father. The problems that had been troubling the patient ever since puberty and were traceable back to the oedipal situation, thus emerged in a new form when she became psychotic.

Factors precipitating the onset of psychosis

According to the simple diathesis–stress theory, propounded especially by genetically oriented researchers (Rosenthal, 1970; Zubin & Spring, 1977), the factors precipitating schizophrenic psychosis are nonspecific, consisting of both psychic and physical stress factors that prove intolerable to the patient. Psychodynamic developmental research shows this notion to be superficial. Even the significance of precipitating factors becomes understandable in the light of patients' life histories—both the evolution of their interpersonal relations and their intrapsychic personality development.

Physical precipitating factors

When the precipitating factors include physical stress, they can be considered relatively nonspecific. This is the case when, for example, the patient becomes psychotic during a fever. But even in these cases the patient seems to have been psychologically predisposed to schizophrenia, with topically diminished stress tolerance.

In some other cases physical and psychological precipitating factors combine in such a way that the nature of the physical stress is more specifically related to a psychological vulnerability. This is frequently the case in schizophreniform puerperal psychoses. Psychodynamically the birth of a baby has frequently been a problematic event, arousing ambivalent feelings in the mother because of her life situation or because becoming a mother has involved a particular psychological strain due to problems connected with the relationship to her own mother.

These problems are sometimes shown in patients' delusions. A patient of mine, who had previously repressed the problems of her difficult mother relationship, developed after her first delivery a puerperal schizophreniform psychosis. She then believed that her own mother had tried to strangle her as a baby. The patient had been an unwanted baby for her then elderly mother, who was living in exceptionally dire conditions at the time. She was greatly helped by psychotherapeutic working-through of the problems of her early mother relationship.

Similar specific psychodynamics may also be observable in postoperative psychoses, often related to the patient's unconscious fears of castration or annihilation. The schizophreniform psychoses manifested during physical stress are frequently—though not always—benign and subside relatively quickly, as the patient recovers strength.

Another group of patients' psychoses are related to the use of *drugs*, especially *cannabis*, and alcohol, though in such a way that they cannot be classified as toxic psychoses. The effect of drugs or alcohol in these cases is best understood as having brought into consciousness anxiety-evoking psychic tendencies intolerable to the weak ego structure, such as homosexual drives. Also, the use of drugs in itself may be an indication of anxiety or lability of the psychic balance. Recently, several reports have described schizophrenic psychoses precipitated by the use of cannabis (Allebeck et al., 1993; Hjort & Ugelstad, 1994; Linszen et al., 1994). The number of such patients seems to be increasing in urban environments.

Psychological precipitating factors

The onset of schizophrenic psychosis is typically associated with problems experienced in adolescence or early adulthood. As pointed out earlier, the precipitating factors are seldom very conspicuous, because they are related to problems or developmental tasks experienced by all young people.

Psychoanalytic researchers have emphasized the *increased drive pressure* at puberty. Maturation of genital sexuality strengthens the needs emanating from the drive base of the personality in a way that appears uncontrollable to the weak ego, which therefore disintegrates, regressing to the narcissistic level and abandoning aspirations towards external objects. This is true of both sexual and aggressive impulses. When Freud (1924a) defined psychosis as a consequence of a conflict between the ego and the outer world, he meant that the ego, attacked by intolerable anxiety due to frustrations of the drive-based aspirations towards the outer world, gives in, abandons reality, and creates a new, delusional internal reality, which, in a psychotic, projective form, is felt partly to coincide with and replace external reality.

Later, psychoanalytic research emphasized the most central early anxiety, called *annihilation anxiety* or *dedifferentiation anxiety* (e.g. Tähkä, 1993). It is the deepest fear of the human being—a threat of death or at least psychological death. It finds its first expression in the baby's vague fear of being rejected, in a state of helplessness from which there seems to be no salvation. At the oedipal stage it is associated with the emergence of castration anxiety. According to Kohut (1977), annihilation anxiety becomes manifest later in life, whenever the individual experiences heavy narcissistic offences or losses of important self-object relations. It is not the only reaction caused by such experiences: depending on the ego's resources, there may alternatively also develop an "empty depression", associated with a feeling that life lacks any purpose, or a rage resulting in violence.

Viljo Räkköläinen (1977), a colleague in Turku, examined the factors precipitating the onset of psychosis in 68 new patients. He pointed out that in most cases the onset of psychosis was preceded by the beginning of an important transitional phase in the patient's life. He especially emphasized two specific areas of affected psychodynamics: narcissistic traumas, or offences to self-esteem—for example, feelings of failure or rejection in love—and unsuccessful attempts to detach oneself from supportive relations, usually with parents, but occasionally transferred to other people. His conclusions combine the intrapsychic and interpersonal viewpoints. Individuals who develop schizophrenia-type psychoses tolerate frustrations and life changes poorly, because they have established or retained as their support concrete unions or bonds with people (serving as self-objects), who are vitally important for them as surrogates for the deficiency of their internal psychological structures. The mental representations pertaining to these self-objects are often of archaic, omnipotent quality, which in itself tends to predispose to frustrations and is particularly painful when the self-object relationship is lost. Räkköläinen also talks about *protective interpersonal structures*, which help to keep together the personalities of many schizophrenia-prone individuals by providing them with the support they need and confirmation for their psychological existence. Protective structures of this kind were also found to be significant for the prognosis of psychotic patients (Räkköläinen, Salokangas, & Lehtinen, 1979).

An insight into this kind of psychodynamics may best help one to understand why such "ordinary" psychosocial stressors as leaving home, migration, and so forth may pave the way to psychotic breakdown. The most obvious psychological precipitating factors consist of *experiences of loss*, as upon the death of someone who has served as an important supportive self-object, or other separation from such a person, or upon a change of the quality of the self-object relations due to the latter's somatic illness, for example. Hence the onset of serious schizophrenia in patients undergoing early adolescence has occasionally a clear—if not necessarily immediate—connection with the death or divorce of a parent.

A girl included in my family study samples fell ill with catatonic schizophrenia at the age of 16. She had been very attached to her father, whom, however, she had lost through death two years earlier. After that, her relationship with the mother—always strained—became increasingly aggressive, at times with violent outbursts. The outbreak of the patient's psychosis was acute and confusional. She had religious experiences, feelings of "emancipation and disappearance of inhibitions", but also end-of world experiences and ideas of reference. She went in a psychotic condition to deliver a speech on her father's and Marshal Mannerheim's graves. In the hospital she declared that all her movements and feelings—like her hate towards the mother—are compelled by an outside force. It also became clear that she had had her first ideas of reference soon after the father's death.

In some other cases the experience of separation may be due to the patients' concrete attempts at leaving home, or situations where there is a change in the external conditions, such as the person moving away to study or into military service.

Although precipitating factors of this kind may be easily discernible, they are often psychodynamically complex and difficult to interpret, owing, for example, to double-bind–type family attitudes. I experienced this poignantly when I was present as a consulting observer in the family therapy session of a first-admitted schizophrenic patient.

The patient was a 26-year-old woman who had become psychotic soon after she had left home and moved to live alone in a flat. She was uncontrollably aggressive towards her parents and vaguely accused them of treachery. Unlike her younger brothers, who were still living at home, she had even previously frequently vented her partly veiled dissatisfaction with her family, which had seemed disruptive in the prevailing "harmonious" atmosphere of pseudomutuality. The patient had, however, tried to control her aggressive feelings and had usually apologized to her parents as soon as she had calmed down.

When her moving away from home was discussed with the family, it turned out that the initiative had been hers, and she had intended to start a "life of her own". The mother, who was the dominant figure in the family, had assumed practical responsibility in the matter and had arranged a small flat for her. It was not considered a particularly good deal by the daughter, but she accepted it because the flat was located relatively close to her parents' home. To the patient's surprise, however, the family, without preparing her in any way, moved soon afterwards to a remote suburban locality. It was after this incident that she became psychotic.

The family therapist asked the patient whether she had felt disappointed when the family moved away. "I guess so", she replied. At that, the mother burst out crying, saying that she visited her daughter frequently and even stayed overnight in her flat when doing night shifts, as she worked quite near. The patient also began to show signs of anxiety and started consoling her mother. Yet it hardly escaped anybody that the mother, while arranging for the daughter's flat, had also considered the family's future moving plans. There ensued an oppressive silence, which was broken by the father, who remarked that the lamp on the ceiling was hot.

Despite the patient's attempt at separation, her relationship with her mother was still dominated by ambivalent dependence. She stated emphatically that her mother was the person to whom she told everything. The mother, in turn, seemed to appeal to her daughter, exploiting the guilt feelings caused by her own anxiety. It also turned out that the patient did not have many contacts outside the family, and that her chances for an independent life were therefore not very good.

After several months of family therapy, the patient started individual therapy. She stayed on in her flat, but, after recovering from the acute stage of the psychosis, developed a reclusive personality, living in a partly psychotic world of her own imagination, which she abandoned only gradually as her therapy proceeded.

Of the life changes taking place at a more internal level, *falling in love* (usually in a way characterized by strong symbiotic features) and the consequent disappointments and injuries to self-esteem probably constitute the most common factor precipitating psychosis. There may be cases of remote love at an imaginary level, but there are also instances of actual dating with attempts to establish an interpersonal relationship at a more adult level than previously. "Symbiotic" reliance and adherence—with an underlying desire to find a self-object relation—and vulnerability due to a developmental lag and childishness compared with the partner are factors that often precipitate failure. From the viewpoint of the patient's self-esteem, the investment is greater than usual and the wound thus inflicted all the more severe.

Even in so-called *homosexual panic*—which refers to the severe anxiety that may be released by the recognition of intense and conflicting emotions felt for a friend of one's own sex—the desire for a self-object usually plays a central role. The idealized friend towards whom the emotions are directed is felt to be a more developed idol or object for identification, who will help to consolidate one's own masculinity or femininity. This is an important underlying factor in an anxiety-evoking attachment leading to intense feelings of jealousy, which ends up in a panic, as the sexual components of the relationship threaten to become conscious.

Precipitating factors of this kind are especially common among young people. But even among people living in a couple relationship, the contradictory feelings involved in falling in love may precipitate psychosis. And the manifestation of psychosis is even more common upon rejection by the partner (Alanen & Kinnunen, 1975).

But it is easy to understand that an irreconcilable conflict between inner imagery and the external reality may lead to gradual isolation from concrete human relationships and to omnipotent phantasies, which are increasingly removed from reality. In such a regressive development, the finding of external precipitating factors may prove to be very difficult.

The onset of psychosis

The connections of schizophrenia with both psychological and physiological events is most obvious at the onset of the psychosis. Especially an acute onset of a psychotic state involves intense psychic anxiety and/or agitation, which is also evident at the physiological level. This development reaches its culmination in catatonic states, which—whether agitated or stuporous—appear to deny the possibility of psychological contact even more than do the other schizophrenic states, though their ultimate prognosis is generally good.

Even when the psychosis develops gradually and the clinical status is dominated by negative symptoms and progressive isolation, the early stages of the process may involve recurrent culminations or leaps, with symptoms of anxiety followed by a deterioration of the patient's condition.

Although the disorganization of psychic functions manifested as psychosis has been investigated from several viewpoints by physiologists, pharmacologists, and biochemists, all that we actually know about the associated biological processes is based on assumptions and postulations.

The *dopamine hyperactivity theory*, based on the observation that the effect of neuroleptic drugs is related to an inhibition of the dopaminergic (esp. D2) nerve paths in the central nervous system (Carlsson & Lindqvist, 1963; Snyder, 1981) is, at least in its simple form, contradicted by the conflicting PET (positrone emission tomography) findings of the density of dopamine receptor sites in the brains of drug-naive schizophrenics (Farde et al., 1990; Hietala et al., 1994, 1995; Martinot et al., 1990; Wong et al., 1986). Seeman (1993) tried to interpret the controversies regarding the differences between the studies with respect to their inclusion of the D4-type dopamine receptor sites in their findings, depending on the radioligand used.

The hypothesis proposed by Marta and Arvid Carlsson (1990) is one example of more complex theories. The central idea is that schizophrenia may primarily be a consequence of the inadequate functioning of glutaminergic pathways resulting in an excessive or uncontrollable flood of information in the cortex. Summarizing their views, the Carlssons write: "Schizophrenias may be looked upon as a syndrome induced by neurotransmitter imbalance in a feedback-regulated system, where dopamine and glutamate play a crucial role in controlling arousal and the processing of signals from the outer world to the cerebral cortex via the thalamus." However, apart from dopamine hyperactivity or glutamate hypoactivity, many other neurotransmitters may also contribute.

Ciompi (1991, 1994), when striving for an integrative explanation, refers more generally to a functional overload of the central nervous system and a disturbed balance, which comes about through the "mutually escalating interaction between the constantly declining ability to adapt and the increasing psychosocial or biologically based emotional–cognitive stressors". These may correspond to normal developmental tasks as well as to hormonal changes, or to the use of drugs. At a critical moment, the psychological–biological system is ultimately jolted out of balance, becomes decompensated, and is forced into a new, structurally disorganized functional constellation, which is psychotic. Ciompi thinks that this development can be understood by means of chaos theory.

In itself, the notion of a disorder of the physiological regulatory mechanism seems quite plausible, even to a psychologically oriented researcher. It is of interest, then, how "tied up" the disorders of the integrative functions are in their biological base and/or how easy it is to influence them psychologically, by means of a therapeutic relationship—or other human relationships—increasing the feeling of safety in the panic-ridden individual. According to my experiences, schizophrenic patients differ much from each other even in this respect.

Pao's five steps

Ping-Nie Pao of the Washington School, in his book *Schizophrenic Disorders* (1979), presented an interesting classification of the development and subsequent course of schizophrenic psychosis as five successive stages or steps, which he viewed from a holistic psychodynamic viewpoint. Pao proposed the following five steps:

1. Certain events in the life situation activate a previously repressed conflict, where erotic or aggressive impulses play an important role.

2. The conflict causes the individual to feel exceptionally intense anxiety, which Pao calls "organismic panic", referring to Mahler's term "organismic distress" (Mahler, 1968). The tension involved in the panic is uncontrollable for the ego and becomes manifest at the physiological level; it is comparable to the uncontrollable ten-

sion of a little infant that can only be relieved by the presence of another person (the mother).

3.   The panic state, which is a relatively brief though often recurrent affective experience, results in a temporary deactivation of all ego functions, an internal catastrophe or shock.

4.   Recovery from the shock involves regression of ego functions, with the internal goal of finding a "best possible solution" at a more primitive level of psychological organization. This leads to activation of more archaic defences as well as such primitive ways of self preservation that imply a loss of previous psychic viability, drive neutralization, and personality organization. A personality change typical of schizophrenia ensues.

5.   Psychotic symptom formation serves the purpose of finding the "best possible solution".

Volkan (1990) agrees with Pao to a considerable extent but points out—quite justifiably—that the latter gives inadequate attention to the schizophrenic patient's internalized object relations. According to Volkan, the purpose of psychotherapy is to activate a recovery process in an order that is the opposite of Pao's stages. A particularly important and critical stage of the therapy is the new, now victorious, return to the representational contents that originally brought about the psychotic panic.

It is interesting to ask to what extent the onset of a psychosis can be seen as having meaningful developmental goals aiming at better adjustment. This possibility has been suggested by some psychotherapeutic researchers of schizophrenia, such as Sullivan (1924).

Larmo discussed this question from a systemic point of view in her monograph on parents' psychosis (1992). She pointed out that a goal orientation of this kind, the "dynamics of re-birth", could be seen in cases where the illness was due to a conflicting triadic relationship. In these cases, the psychosis is an indication of the family's developmental crisis at a certain stage of life—the stage when the children grow up—showing that the intrafamilial relations had become stuck at a critical juncture. The psychosis and its influence on the family members could be conceived of as an attempt to re-activate development. The other group analysed by Larmo, which typically suffered from symbiotic dyadic relationships, showed no signs of such meaningfulness but was exclusively dominated by the "dynamics of regression".

The psychosis of an adolescent attempting to separate from his or her family or to establish an age-appropriate heterosexual relationship can certainly also be interpreted as a developmental effort that fails, resulting in the onset of the psychosis. Relatively few young people, however, have sufficient personal resources—as did Sullivan (1924), who is said to have experienced his own crisis at adolescence as a developmental victory. It is more often the case that problem solution at a psychotic level leads to a regressive representational world. Even when the psychosis is over, it is still felt to be a loss that further impairs self-esteem. Things may, however, turn out differently if the patient at this stage receives psychotherapeutic support for his or her development.

Is schizophrenia a uniform illness?
Integrating remarks

I have not been able to identify any one single causative factor that would be specific for schizophrenia—that is, would always be present in its background and would also be restricted to it. Instead, I have presented several factors contributing to the emergence of schizophrenia.

My conclusion is that the causes of schizophrenia are multifactorial, both multi-faceted and multi-layered. These factors are differently weighted in different cases. Clinically, schizophrenic conditions can be described as a *heterogeneous continuum*, with severe psychoses due to extensive and deep-rooted developmental disorders at one extreme and prognostically benign, reversible psychotic states at the other.

Since even the aetiologic subfactors are differently weighted in different cases, some researchers have been ready to postulate that schizophrenia is actually a group of diseases consisting of two—or even several—disorders with different aetiologies. Is it possible, for example, to separate cases of schizophrenia that involve structural brain abnormalities from others as a sub-group with definite organic causes? There are also clinical reasons for such assumptions because negative symptoms are more frequent in this type of patients than in the others, and their prognosis is also poorer than the average. But even here the boundaries are blurred rather than clear, and not even the symptomatological differences are sufficient to permit a precise clinical discrimination among patient groups. This becomes even more obvious when we recall that corresponding brain abnormalities are found in some schizoaffective and bipolar affective disorders (Hauser et al., 1989; Rieder et al., 1983).

•   The theory that schizophrenia would comprise two or more different disorders is not new. Even Sullivan (1954) proposed, based on his psychotherapeutic experiences, that "schizophrenia simplex"—a clinical condition totally restricted to negative symptoms—should be separated from the psychologically based "essential" schizophrenia as an organic illness process appropriately called dementia praecox.

Among the newer conceptions, the hypothesis of two types of schizophrenia by Crow (1985) may be mentioned. Type I is characterized by the predominance of positive symptoms and would, according to him, be due to an overactivity of the dopaminergic system. Type II is based on cellular loss in the brain structures and shows predominantly negative symptoms. Still, Crow does not regard these types of disorder as totally separate entities, but, rather, as different manifestations of the same disease, which might overlap.

Furthermore, even if the predisposition to negative symptoms is probably influenced by biopsychiatric factors—to variable degrees in different patients—psychological factors contribute to their appearance. Strauss, Rakfeldt, Harding, and Lieberman (1989) enumerated as many as ten different factors that may cause the patient to withdraw into isolation dominated by negative symptoms, some of them being the psychic suffering due to the recurrence of positive symptoms, the loss of hope and self-esteem, the presence of guilt feelings for previous psychotic behaviour, the threat evoked by social situations, and the effects of institutionalization, including the stigma of being diagnosed as schizophrenic.

As far as I can see, it is more appropriate to speak of a heterogeneity in the case-specific weighting of aetiological factors than to assume that the aetiological factors might be completely different in the different cases. Along similar lines, a proposal for an integrated three-dimensional (genetic, brain-damage, psychosocial) aetiological view of the schizophrenias was presented by the Swedish psychoanalyst Johan Cullberg (1993a, 1993b).

It is interesting to note, from an integrative viewpoint, that the biomedical findings indicating the heterogeneity of schizophrenia and the psychoanalytic theories show some parallels. The group of schizophrenias with the poorest prognosis involves most structural brain anomalies, and patients with this diagnosis suit the psychoanalytic deficiency theory, which assumes schizophrenia to be due to a massive and early disorder of personality development. The prepsychotic development of this group of patients is clearly more seriously disturbed than that of those patients—often with a better prognosis—whose psychosis is more obviously associated with topically exacerbated conflict situations (and who are thus compatible with the notion of the psychodynamics of schizophrenia based on conflict theory).

The causal chain between the predisposing biological factors and their effect at the psychological level is a question that has not yet been solved, or even thoroughly investigated. According to most researchers, the answer probably lies in the functional impairment of the integrative information processes between the different brain centres. It is assumable that biological and psychosocial factors are here closely interrelated. Stephen Fleck (1992) is one of the proponents of such a theory. Fleck refers to a "co-evolution" of the neurophysiological organization and the family (social) interactions, and he believes that schizophrenia is best conceptualized "as a mixed maldevelopment of the neurological, psychological and social dimensions of personality, rooted in early or inborn weakness of neuromodular organization which is compromised further by aberrant and contradictory social inputs". This leads to a multifaceted developmental aberration, including deficient heterarchical (Grigsby & Schneider, 1991) neural organization, transmitter instability and inhibition failures, unstable, poorly structured affective–cognitive systems of reference (vulnerable premorbid personality, "weak ego"), deviant information processing, abstract conceptualization, and relationship difficulties.

The interrelated processes proposed by Fleck (1992) as well as others (including this author) should—and probably will—be one of the crucial targets of future schizophrenia research. And the scope of research should not be restricted to the development of vulnerability, but should also include a comprehensive examination of the effects of the on-going illness on the bio–psycho–social dimensions.

Of the family-dynamic interactional factors, I have emphasized the importance of both the earliest stage of development and the persistence of the disturbed context. The multi-layered aetiological factors make up a temporal continuum in which the development during the earliest years and during puberty and adolescence—"the second separation–individuation phase"—are of the most crucial significance. Stern's (1985) theory, which indicates that the developmental stages begin at different times but continue as parallel psychological processes of development, seems to agree well with this notion. From the individual–psychological point of view, the problems pertaining to dyadic relationships appear to be of central importance, but they should be seen as part of a larger, systemically functioning whole. I demonstrate in chapter five the importance of a broader systemic view to be applied when the treatment of a schizophrenic patient is planned and put into practice.

The classical studies by Wynne and Singer (Singer et al., 1978; Wynne et al., 1977) underlined the importance of deviant communication in the transmission of disorders from one generation to the next. We may conclude that the intrafamilial communication disorders—as well as the cognitive defects seen prepsychotically in many severely ill schizophrenic patients—contribute in an important way to the predisposition to schizophrenia. The emphasis on their family-dynamic specificity may, however, have been slightly misleading. I believe—like Ciompi (1982, 1994) and most psychoanalysts—that emotional problems are of more primary significance than are those at the cognitive level, even if they are more difficult to study in a systematic and empirical way. I will here refer to the significance of panic-like anxiety for the outbreak of psychosis.

The most crucial psychological factor predisposing to schizophrenia consists of problems in the formation of a symbiotic interactional relationship and the detachment from it. I have related these issues to the significance of self-objects relationships for personality development and its disorders. These factors also seem to make up the most "specific" and common—though aetiologically variable—cluster detectable in the pathogenesis of schizophrenia. The disordered development of the self-object relationships and the concomitant lack of psychological individuation can be seen as an integrative theory, within the framework of which the inner problems featured by projective–introjective processes may be placed. Accordingly, self psychology does not substitute or exclude other psychoanalytic concepts based on different approaches, such as projective identification, which is very useful for understanding both the individual and the family dynamics of schizophrenia. The term self-object provides us with an umbrella under which a more detailed psychoanalytical approach is needed.

From the viewpoint of family research, it is easy to agree with Kohut's opinion that self-object relations are of greater significance than is drive gratification in developmental psychology (Kohut, 1971). Although the problems of aggressiveness, in particular, are clinically very important in schizophrenia, their culmination can be seen as a secondary

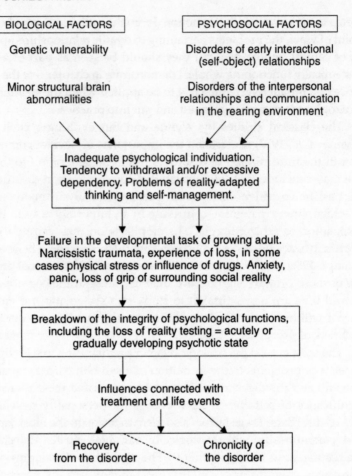

FIGURE 3.2.   Development and course of schizophrenic disorder (partly modified from Ciompi, 1982).

consequence of a deficient neutralization capacity (see Hartmann, 1953), as well as of the great pressure of symbiotically tinged needs for self-objects, deriving from experienced lack of empathy and injuries to one's self-esteem. This view gets support from the fact that the crucial psychological changes in schizophrenia occur in the integrative ego functions.

Even with regard to the problems connected with self-object relationships, schizophrenic patients present a continuum. At one extreme are those who have found it difficult to establish relations in the first place, while at the other extreme are those whose problem is their inability to detach from the symbiosis and achieve independence. These problems have an interactional, circular background; they are influenced both by the qualitative features of the parental personalities and by the inborn qualities of the children. I have proposed that children with structural brain abnormalities may present exceptional problems in establishing relations with their earliest self-objects, and/or—as soon as such relations have been established—a tendency to adhere to them tenaciously. It is also probable that the parents of such children, for reasons of interactional stimulation, tend more often than other parents to maintain continuous symbiotic relationships with them.

Luc Ciompi has designed a good chart of the onset and course of schizophrenia (1982). I present it here in Figure 3.2, with some added specifications. The most notable change compared with the original is that I describe in greater detail the factors precipitating the onset of psychosis, which were labelled as "excessive strain through nonspecific stress" in Ciompi's original chart.

It is important to note that *not all* of the factors are present in *every* case. This is especially true of the biological and psychosocial predisposing factors (top of the chart) and the precipitating factors.

Schizophrenia can be conceived of as the deepest and, as such, the most tragic resolution to the problems of human life, where one can end up through many parallel routes.

As the bottom of the chart clearly indicates, the factors pertaining to the patient's life course and treatment are significant for the outcome. The psychotic solution does not necessarily remain unchanged—rather, there are chances of recovery and renewed development after the onset of the illness.

CHAPTER FOUR

Contemporary ways of treating schizophrenia and psychotherapy research

Introductory remarks

The treatment of schizophrenia in a way that genuinely combines psychological and biological approaches—as based on the illness models described in Exhibit 2.1 at the end of chapter two—is still a rarity. Clearly, the most common method of treating schizophrenia is neuroleptic medication, more or less combined with rehabilitative measures.

The neuroleptic era came into existence in a symposium of French psychiatrists and neurologists in 1952, when Jean Delay, Pierre Deniker, and J. M. Harl (1952) reported the good results they had obtained with chlorpromazine, a phenothiazine derivative, in the treatment of schizophrenia and other psychoses. The popularity of neuroleptics is easy to understand. They are relatively easy to administer to large numbers of patients, including outpatients. This medication, together with the progress of rehabilitative activities, made it possible gradually to shift the focus of schizophrenia treatment from inpatient to outpatient care in the 1960s.

Psychoanalytically oriented psychotherapy has not become general in the treatment of schizophrenia. Still, it has a long history behind it.

Jung and Federn treated psychotic patients at the beginning of this century. In America, the psychotherapy of schizophrenia developed from the psychobiological approach introduced by Adolf Meyer. The most fruitful period of the Washington School, which developed under the influence of Sullivan and Fromm-Reichmann, lasted from the 1940s until the 1960s. During this period there arose a generation of American psychosis therapists, who created a foundation for the psychological understanding of schizophrenia and hence for individual psychotherapy and community therapeutic treatment of schizophrenic patients. At the same time, two centres of psychotherapy came about in Europe, one in Switzerland (Sechehaye, Benedetti, and Müller with their students) and the other in Britain, where the psychoanalysts of Melanie Klein's school analysed the archaic and deep-rooted defence mechanisms of schizophrenic patients.

This tradition has not died out in the United States. L. Bryce Boyer (1983, 1986, 1989) and Vamik D. Volkan (1990, 1995), especially, have broadened the work of the Washington School, also stimulated by the British object relations school; the recent book by Michael Robbins (1993) represents a psychoanalytic approach based on a biopsychosocial model. But the position of psychotherapy in the treatment of schizophrenia has clearly declined over the past two decades, as has the number of psychotherapists interested in schizophrenia.

On the other hand, during the same decades, interest in the psychotherapy of schizophrenic patients has been increasing in some European countries, including Finland, Norway, Sweden, and Italy (and, as far as family therapy is concerned, in Poland). Research on individual, family, and community therapy has been stimulated by a series of international symposia on the psychotherapy of schizophrenia, which were initiated by Benedetti and Müller. Twelve symposia have now been held: 1956, 1959, 1963, and 1978 in Lausanne (Switzerland), 1971 in Turku (Finland), 1975 in Oslo (Norway), 1981 in Heidelberg (Germany), 1984 in New Haven, CT (United States), 1988 in Turin (Italy), 1991 in Stockholm (Sweden), 1994 in Washington, D.C. (regarding their history, see Benedetti, 1992); and 1997 in London, organized by the International Society for the Psychological Treatments of Schizophrenia and Other Psychoses (ISPS).

The general interest in the treatment of schizophrenic patients has also been stimulated by the development of family therapy from the 1950s onwards. But even family therapy has been drifting away from the psychodynamic frame of reference. In the 1980s psychoeducational treatment attracted most research interest and was practised most frequently (Steinglass, 1987). This is partly related to the obvious—and frequently recognized—connection between the psychoeducational approach and the biomedical schizophrenia concept.

The same is also true of rehabilitative activities, which developed remarkably in the 1960s and 1970s. During the past decade, however, the development of rehabilitation began to suffer from the effects of the growing political demand for a curtailment of public social and health care expenditure, which in many countries has been further enhanced by the economic recession. However, good examples of the development of community-based services with profitable results can be found (e.g. Hoult et al., 1983; Sledge et al., 1996; Stein, 1993; Stein & Test, 1980; Tuori, Lehtinen, Hakkarainen et al., 1997).

Psychotherapy of schizophrenia— a rarity, but why?

The disproportionate popularity of the biomedical modes of treatment compared with psychotherapy is due to many different reasons, some of which are presented below:

- Medical research and education have been committed to the natural–scientific ways of thinking, which often make it difficult to understand and appreciate the work of researchers representing a different theoretical outlook.
- There has been a boom of biomedical schizophrenia research, which has nurtured and enhanced the belief of many biomedically oriented researchers and psychiatrists in the organic nature of schizophrenia and the possibilities of treating it exclusively on this basis.
- Drug manufacturers have notably and usually one-sidedly influenced the doctors' ways of thinking.
- It has been generally believed that psychotherapeutic work requires extensive staff resources, and that widely applied psychotherapy would therefore not be possible in public health care, at least for psychotic patients.
- The results of "controlled" treatment trials have not been particularly promising, especially with regard to the effects of individual psychotherapy of schizophrenia.

• Classical psychoanalytic theory has engendered a pessimistic attitude towards psychotherapeutic treatment of schizophrenics, and
schizophrenic patients are rarely suited to formal intensive psychoanalytic treatment. Psychosis psychotherapy is rarely included in
psychoanalytic training programmes.

• Studies of the psychological causes of schizophrenia arouse anxiety
and resistance, especially when they are (erroneously) perceived as
an accusation of the parents for their child's illness.

• There have been sociopolitical ideologies that have slowed down or
eliminated intensive public health care and social welfare that are
essential for the comprehensive treatment of psychotic patients.

In the following sections I touch upon and discuss in greater detail
the effects of most of these factors and the ways in which we should
address them.

Psychopharmacological treatment

The effectiveness of *neuroleptic treatment* in relieving psychotic symptoms has been verified conclusively: as early as 1969, Cole and Davis
reviewed a hundred studies in which their effectiveness in schizophrenia was compared with placebo groups, using double-blind
procedures. In 86 of the studies the medication alleviated the psychotic symptoms more effectively than did placebos. The multiple
centre research organized in the United States by the National Institute of Mental Health and headed by Cole yielded most conclusive
results: the condition of 70% of the patients improved essentially
within 6 weeks, while the corresponding figure in the placebo group
was only 25% (Cole & Davis, 1969).

Nevertheless, the effect of neuroleptics is not specific for schizophrenia, though schizophrenia is a main indicator for their use. Neuroleptics act on several different psychotic conditions, and their effect tends
to be the more pronounced, the more distressed and/or restless the
patient is. They do not cure schizophrenia, but they have a clearly favourable alleviating and anti-psychotic effect on about two thirds of
schizophrenic patients (Cole & Davis, 1969; Wiesel, 1994). They act most
effectively on the positive symptoms (thought disorders, hallucinations,
delusions), and they also help the patient to control such symptoms in

the long term. Their effect on the negative symptoms (isolation, passivity, affective blunting), however, is less obvious. Especially in acute states, they often help to eliminate the symptoms completely. In chronic cases the effect is less spectacular, and sufficiently long follow-up studies—see chapter two—indicate that the number of patients who have become permanently cured of their psychotic symptoms has not changed markedly since the introduction of neuroleptics. However, with the help of these drugs, the symptoms of the chronic patients are now less severe, reducing the need for inpatient treatment.

The *effective mechanism of most neuroleptics*—especially the phenotiazine and butyrophenone derivatives—on psychoses is due to their blocking the transmission of nerve impulses between brain cells by means of the dopamine 2 (D2) transmitter (Carlsson & Lindqvist, 1963; Snyder, 1981). Positron emission tomography (PET) studies have shown that relatively low doses of neuroleptics are enough to achieve this. Blocking at a 65–85% level is considered sufficient, and this level is reached with relative low dosage (Farde, Wiesel, Halldin, & Sedvall, 1988). A higher dosage, which has often been recommended, is a misguided choice, as it no longer improves the outcome of the treatment but, rather, increases notably the number of adverse side-effects (drug-induced parkinsonism, tardive dyskinesia, passivity, and anhedonism). Many leading psychopharmacologists have recommended the use of low or moderate doses instead of high ones (Baldessarini, Cohen, & Teicher, 1988; Donaldson, Gelenberg, & Baldessarini, 1983; Marder et al., 1987; Van Putten et al., 1993).

PET imaging has shown that the blocking of dopamine functions begins after the first few doses of neuroleptics. Because of the difference between the time-course of receptor occupancy and the time-course of antipsychotic effect, researchers (e.g. Wiesel, 1994) have postulated that the antipsychotic effect of neuroleptics is not exclusively due to the blocking of dopamine functions, but includes more complex interactions among several different neuronal systems. One may suppose that the adjustment "on a low flame" of central nervous system functions, associated with the neuroleptic effect, may also have psychological influences that help the patient's ego to resume the internal psychic balance.

Clozapine holds a special position among neuroleptics. Its effect on the blocking of dopamine 2 receptors is only about half that recorded for other neuroleptics, but its alleviating effect on the symptoms of chronic patients in particular is, nevertheless, better. This has been tentatively ascribed to the more extensive action of clozapine on the functions of other transmitters, but we do not know for certain what mechanisms are involved in it. Serotonin (5-HT2) antagonists as well as blocking effects of dopamine 4 (D4) receptors have been proposed as plausible possibilities (Lieberman, 1993; Seeman, 1993; Van Tol et al., 1991). The use of clozapine is restricted by potentially fatal consequences due to severe leukopenia (Idänpään-Heikkilä et al., 1977). The risk of haematological changes is present in about 1% of all cases (Alvir et al., 1993) and is greatest in the first several weeks to three months of treatment.

Recently, a number of compounds currently in development—such as risperidone—with combined serotonin (5-HT2) and D2 antagonist properties, have demonstrated impressive antipsychotic efficacy (Lieberman, 1993).

The attitude of psychiatrists towards neuroleptic medication is mostly related to their theory of schizophrenia: some consider neuroleptics a necessary basic medication that should be administered regularly and continuously, while others—myself included—see neuroleptics as important agents to be used with moderation to support psychotherapeutically and psychosocially oriented therapy.

Of the other psychoactive drugs used in the treatment of schizophrenia, *benzodiazepine derivatives* are the most common. Wolkowitz and Pickar (1991), in their review of the studies on the use of benzodiazepines in schizophrenia, concluded that benzodiazepines alleviated schizophrenic symptoms in one-third to half of patients. The most typical indication for the use of benzodiazepines is the need for additional rapid tranquillization along with neuroleptic medication. *Antidepressive drugs* are also occasionally used as auxiliary medication for patients of the schizophrenia group on a neuroleptic regime, most justifiably in the depressive conditions associated with schizo–affective psychoses. Patients with typical schizophrenia also often feel depressed after an acute psychotic episode, when their sense of reality has recovered and they are faced with the fact of being ill. However, psychotherapeutic work with the patient is generally a better alternative in these cases than antidepressive medication.

Is medication necessary? This question sounds strange to most psychiatrists, not least to those who—like myself—remember how distressing, restless, and noisy was the atmosphere on closed psychiatric wards before the introduction of neuroleptics. There are, however, findings that justify this question.

Thus, for example, Carpenter, McGlashan, and Strauss (1977) carried out a therapeutic trial in the National Institutes of Health Research

Center (NIH) in the United States in the 1970s, where 49 patients with acute schizophrenia were treated with intensive and extensive psychotherapy (individual therapy sessions 2–3 times a week, group therapy sessions once a week, and often supplementary family therapy) in an effort to avoid medication. The outcome was that just over half the patients managed without medication, while 22 patients started a neuroleptic regime 3 weeks after the beginning of the treatment but discontinued it well before they were discharged from hospital after an average stay of four months. When the prognosis of these patients was compared one year later with the prognosis of a matched patient group treated elsewhere with medication, the results of the multi-dimensional follow-up were slightly in favour of those treated at the NIH. There were, however, no differences between those treated with and those without medication within the NIH population.

Carpenter, Heinrichs, and Hanlon also found out in a later study (1987) that there were no differences in a two-year follow-up between schizophrenic patients on continuous medication and patients who were given a brief, symptom-specific neuroleptic regime combined with psychosocial intervention, although the need for hospitalization was initially lower for patients on continuous medication.

Rapaport et al. (1978) studied a Californian series of 80 young male schizophrenics, half of whom were treated with chlorpromazine, the other half with a placebo. As could be expected, the results of pharmacotherapy were better. The follow-up examinations, however, revealed a group of patients who had not received medication either in the hospital or afterwards and had a better prognosis than any of the other groups. These patients belonged to the category with a "good premorbid prognosis", and their clinical picture was predominantly paranoid.

In the Kupittaa Hospital in Turku, a pilot project was launched under the supervision of Viljo Räkköläinen in 1989, with first-admission patients of the schizophrenia group being treated without neuroleptics, one reason being that they also originally underwent PET scanning, whose results would be distorted by neuroleptic medication. The treatment is characterized by an intensive and versatile psychotherapeutic orientation, with the principles of the need-adapted treatment described in chapter five. When necessary, patients' anxiety is controlled with benzodiazepines for a short time. A case report of this series (Catherine) is presented in this book in chapter six.

According to follow-up findings over 2–5 years (Räkköläinen et al., 1994; Vuorio et al., 1993), only 8 of the 19 first-admission patients had to resort to neuroleptics. Despite the lack of medication, the outcome of the patients could be considered quite satisfactory. Of the 11 patients treated without neuroleptics (8 of whom had a DSM–III-R diagnosis of schizophrenic disorder, and 3 of schizophreniform disorder), 8 had no psychotic symptoms at the latest follow-up. There was, however, the drawback that the hospital episodes of some patients were relatively long. According to later experiences, a change towards shorter hospital episodes has been developed.

Räkköläinen and colleagues think that the neuroleptic treatment should be regarded unnecessary with acutely ill schizophreniform patients treated with comprehensive psychotherapeutic measures. On the other hand, benefit from neuroleptic treatment was derived by severely ill, already chronic patients as well as moderately ill schizophrenic patients with underlying borderline personality structure, as defined by Kernberg (1975, 1984).

In Finland, the experiences of the Kupittaa Project led to a larger multicentre study of the indications of neuroleptic and non-neuroleptic treatment of first-admission schizophrenic patients (V. Lehtinen et al., 1996). It was thought that there may be certain benefits involved in not medicating these patients. These benefits should be taken into account whenever the therapeutic resources and the benignity of the patient's clinical condition permit it. Not only can the initial assessment be made without drugs, but possible side-effects as well as the danger of a needless maintenance medication will also be avoided.

Chronic schizophrenic patients benefit from maintenance neuroleptic treatment. With these patients, drug discontinuation may exacerbate psychotic symptoms, provoking a recurrent need for hospitalization. On the other hand, the follow-up results of the psychotherapeutically oriented Scandinavian NIPS Project (Alanen et al., 1994; see chapter five) very clearly indicated that a continuing maintenance treatment is not necessary for all patients diagnosed as schizophrenic.

Individual psychotherapy

The psychotherapeutic literature on schizophrenia long consisted of individual case reports written up by therapists. They generally described patients who had, through a successful long-term dyadic therapeutic relationship, undergone a developmental process that not only resulted in a disappearance of psychotic symptoms, but also involved internal growth of personality and improvement in the patient's interpersonal relationships. As a young psychiatrist, I found the descriptions by Sechehaye (1955), Johansson (1956), and Will (1961) of their experiences especially impressive.

In the individual therapy of schizophrenic patients, psychoanalytic principles are applied, though the actual psychoanalytic technique is rarely used. The treatment is therefore usually called *psychoanalytically oriented* or *psychodynamic psychotherapy*, thus making a distinction between it and actual psychoanalysis. The more central to the treatment are the analysis of the transference emerging in the patient–therapist relationships, the observation of the countertransference reactions of the therapist, and the processes related to these phenomena, the more psychoanalytic the technique. The treatment practically always includes supportive elements whose role is most conspicuous in therapeutic relationships with infrequent sessions and/or less psychoanalytically oriented or trained therapists.

Some talented psychosis therapists, such as Boyer (1986), Johansson (1985), and Robbins (1993)—as well as Benedetti (1975), describing the patients of his student, Bertha Neumann—have published summaries of therapy outcomes. These accounts have reported a good or satisfactory outcome in 50–60% of the patients. Boyer based his data on as many as 106 patients suffering from or prone to psychosis. Johansson stated, based on catamnestic data up to 30 years, that the patients' satisfactory integration, verifiable in psychodynamic, clinical, and psychosocial terms, was achieved in 50% of the 40 schizophrenic patients treated by him for a period of at least one year with intensive psychoanalytically oriented psychotherapy. Neumann had 20 patients, of whom 10 were fully socially recovered and 6 others remarkably improved, with good social adaptation. Robbins had positive outcomes with 9 of 18 patients who satisfied DSM–III criteria for schizophrenia; of those with negative outcomes, 7 treatment efforts had failed after less than 2 years of psychotherapy.

We can also include in this group the therapeutic results achieved by Barbro Sandin (1992), who worked with seriously schizophrenic male patients in the Säter Hospital in Sweden. Rolf Sjöström (1985) carried out a follow-up of these patients and a control series collected from the same hospital. Two of Sandin's 14 patients had committed suicide, but the others were in a markedly and statistically significantly better condition than the controls. There was a particularly great difference in the patients' need for medication after a six-year follow-up; most of the patients who had been in psychotherapy had no medication 6 years later, the mean dosage in this group being 25 mg/day of chlorpromazine equivalents per patient, while the corresponding figure in the control series was 400 mg/day. An average of 200 hours of psychotherapy per patient had been provided in this series.

These outcome results were limited to groups of selected patients and therapists with an aptitude to work with psychotic patients. Poorer results were obtained in the more extensive follow-up studies carried out by Christian Müller (1961) on psychotherapeutically treated schizophrenic patients of the Burghölzli Hospital from 1950 to 1958 and by T. McGlashan (1984) on the prognosis of the schizophrenic patients of the Chestnut Lodge Hospital (a vast majority of them being already chronic at the time of admission). Despite the less favourable general tendency, however, these follow-up findings also revealed some quite unexpected recoveries of typical schizophrenic patients.

In the 1960s, the empirical natural–scientific methods that had often been applied to drug trials were introduced into psychotherapy research. According to these principles, the patient series were to be unselected and given randomized treatment. This meant, for example, that every second or third patient was given one type of treatment, while the other patients went without treatment or were given some other kind of strictly defined treatment.

In the United States, results have been published on four major controlled psychotherapy trials with individual therapy of schizophrenic patients. The most cited of these studies is the one from Camarillo Hospital in California under the guidance of Philip R. A. May (1968; later follow-ups: May, Tuma, & Dixon, 1981; May et al., 1976). The series consisted of 288 first-admission schizophrenics. Subjects with the best and poorest predictive prognosis were excluded. The series was divided in a random fashion into five groups receiving different kinds of therapies: (1) individual therapy, (2) pharmacotherapy (trifluoperazine), (3) individual therapy combined with pharmacotherapy, (4) electroshock treatment, and (5) "milieu therapy". The amount of treatments considered as successful in these groups were 65%, 95%, 96%, 79%, and 58%, respectively.

The findings of this "five-treatments trial" have, understandably, been eagerly quoted by the psychopharmacologically oriented researchers, who have taken them as objective proof for the superiority of psychopharmacological treatment over psychotherapy. Usually they have ignored the weaknesses of this work, of which the major ones were the following. (1) The psychotherapy was carried out by residents without psychotherapeutic training, who were supported by guidance and supervision but worked in a milieu sceptical about psychotherapy with schizophrenics. (2) The criterion for the statistical data of outcome was whether the patient could be discharged from the hospital or whether he/she had been in hospital continuously for 6–10 months, after which time both therapist and supervisor decided that the treatment had failed. Furthermore, the psychotherapeutic relationships were relatively short (an average of 46 hours per patient) and were only maintained for as long as the patients were in the hospital. The findings clearly confirm the shortening effect of psychopharmacological treatment on the duration of hospital episodes, but they do not provide an adequate basis for conclusions on the effects of competent and long-term psychotherapy continued in the frames of outpatient treatment.

Another project with negative results regarding psychoanalytically oriented psychotherapy was conducted at Harvard University (Grinspoon, Ewalt, & Schader, 1972). The therapists involved in the study were more competent, but the patients were seriously ill, consisting of 20 male patients with chronic schizophrenia, who had been inpatients at the Boston State Hospital for at least 3 years without interruption. They were brought to the Massachusetts Mental Health Center for 1 or 2 therapy hours weekly—that is, there was no milieu programme. According to the authors, psychotherapy combined with medication alleviated the patients' symptoms to a limited extent, while psychotherapy alone helped these patients "little or not at all". The book on the findings of this project also includes the therapists' descriptions of their work, which they considered partly beneficial even for some patients of the latter group.

Karon and VandenBos (1972, 1981) carried out a project at Michigan State University. Most of the patients belonged to the lowest social group; two thirds of them were hospitalized for the first time, and the others were also regarded as relatively recent cases of schizophrenia. The project included three groups of patients, the first of which underwent psychoanalytic psychotherapy with "direct" interpretations and without medication, while the second received "ego-analytical" (also psychoanalytically oriented) psychotherapy combined with small or moderate doses of chlorpromazine, and the third group was given only moderate or large doses of chlorpromazine. The psychotherapies were started rather intensively and were continued with longer intervals for altogether 20 months, including outpatient status. Follow-up examinations carried out 2 years after the termination of therapy, including both psychiatric interviews and psychological assessments, indicated that there was a significant difference in favour of the psychotherapy patients, both as regards the duration of hospitalizations and the patients' clinical status. The results achieved by the experienced therapists were better than those of the less experienced.

This study by Karon and VandenBos was at the other end of the spectrum from May's survey, but it was largely overshadowed by the latter in reviews. It has also been criticized for the small numbers of patients (altogether 36 patients) and the difference between the therapeutic milieus: the medication group was treated in a hospital whose general standard was lower than that of the wards where the psychotherapy patients resided.

The most interesting of the U.S. studies is the extensive and methodologically sophisticated project conducted by Stanton and Gunderson in MacLean Hospital in Massachusetts—a milieu favourable for psychotherapy—in the 1970s and 1980s (Gunderson et al., 1984a, 1984b). Its purpose was to compare two individual therapy approaches; both groups were also given standard doses of medication. The approaches were, respectively, explorative, insight-oriented (EIO) psychotherapy (two sessions weekly), and reality-adaptive, supportive (RAS) psychotherapy (averaging less than one session per week). Treatments were provided by experienced therapists, and the intent was to continue therapies for at least two years, including outpatient care. The series included 186 schizophrenic patients. As in the May study, the most severely and mildly disturbed patients were left out of the sample.

The most important result of this project was that no great difference was found in the outcome of the two groups, even if there were some differences in the direction of the findings. According to the two-year follow-up, the EIO patients benefitted somewhat more from their therapies with regard to ego functions (improvement of thought disorders, development of insight), while the result was clearly better in the RAS group concerning social functions (especially occupation).

The project yielded some significant subsidiary findings. These included the notable number of psychotherapy dropouts in both groups. As early as six months after the beginning of the trial, 42% of the 186 patients initially included in the series had dropped out, and only 51 (31% of the original) patients attended final evaluative sessions two years later. It was also noted that these dropouts had received relatively frequent psychiatric treatments elsewhere, and that their outcome was not essentially poorer than that of the other patients in the series.

Additional analyses of the tape-recorded sessions (Glass et al., 1989) indicated that the patients' outcomes had interesting and statistically significant connections with the methods and procedures used by the therapists. According to these follow-up findings, a "skilful psychodynamic exploration" by the therapist, including a sensitivity to the patients' subconscious "deep currents" and appropriateness of the technique (in the case of the EIO therapies)—was statistically significantly related to a decrease of global psychopathology, especially denial of illness and the absence of negative symptoms. On the other hand, however, the patients' anxiety and depression increased when they emerged from their apathy and isolation. Active support given to the patient— which was even more important in the RAS therapies—correlated with a decrease of anxiety and depression.

Of the European studies, I have already mentioned Sjöström's follow-up of Sandin's patients. In 1980, Sjöström initiated a new project, aimed at finding out whether other therapists were able to reproduce Sandin's results. The project suffered from a scarcity of patients: there were only 8 therapy patients, all of them male, and a 6-year follow-up revealed no differences between the patients and a control series of the same size, even if the mean prognostic development slightly favoured the therapy patients. Still, the results may rather be interpreted as a negative answer to Sjöström's question (Sjöström, 1990).

In Oslo, Endre Ugelstad (1978) studied the effects of psychotherapy with 30 chronic male schizophrenics, who had all been in the hospital for at least 3 years and had been treated in Gaustad Hospital for at least 1 year without a break. The psychotherapy group consisted of 12 patients, of whom 6 were involved in intensive psychoanalytically oriented individual psychotherapy and 6 in active milieu therapy on a small ward established for this purpose. A control group consisted of 12 patients with jobs or doing sheltered work outside the hospital, even though they were still inpatients. A minor control group consisted of 6 patients receiving less-specific milieu therapy. An evaluation of the patients' psychic condition by means of a quantifying method indicated that the patients in the therapy group were clearly more seriously disturbed initially than the patients in the larger control group. The follow-up results indicated a better outcome for the therapy patients according to the Rockland–Pollin scale, psychological tests, and discharge data. Later follow-ups covering up to 10 years (Haakenasen & Ugelstad, 1986) demonstrated, however, a levelling of the difference between the therapy and control groups, especially with regard to the psychosocial outcome, while the patients given individual psychotherapy still showed a greater reduction in psychotic symptoms. The authors emphasized the significance of the rehabilitation connected with social factors (work and dwelling) for the achievement and permanence of therapeutic results.

Another Norwegian study published by Varvin (1991) revealed clear improvements in one-third of 27 patients treated on a special psychotherapeutic ward in Oslo with a combination of intensive individual therapy and milieu therapy. All the patients with a good outcome were female, and the good outcome for half of them was found to be connected with a better preadmission level of global functioning.

Active non-controlled projects on individual psychotherapy of schizophrenia have also been conducted in Italy (see Borri & Quartesan, 1990: Furlan, 1993).

Despite their ostensible objectivity, controlled psychotherapy trials involve quite significant limitations, which have not been generally recognized. These limitations only become apparent when they are evaluated from a wider clinical viewpoint. The first of these limitations is due to the clinical heterogeneity of schizophrenia. The patients therefore differ in both their motivation for treatment and their therapeutic needs. Both Gunderson's project and our experiences in Turku (see chapter five) indicate that patients differ greatly in their ability to benefit from individual therapy. But if individual therapy is successful and results in a good outcome only in a portion of patients, being unsuitable for others, the good and bad results cancel each other out in the statistical analysis of unselected patient populations. Even so, a mode of treatment cannot be considered ineffective if it only benefits some of the subjects. Rather, one should try to investigate for which patients the treatment should be recommended.

The second limitation is due to the fact that the treatment of most schizophrenic patients requires an integrated approach, where several modes of therapy are optimally combined. The investigation of a single mode cannot give a view of the possibilities of comprehensive psychotherapeutic treatment in schizophrenia.

The third limitation of great significance is the psychotherapist's personality in the treatment of schizophrenia. The treatment requires long-term motivation in both patient and therapist. Their personalities need to be mutually compatible. This point should be given more attention at the initial stage of therapy than occurs at present.

Our Turku team has repeatedly brought out these points when presenting our findings and experiences (Alanen, Räkköläinen, Laakso, &

Rasimus, 1980; Alanen, Räkköläinen, Laakso, Rasimus, & Järvi, 1983). In our opinion, the focus should shift from method-oriented studies to problem-oriented (or need-oriented) ones. The patients' needs and not the researchers' needs should be used as the starting-point. Armelius et al. (1989), in a review they presented to the Swedish National Board of Social Welfare, doubted the value of research projects employing unselected series, pointing out that we should rather try to find out in the future what takes place in successful and unsuccessful therapies. They claimed that the time for new controlled trials will only come after we have found out more about the factors that promote and sustain the therapeutic relationships.

The *cognitive–behavioural approach* to schizophrenia has been aptly reviewed by Birchwood and Preston (1991). Based on learning theories, the cognitive methods are directed more towards those factors that maintain the schizophrenic symptoms than towards factors related to psychological origins. In the *cognitive–analytical approach*, cognitive-based methods and psychodynamic viewpoints are combined. The most widespread application of cognitive methods has emerged in the field of family therapy (see below). Perris (1992) described a comprehensive cognitive psychotherapy programme as it is applied in an integrated milieu and individual therapy in small, family-style treatment units.

Family therapy

Family therapy began to develop later than individual therapy, because our therapeutic culture had been so exclusively dominated by the individual therapeutic approach in all of medicine. Psychiatrists and other mental health field workers first became interested in family therapy after the Second World War, and their interest has continued to grow ever since. According to our Finnish findings (Aaltonen, 1982; Alanen, Lehtinen, Räkköläinen, & Aaltonen, 1991), the motivation of the families of schizophrenics to participate in joint discussions is good, especially if they are invited to attend right at the beginning of the treatment.

Family research on schizophrenia gave a crucial stimulus for the development of family therapy. Ever since the introduction of family therapy, schizophrenia has been one of the major indicators for its use. One reason for this is found in the dependency bonds between these patients and their families, which are reinforced and even exaggerated as a consequence of their illness. Many individual therapists—beginning with Federn (1943, 1952)—have also pointed out that the inclusion of the patient's family in the treatment, in one way or another, is necessary in schizophrenia. Johansson (1956, 1985) and Robbins (1993) combined family meetings or therapy in their approach at some stage during the individual therapy, in order to safeguard the patient's efforts towards independence.

Another reason for the increase in family therapy and, more generally, family-oriented treatment has been the families' need for support to relieve the strain experienced by the outbreak of psychosis and by the often continued psychotic behaviour of the patient. This has become an intensely crucial question over the past few decades, as the focus of schizophrenia treatment has shifted from inpatient to outpatient care. The burdens and responsibilities felt by the families of schizophrenics have increased (Kuipers, 1993; Winefield & Harvey, 1994). This situation has presented a new challenge to the therapeutic system and has also stimulated the development of new therapeutic orientations. Furthermore, when supported by the therapeutic team, many families can give an important positive impact on the therapeutic activities.

Many of the first family therapists of schizophrenics based their work on family research, closely combining research and actual therapy. Experiences were published, for example, by Jackson and Weakland (1961), Boszormenyi-Nagy, Bowen, Framo, Whitaker, and Wynne (see the papers of these authors published in Boszormenyi-Nagy & Framo, 1965), Scott with co-workers (Scott & Alwyn, 1978; Scott & Ashworth, 1967), Stierlin (1972, 1974, 1976), Kaufmann (1976), and Alanen (1976). Most of the therapies were *psychodynamically oriented family therapies*, with the goal of stimulating an intrafamilial developmental process (as in the case of Paula, in chapter one). The focus of therapeutic attention in these cases is on the relationships among the family members and not, as in individual therapy, on the internal development of the schizophrenic family member, though it is hoped that the developmental process taking place in the family might also stimulate his/her individual development. Another difference between individual therapy and family therapy has been aptly described by Wynne (1965), stating that family therapy prefers to point out things that are visible, but not recognized, while individual therapy points out things which can be inferred, but of which people are not conscious.

Although the published experiences were generally favourable, psychodynamic family therapy was gradually overshadowed by the development of two other orientations. One of these is systemically oriented—often called systemic–strategic—family therapy and the other psychoeducational family therapy. There are also many other family therapy orientations in field use, but they are not particularly significant for the treatment of schizophrenics.

One of the important pioneers of the *systemic–strategic family therapy* of schizophrenics was the Milan Group (Selvini Palazzoli et al., 1978, 1980), which also influenced the thinking of another important European pioneer, Helm Stierlin. He has related that his shift from psychodynamic family therapy to the systemic–strategic orientation was influenced by his observation that the latter type of therapy was feasible far more often than was psychodynamic therapy, which tends to arouse resistance in many families of schizophrenics (Stierlin, 1983). Stierlin's team has especially studied family therapy of schizo–affective and manic–depressive psychoses (Retzer et al., 1991).

When the technique of systemic–strategic family therapy is applied, a team is used instead of a single therapist, the sessions are closed by giving the family strategic messages, and the sessions are held at relatively long intervals. The purpose is to alter the family's psychological balance in a way that is favourable for both the patient and the other family members. Although technical details differentiate this orientation from the older type of psychodynamic family therapy, the psychological understanding of family situations is essential for success in both. This point should be emphasized in order to prevent too radical systemic–strategic interventions sometimes based on inadequately grounded conclusions.

The *psychoeducational family therapy* orientation, on the other hand, has grown from different premises. Most of the proponents of this approach, whose frame of reference is primarily based on learning theories, generally perceive schizophrenia as an organic disease, in accordance with the vulnerability–stress theory. Usually this notion is also pointed out during the therapy, and the goal—for both the schizophrenic patient and the family members—is to learn to live with the illness rather than to work towards a developmental recovery process. For the patient's parents, this orientation has the benefit—but also the restriction—that the conscious or subconscious feelings of guilt associated with the child's illness are suppressed.

These premises are compatible with the biomedical orientation that dominated schizophrenia research in the United States and Britain in the 1980s. The editor of *Family Process*, Peter Steinglass (1987), stated in late

1980 that he considered the emergence of this approach the most important advance in family therapy over the past 20 years. He especially emphasized the importance of *Schizophrenia and the Family*, published by Carol Anderson and her co-workers in 1986. Family therapists can learn many things from this book, especially about the empathy to be shown towards the parents of schizophrenic patients (which seems inadequately outlined in Selvini Palazzoli's reports, for example) as well as the willingness to establish a cooperative relationship with them. But the same authors also emphasize the hypothetical hereditary–biological aetiology of schizophrenia—which they present as a proven fact to both the patients and the families—while ignoring the developmental–psychological background (Anderson, Reiss, & Hogarty, 1986).

Of the *controlled family therapy trials*, we might first mention the pioneering project carried out by Donald G. Langsley and his co-workers in Denver, Colorado, in the late 1960s (Langsley, Machotka, & Flomenhaft, 1971; Langsley, Pittman, & Swank, 1969), where the primary goal was to avoid hospitalization by providing prompt crisis intervention on a family basis.

Their series consisted of 150 families who had been seeking admission for one of their members with a serious psychic disorder. About half the patients suffered from psychoses of the schizophrenia group. Instead of admitting the sick member to a hospital, the families were introduced to crisis therapy conducted by Langsley's team as outpatients. The trial included a control group of the same size, where the sick members were admitted into hospital. The outcome was that only 13% of the study families had to resort to hospitalization during the six-month follow-up, while in 29% of the control families the sick member who had been initially hospitalized was *re*hospitalized within the same period. Repeated follow-up checks 12 and 18 months later indicated that the differences in the two groups' needs for hospital treatment and their social coping abilities had gradually begun to level off. Langsley et al. therefore emphasize that the opportunities for family crisis treatment should be made permanent.

There have been four pioneering groups working on therapeutic trials that can be classified as psychoeducational family therapy of schizophrenia. These are the teams led by Michael Goldstein and Jerry Doane (Doane et al., 1986; Goldstein et al., 1978), Julian Leff (Leff et al., 1982, 1985), Gerard E. Hogarty and Carol Anderson (Hogarty et al., 1986, 1991), and Ian R. H. Falloon (Falloon et al., 1982, 1985). They all published reports on family intervention projects using the controlled trial arrangement in the early 1980s (Goldstein in 1978). These projects shared the following features: the intervention had been planned in advance, the outcome was measured with the number of relapses and/or rehospitalizations, and the basic treatment of both the study and the control patients consisted of neuroleptic medication.

The family interventions differed somewhat. Goldstein and his co-workers emphasized that both the acutely ill patient and the family members had to accept the existence of the psychosis and to try to identify and thereafter avoid the stress factors that seemed to make the disorder manifest. Leff and colleagues, whose series consisted of more chronic patients, combined lectures given to the families on the nature of schizophrenia, family members' groups, and family therapy sessions with the goal of lowering the high parental EE values, which were postulated to precipitate relapse. Hogarty's team combined psychoeducational family therapy with social skills teaching with good success. Falloon employed the most straightforwardly behavioural methods—he even called his programme "family management"—with the goal of educating the families to find jointly acceptable solutions to problematic situations.

The outcome findings of these projects were promising: rehospitalizations and relapses or aggravated symptoms were only seen in 0–9% of cases in the study group and in 44–50% of the control cases. The combination of family intervention and medication—and, as in Falloon's project, individual-oriented management—hence clearly improved the patients' prognosis. In Goldstein's first series—where intervention consisted of six sessions only—the differences appeared to level off over a longer follow-up period (Goldstein & Kopeikin, 1981). The other teams, who followed their families for longer, reported that the differences between the study and control groups were still observable two years later. Parallel results have also been reported by some other research teams applying psychoeducational family therapy (e.g. Tarrier et al., 1989).

There has been less research on systemic–strategic and psychodynamic family therapies of schizophrenia, and their results have been evaluated differently. We might, however, mention the pilot study by the Canadian team of Levene (Levene, Newman, & Jefferies, 1989) on two modes of family therapy in a group of ten patients whose response to neuroleptics was poor. Both psychodynamic family therapy with a focal problem orientation and supportive therapy approaching psychoeducational principles—which were continued for six months after discharge from the hospital—were shown by a one-year follow-up to have clearly improved the patients' social skills. Symptoms were significantly fewer and less serious in the group that had been in psychodynamic family therapy.

Timo Tuori (1987), in Finland, evaluated the outcomes of systemic family therapy among schizophrenic patients who had been married at the time their illness became manifest ($n = 24$), using the non-psychotic married patients admitted during the same period as a control group. He found out that both the motivation for family therapy and its outcome were better in the former group than in the latter. The therapy appeared to diminish the need for rehospitalization among the first-admission patients, while no similar effect was observable in the group of rehospitalized patients. Tuori considers family therapy especially necessary whenever the manifestation of psychosis is clearly associated with the family or marital situation or when the couple has a child who has either been involved in the psychotic symptoms or been ascribed the role of a scapegoat or has become an object of parental quarrels. These observations also point to the significance that family-oriented work may have in preventing mental disorders in children.

Favourable results from systemic–psychodynamic family therapy in the treatment of schizophrenic adolescents have also been reported, for example, by Malkiewicz-Borkowska and Namyslowska (1991) as well as by Pietruszewski (1991) from Poland. Guntern (1979), in Switzerland, became a pioneer in the application of systemic family and milieu therapy to the psychiatric treatment of the whole population in a given area. In the Western Lapland Project (Tornio, Finland), the establishment of family therapeutic training to practically all mental health workers in the district led to similar development (Aaltonen et al., 1997; Keränen, 1992; Seikkula, 1991).

Groups and communities

Group therapy has longer traditions in the treatment of schizophrenia than does family therapy. Reports on it were already published in the 1920s and 1930s (Lazell, 1921; Marsh, 1933). The development of outpatient care and the increase of therapeutic communities in both hospitals and outpatient units have further promoted the interest in both group therapy and more general group functions. In therapeutic communities, group functions play a central role.

Group therapy in the treatment of schizophrenia has a number of important benefits: it stimulates patients with marked isolative tendencies, gives them practice in making contacts with other people, and improves their social skills. As an additional benefit, group therapy costs less than individual therapy. Several reviews—for example, by Parloff and Dies (1977), Mosher and Keith (1979), and Kanas (1986)—emphasize the significance of group therapy in these respects. González de Chaves Menéndez and Garcia-Ordás Alvarez (1992) pointed out that the atmosphere in a group therapy situation is realistic and characterized by equality and thus promotes the growth of self-esteem and stimulates the totality of psychotherapeutic functions. Alleviation of symptoms and a decline in the need for neuroleptic medication have also been reported as consequences of group therapy. The overall conclusion is, however, that the improvements of patients' clinical condition are more modest than are the psychosocial effects.

The field of group therapy also has several orientations, some based on psychodynamic and others on a psychoeducational frame of reference. Of the former type, particularly noteworthy is the extensive experience collected by Frank Schwarz (1982) at the Max Planck Institute in Munich in a programme that combines group and individual therapy and has also integrated a psychoanalytic family therapy orientation.

Controlled trials on the effects of group therapy in schizophrenia compared with patients treated with other methods have been made by, for example, O'Brien et al. (1972), Claghorn et al. (1974), Lindberg (1981), and Malm (1982). All of them noticed a greater effect on the improvement of the patients' social and interpersonal skills than on their clinical symptoms. In Malm's study, for instance, the group therapy results showed improvement in items related to emotional communication, increased leisure activities, and entries into the social field.

The concept of the *therapeutic community* was introduced into psychiatry after the Second World War by two British innovators, Maxwell Jones and T. F. Main. Their goal was to turn the psychiatric hospital wards, which had, up until then, closely resembled general hospitals, into communities that were more suited to their purpose and actively promoted the patients' psychological skills. Jones (1953) especially emphasized the need to involve the patients in the responsibility of planning and implementing functions. The decision-making power in the community was held by the joint meetings of patients and staff. Main (1946), who coined the term "therapeutic community", was a psychoanalyst and tended to consider psychotherapeutic goals as the most important.

Neither of these innovators, however, worked mainly with psychotic patients. Main was mostly interested in neurotic patients and Jones initially in the war-time shock reactions and later in character disorders, though he was later acting as the director of a large Scottish mental hospital. When we speak of the therapeutic communities for psychotic patients, we should remember the earlier pioneer, H. S. Sullivan, who as early as the 1920s developed the principles of community treatment suitable for schizophrenic patients at Enoch and Sheppard Pratt Hospital in Maryland (Sullivan, 1930, 1931; see also Sullivan, 1962). An important American pioneering work dealing with therapeutic milieu in a mental hospital was published in the 1950s by Stanton and Schwarz (1954).

The purpose of applying therapeutic community principles to the psychiatric ward is to establish the supportive structure that is necessary for psychotherapeutic endeavours in the context of institutionalized care. Clinical experiences on wards treating psychotic patients following psychoanalytically oriented principles have been described, for example, by Schulz and Kilgalen (1969), Simo Salonen (1975), and Murray Jackson (Jackson & Cawley, 1992; Jackson & Williams, 1994). Our approach of psychotherapeutically oriented ward communities treating newly admitted schizophrenic patients is described in chapters five and six.

Therapeutic communities for schizophrenic patients have been developed and their effects investigated from several different viewpoints. Paul and Lentz (1977) divided their series of chronic schizophrenic inpatients into three groups, of which the first underwent a precisely structured behaviour-therapeutic programme (including token economy), the second was treated in accordance with more conventional therapeutic community principles, and the third served as a control group receiving conventional mental hospital treatment. Within three years, 96% of the patients in the first group could be discharged, the corresponding figures being 68% in the second group and 46% in the control group. The results thus clearly indicate that behaviour-therapeutic programming, which was the method most familiar to the researchers, was effective.

In Scandinavia, an important pioneering work in this field was executed by the Sopimusvuori therapeutic communities in Finland. These communities were originally founded by Erik E. Anttinen and his co-workers in Tampere in 1970 to promote the rehabilitation of chronic mental patients discharged from the hospital (see chapter seven). The aim is to create as normal a living environment as possible, observing psychodynamic and humanistic principles. A cooperative spirit based on interpersonal contacts among the clients and an improvement of self-confidence is considered to have an important role in the rehabilitative process (Anttinen, 1983; Ojanen, 1984).

According to follow-up data (Anttinen, 1992), 48% of the first 236 clients of Sopimusvuori—of whom 50% had been in a mental hospital for more than 10 years and 66% for more than 5 years—had been able to move to dwellings outside the Sopimusvuori communities, 17% had remained to live there permanently, 25% had been rehospitalized, and 7% died.

Therapeutic communities functioning outside hospitals have recently come to have a role of their own even in the treatment of acutely schizophrenic patients. One London pioneer in this field was R. D. Laing, who founded residential homes that are still operating. He himself, however, preferred to call them antipsychiatric asylums rather than therapeutic communities. (When I asked Laing in the early 1980s what he considered the most important treatment of schizophrenia, he said he preferred to teach persons called schizophrenic *aikido*—a Japanese self-defense skill emphasizing nonviolence). Well-defined therapeutic goals combining the psychoanalytic and family-oriented approaches began to be observed in the ward community Villa 21, established in the Shenley Hospital near London in the late 1960s after Michael B. Conran was appointed its head (Conran, 1972).

The reports by Loren R. Mosher and Alma Z. Menn (1978, 1983) on the therapeutic results achieved outside the hospital in the Soteria home are well known. They founded Soteria in California in the early 1970s. The leading principle for the patients in this home was to experience the psychotic regression as growth and development under the guidance of lay staff without professional training but devoted to their work, in a home-like milieu, and with as little medication as possible.

In the follow-up studies the controls were similar patients treated in regular, well-staffed psychiatric hospitals. There was also the further difference that the period of hospitalization defined as "brief and effective" lasted for only 21 days, whereas the average period spent in the Soteria home ranged from 5 to 6 months. A two-year follow-up indicated that the Soteria clients had been coping slightly better than those who had been in the hospital with regard to both subsequent need for treatment and social and interpersonal life course.

The starting-points were largely similar in the "Soteria Berne" Project launched by Luc Ciompi and co-workers (Ciompi et al., 1992). They also have a small nursing-home that resembles a normal living milieu, where the staff consists of half professionals and half carefully selected lay persons. Schizophrenia is perceived as a regressive crisis experienced by specifically predisposed young people in problem situations during their life course.

The treatment in "Soteria Berne" is divided into four successive phases. During the first phase the patient is placed in a "soft room" together with a maternally protective and soothing staff member, where his/her condition is normalized. Patients then resume their daily activities and return to address their problems at a realistic level with other staff members. At the final stages, the patient is rehabilitated socially, the problems implicit in leaving the Soteria home are discussed, and the after-care is planned, emphasizing the strategies for preventing recurrence of the illness. The use of neuroleptics is restricted to especially threatening situations or is started with low doses after 4–5 weeks without signs of improvement.

A two-year follow-up, where the control group consisted of similar patients treated in four psychiatric hospitals, revealed no differences in subsequent coping, with the exception that the patients who had been living in the Soteria home had moved to live separately from their parents significantly more often than had other patients. Ciompi and colleagues, however, emphasize that both the Soteria patients and their families felt the atmosphere of the Soteria home to be friendlier and less labelling than the hospital milieu, and that the therapeutic environment in these homes—including the lack of medication—had helped them to "remain themselves" better and to integrate the psychotic experiences into the totality of their lives.

Community psychiatric developments

The *rehabilitation* of psychiatric patients involves ways of improving their psychic as well as their physical condition and particularly of promoting their social skills and occupational abilities with the objective of improving the quality of their lives and helping them to adjust to society. Rehabilitation is provided mostly for chronic patients but is also needed more often than is generally realized at the acute stage of schizophrenia.

The rehabilitation of chronic patients usually proceeds along two tracks, one of which helps the institutionalized patient to learn to live outside the hospital, while the other supports his/her progress towards work life (see Figure 7.1, p. 250, describing the rehabilitative system established in connection with the Sopimusvuori therapeutic communities in Finland).

The pioneering period in the development of rehabilitative work took place in the 1960s. At that time, rehabilitation of the working capacity was considered the most important task, and it was promoted by the development of "industrial therapy" in hospitals (pioneered by Early, 1960, and Freudenberg—described by Wing, 1960—in Britain) and the foundation of sheltered workshops (e.g. Speijer, 1961) and jobs outside hospitals.

When I was enabled by a WHO scholarship in 1969 to travel to Holland and Britain to visit units of social psychiatry, I saw the great majority of the patients in many mental hospitals working in large industrial therapy halls for most of the day, doing subcontracting work and thus labouring for the common good. I felt somewhat dubious about this development, though I was repeatedly assured that the patients' ego functions were thus supported and that they were being prepared for working outside the hospitals. Someone did remark, however, that the foremen were occasionally reluctant to give up a good worker.

Things changed in the 1970s, when the employment situation turned from a lack of labor to unemployment. By that time it had also been realized that in order for rehabilitation to be successful, the patients had to be helped more generally, improving their interpersonal skills, not only their work capacity. The focus now shifted to rehabilitation that promoted living outside the hospital and support for the patients' other living skills. But there have also been difficulties in these efforts, especially in the 1980s, when the social political ideologies prevailing in the Western world emphasized the removal of mental patients from hospitals for financial reasons but failed to provide adequate community services.

The good outcome results achieved by the rehabilitative Vermont project (Harding et al., 1987) were referred to in chapter two. A matched comparison of the outcome of Vermont subjects with those in Maine who were treated more traditionally indicated that the good outcome of the Vermont patients was due to the rehabilitation programme, including an earlier opportunity for community life (De Sisto et al., 1995).

Apart from the functions of the rehabilitative system, there are also semi-institutional modes and units of treatment, such as *day-and-night hospitals* and other types of part-time hospital care, as well as different crisis and activity centres for outpatients. *Psychiatric home care* has been found to be an expedient method of taking care of chronic patients. The works published by Anttinen, Eloranta, and Stenij (1971), Davis, Dinitz, and Pasamanick (1972), Fenton, Tessier, & Struening (1979), and Hoult et al. (1983) are good examples of investigations of the use of intensive home care combined with various supportive social activities as an alternative to hospital treatment. They all reported a notable decrease in the need for hospital treatment, as well as beneficial effects on the patients' social and clinical development.

The Dane County Project conducted by Stein and Test in Wisconsin in the 1970s (Stein, 1993; Stein & Test, 1980) is generally regarded as a classic effort to establish an *integrated, community-based system of care* as an alternative to psychiatric inpatient treatment. The emphasis of the work has been on patients recommended for admission into hospital, including chronic mental patients. Teams created for the project supported these patients in many ways, such as by taking care of their material needs. In the first phase (Stein & Test, 1980), the central part of the project consisted of a programme called "Training in Community Living", and its purpose was to promote the patients' ability to manage independently in their daily activities and more generally in life.

The project was found to have diminished greatly the need for hospital treatment and to have promoted the patients' abilities to cope. But when the project was discontinued 14 months later, most of the benefits were lost, and the need for hospital treatment increased sharply. The work was resumed later, now based on the conclusion that the care must be continuous and must provide a wide variety of services needed by patients in order to achieve a stable adjustment to the community (Stein, 1993). Comprehensive community services now include crisis resolution services, a mobile community treatment team—especially for young adults with chronic schizophrenia who are, at times, unwilling to come in for services and must be contacted at home—a psychosocial rehabilitation programme, and living arrangements visited by the staff, in a continuum from highly structured to minimally structured.

Stein (1993) states that in the United States, on the average, 70% of mental health dollars go to support hospital services, leaving only

30% for community services. In contrast, Dane County allocates 20% of mental health dollars for inpatient care while 80% supports community-based services.

Some of the other reports on innovative community psychiatric projects should be mentioned. Sledge et al. (1996) compared a conventional inpatient programme in Connecticut for urban poor severely ill voluntary patients who usually require hospitalization to an alternative experimental programme consisting of a day hospital and linked to a crisis respite community residence. The experimental programme had the same effectiveness as an acute hospital: according to follow-ups, the experimental programme had a slightly more positive effect on measures of symptoms, overall functioning, and social functioning.

Muijen et al. (1992) applied the controlled trial method in London to study the effects of social skills training (The Daily Living Programme), combined with many other kinds of outpatient support. During a follow-up period of 10 months, the study patients in the sample—including both schizophrenic and affective psychosis patients, all in need of hospital treatment—were in hospitals for an average of 14 days, while the controls spent an average of 72 days on wards. Opposing the possibly overoptimistic—and injurious—hopes of easy money-saving, the authors emphasize that the total cost of the treatment per patient was, nevertheless, the same for the two groups. Dean et al. (1993) similarly compared a community-based service, including outpatient care, day treatment, and social services, with hospital-based service. The former appeared to be as effective as the latter and was preferred by the relatives. It was also more effective in keeping people in long-term contact with psychiatrists.

The situation in Italy has been interesting, because legislation ratified in 1978 permitted a complete abolition of the mental hospital network. The law has not been enforced very consistently, at least in southern Italy, and it also involves drawbacks: many of the psychotic patients, for example, are now being treated in the mental hospital wards of prisons. In many places, however, this innovation resulted in a vigorous activation of outpatient care. Favourable experiences have been reported from Verona, Trieste, Arezzo, and Perugia (Pylkkänen & Eskola, 1984).

With regard to *early case finding* and *prevention*, extremely interesting even if very preliminary results with regard to the prevention of schizophrenic episodes were reported by Falloon in 1992. Appointed the head of the mental health organization in a catchment area with a population of 30,000 in the county of Buckinghamshire, England, he began a case-finding programme to be able to identify and work with schizophrenic patients at an early stage of the illness (or actually before that). The work mainly consisted of explaining the early symptoms of schizophrenia to the general practitioners and public health nurses and summoning the family crisis team immediately to work out situations reported by doctors or nurses. He reported that the incidence of new cases diagnosable as schizophrenia dropped to one tenth of what it had been earlier: during a period of four years, only one patient in this area became so seriously disturbed as to fulfil the DSM–III-R criteria for schizophrenia (Falloon, 1992).

Falloon underlines that the family-centred therapeutic programme, with an intervention by the team in any crisis within 24 hours, must be carried out on an emergency basis. Though he thus implies that the schizophrenic disorder can be prevented, Falloon continues to consider schizophrenia to be organic in origin, based on the vulnerability–stress hypothesis.

The paradigm of early intervention has also been emphasized by Birchwood and Macmillan (1993), and new projects aiming at the prevention of schizophrenic episodes have been put in practice, for example, in Sweden and Norway (André, 1995; Larsen, 1994). In Finland, the comprehensive family- and network-centred Western Lapland Project has led to a marked decrease in the annual incidence of first-episode schizophrenic patients (DSM–III-R), while the admission rates for patients suffering from prodromal symptoms have increased (Aaltonen et al., 1997). This area of development will undoubtedly receive increased attention in the near future, because of the improved prognostic prospects connected with early therapeutic intervention.

CHAPTER FIVE

Need-adapted treatment of schizophrenic psychoses: development, principles, and results

I n this chapter, I describe our experiences and findings over the past two decades in the Clinic of Psychiatry in Turku, which led to the treatment orientation called *need-adapted treatment of schizophrenia-group psychoses*. We had a chance to apply our approach more widely when a national programme for developing research, treatment, and rehabilitation of schizophrenics was carried out in Finland in the 1980s under my leadership as well as in connection with the Inter-Scandinavian NIPS Project (Nordic Investigation on Psychotherapy of Schizophrenia). I hope that these experiences may be of benefit to those doing developmental work of a corresponding nature elsewhere, despite the differences in the structure of mental health organizations.

The Turku Schizophrenia Project

"Turku Schizophrenia Project" denotes the research and therapeutic activities undertaken in the Turku Clinic of Psychiatry from 1968 onwards to devise optimal treatment of schizophrenia and functional psychotic disorders related to it. The overall goal of the project was to develop a treatment of psychoses belonging to the schizophrenia group that is predominantly psychotherapeutic and can also be applied more generally to public psychiatric health care. To reach this goal, it was necessary to integrate the activities and to make them as versatile as possible.

Since the beginning, our efforts have been towards team-work, with the central goal of enabling all staff members to do active, increasingly independent therapeutic work suited to their personal inclinations and abilities. To this end, supervision and training activities were included in the developmental project as essential elements. As far as I can see, it is not—and will not—be possible to meet adequately the population's needs for therapeutic relationships by providing only psychiatrists' and psychologists' services; rather, it is necessary to involve in this effort other staff persons, including nurses, who are numerically the largest group, especially in hospitals. These goals were particularly important in the Turku Clinic, where the staff was numerically small: the staff/ patient ratio remained within 0.4–0.6 for a long time; it rose to 1.0 on the acute ward only in the late 1980s.

The Turku Clinic of Psychiatry, founded in 1967, is both a university hospital and a part of the community psychiatric system of the town of Turku, the Turku Mental Health District. Together with other units of the district—the Kupittaa Mental Hospital and the Turku Mental Health Office (the centre for psychiatric open care)—the clinic has been in charge of providing psychiatric services for the town of Turku, located in the southwestern part of Finland.

Turku (population 160,000) is the administrative and commercial centre of the area and is known as a university town; the total number of students at the three institutions for higher education is approaching 20,000. For this reason, the incidence of new psychoses is somewhat greater than among the indigenous population of the town. The Mental Health District is part of the General Health service organization of the town, with close connections to the basic health services. The urban character of the catchment area, with short distances between the homes of the patients and service units, facilitates family- and environment-centred activities. The psychiatric health services are quantitatively not well financed, but they are strengthened by qualitative resources through cooperation with the university department.

Our goal was divided into two sub-goals—a developmental objective and a research aim:

1. *To develop the treatment of schizophrenia-group patients* with an integrated but psychotherapeutically oriented approach, emphasizing:

   • a basic psychotherapeutic attitude,

   • development of hospital wards into psychotherapeutic communities,

   • development of family therapy and other family-centred activities,

   • development of individual therapeutic relationships,

   • appropriate use of pharmacotherapy as a mode of treatment supporting psychotherapy, and

   • active participation of all professional groups in the therapeutic work.

2. To find out, by means of *follow-up investigations of cohorts,* including all first-admitted schizophrenia-group patients from the Turku catchment area and representing different stages of development of our approach:

   • how widely it has been possible for us to employ psychotherapeutic activities with this group of patients,

   • which are the indications for different treatment modes (that is, which kind of treatment do the patients need), and

   • how the development of our therapeutic orientation affects the outcome of treatments.

Our project was carried out as action research. We consciously abandoned the methods applied in the kind of controlled psychotherapy trials I described in chapter four. The main reason for this was the priority of the developmental goals, but ethical considerations also played a role. If we had divided the patients into randomized groups and strictly pre-defined the kinds of treatment to be given to each group, we would have tied our hands in a way that would have prevented the development of the treatment to meet each patient's personal needs. Such a starting-point would also have discouraged the attitudes we tried to foster among members of our therapeutic communities and would therefore have been destructive to the therapeutic work in these communities. Other weaknesses of controlled psychotherapy trials were pointed out in chapter four.

Patient cohorts

Instead of randomizing the patients, we decided to analyse the results of our work by comparing the patients' outcomes at different stages of our therapeutic approach. This was done by collecting patient cohorts at different times. The years of admission of our cohorts, the number of patients included in each, and the initial and follow-up studies are presented in Table 5.1, which also shows the developmental stage of the therapeutic orientation at the time of the patients' admission.

Each cohort included all the patients aged 16–45 years who lived in Turku and were admitted for the first time due to a schizophrenia-group psychosis to the various units of the Turku Mental Health District within a certain period. These units included two hospitals, the Turku Psychiatric Clinic and the Kupittaa Hospital, as well as the Turku Mental Health Office, which was responsible for outpatient care. Two other outpatient clinics were taken into account: those in the Turku University Central Hospital (this hospital did not have any psychiatric wards until 1984) and the local health care organization of the university students. Their share of schizophrenic patients remained small.

The diagnostic limits of the schizophrenia group were originally defined widely, because this suited our developmental goals. However, the patients were divided into different diagnostic subgroups, following the International Classification of Diagnoses (ICD 8) and the Scandinavian principles of differentiating typical schizophrenia from other psychoses included in the schizophrenia group (Achté, 1961, 1967; Langfeldt, 1953). The patients in Cohort IV were diagnosed according to the DSM–III-R classification, and this classification was retrospectively also applied to Cohort III.

Comparability between the initial and follow-up data was ensured by using structured schedules (research forms) in which the information on the basic clinical, demographic, and psychosocial items or variables

TABLE 5.1
The Turku Schizophrenia Project.
Cohorts and follow-up studies

Cohort	Year of admission	Number of patients	Development of psychotherapeutic approaches	Follow-up studies
I	1965-67 (24 mos.)	100 (50)	single patients in individual therapy, approach hospital-centred	1973-74
II	1969 (12 mos.)	75 (39)	single patients in individual or family therapy, psychotherapeutic communities initiated	1971, 1977
III	1976–77 (19 mos.)	100 (56)	individual therapy and psychotherapeutic communities, well-developed open care included	1978–79, 1981–82
IV	1983–84 (12 mos.)	30	need-adapted approach with initial family-centred therapy meetings, family therapy well developed	1985–86, 1988–89
V	1995–	?	need-adapted approach, continued sectorization lowers the barrier between open care and the hospitals	1997–2000

The numbers in parentheses (Cohorts I–III) refer to patients diagnosed as "typical schizophrenia". In Cohort IV, the DSM–III-R classification was applied. This classification was retrospectively applied also to Cohort III (cf. Table 5.4).

was gathered in a way that had been designed at the beginning of the project.

Below, I first describe our developmental experiences and then discuss our results in the light of comparative findings on the different cohorts. The most important of these surveys are:

• The comparison between the seven-and-a-half-year follow-up of Cohort I (year of admission 1965–67) and the eight-year follow-up of Cohort II (year of admission 1969) by Raimo Salokangas (1977, 1986).

- The two- and five-year follow-ups of Cohort III (1976–77) by our team (Alanen et al., 1983, 1986).

- The two-year follow-up by our team (Alanen et al., 1991) and the five-year follow-up by Klaus Lehtinen (1993a, 1993b) of Cohort IV (1983–84), comparing the findings with those made on Cohort III.

Development of psychotherapeutic communities

We use the term "psychotherapeutic community" to differentiate our units from the therapeutic communities of Maxwell Jones (1953). Jones's pioneering activities, which aimed at changing the old-fashioned mental hospital milieus, primarily emphasized efforts to achieve maximal equality among the various staff categories and between staff and patients. We also made efforts to bring the ward atmosphere closer to normal living milieus by diminishing hierarchy and allowing both staff and patients to wear informal clothing. However, the line drawn between the staff and the patients was not compromised: the staff members were therapists and the patients were receiving therapy, and the central task was to create a psychotherapeutic attitude and to establish therapeutic relationships.

The goals and activities of the psychotherapeutic community at the acute psychosis ward can be divided as follows (Alanen, 1975):

1. *Shared empathic basic attitude towards the patients.* The main instruments in creating such an attitude were the supervision activities and case meetings, in which treatment plans were arrived at by common consent.

2. *Open mutual communication,* both with patients and among staff members. Of special significance was a staff meeting at the end of the week in which all the members in the shift participated and the actual problems were discussed.

3. *Various group processes and activities.* We do not have ordinary group therapy on our acute psychosis ward, but other group activities—such as the morning meetings, doing various things together, as well as excursions—are usual. Among the meetings of process-like character, the therapy meetings described later have a special position.

4. *Development of therapeutic relationships* within the therapeutic com-

munity. Every patient, including those whose treatment may be focused in family therapy, has a *personal nurse*, whose primary responsibility is to form an empathic relationship with him/her. Some of these relationships progress in a later phase to individual psychotherapy, based on a therapy contract, which may continue after the patient has been discharged from the ward. A prerequisite is the personal supervision, which was gradually made available to all staff members.

5. The importance of *family therapeutic activities* has greatly increased in the course of years, and they are often continued after the patient has been discharged from the ward.

6. *Taking care of the patients' continuing contacts outside the hospital ward.* In addition to the family-centred work, this also includes support given to the patient's other important relationships, as well as—if needed—contacts with the working environment, for rehabilitative purposes.

It is natural that working in a therapeutic community of this kind is more demanding for the members than is work that merely consists of observing the patients' symptoms and obeying the superiors' orders. Openness and empathic qualities are needed, together with a readiness for increased self-knowledge. After coming to work on the ward, many of the community members undergo a personal developmental process, which leads to the emergence or confirmation of a new kind of theory of humanity. Quite a few end up improving their professional competence through personal psychotherapy and psychotherapy training. Others may decide to find a job better suited to their inclinations. But those who stay in the community find their work notably more rewarding than the previous routine work on hospital wards.

In his comparative study, Salokangas (1986) found the average prognoses roughly similar in Cohorts I and II, with the exception that the need for pensions and hospitalizations was somewhat greater in Cohort II than in Cohort I (see Tables 5.2 and 5.3, pp. 154, 155). One reason for this may have been the fact that Cohort II included an unusually large number of young, seriously ill male patients, whose prognosis is generally poorer than that of female patients. The most essential difference between the cohorts was, however, crystallized by Salokangas as follows: patients in Cohort II were more content with their inpatient treatment than were patients in Cohort I, but they also stayed longer in the hospital.

Salokangas (1986) emphasized the need to increase outpatient and rehabilitative services. This criticism was doubtless justified and pointed out the major problem of the early stages of our therapeutic approach—the excessive inpatient orientation due to a lack of outpatient facilities. When the clinic was founded, no outpatient staff was employed, because the town health care officials assumed that the outpatient activities would be totally carried out in the Mental Health Office. Already in early 1970s, we tried to improve the situation by increasing the patients' after-care visits to hospital staff and encouraging cooperation with the Mental Health Office—for example, through psychotherapeutic supervision—and with private psychotherapists. Hospital treatment was defined as an intermediary stage, with the purpose of planning for the subsequent outpatient treatment with the staff responsible for it.

These findings on the early phase of our activities may have given rise to doubts as to whether inpatient therapy of this kind would have any significance for the subsequent prognosis of the patients. The findings on subsequent cohorts, however, proved these doubts to have been premature.

The benefits derived by the patients from psychotherapeutic community treatment were observable in the follow-up findings on Cohort III (Alanen et al., 1983, 1986). Although the first inpatient periods in the clinic were, at that time, still clearly longer than were those of patients in the Kupittaa Hospital (73 days vs. 27 days), the average duration of the subsequent inpatient episodes was shorter from the second follow-up year onwards among those patients admitted into the psychotherapeutic community of the Clinic than for the patients first admitted into the Kupittaa Hospital, where treatment then consisted mostly of psychopharmacological medication. A statistical analysis indicated that the difference was not due to other clinical or psychosocial background factors affecting the patients' prognosis (Alanen et al., 1986).

Development of individual therapy

The focus in the development of therapeutic relationships at that time was clearly on *psychodynamically oriented individual therapy*. This was also clearly reflected in the five-year follow-up findings. Of the 100 patients in Cohort III, 26 had undergone individual therapies for at least two years, consisting of 80 or more sessions, 31 other patients had each had a shorter therapeutic relationship defined as individual therapy, 15 patients had had 12 or more joint family therapy sessions over at least 6 months, while 10 others had had at least 3 joint sessions (Alanen et al., 1986).

The results of individual therapy were more rewarding than those of family therapy. Most therapists, however, lacked proper therapeutic training; two-thirds of them were given supervision for their work with at least one patient. More than 40% of the therapies were conducted by nurses. Many psychiatric nurses who came to know the problems of psychotic patients in their work attained, with the help of supervision, good results as therapists of schizophrenic patients able to benefit from individual therapy (see Aaku, Rasimus, & Alanen, 1980). In addition to being naturally inclined to this kind of work, many of them also undertook formal training in psychotherapy later on. Untrained therapists met with more problems in family therapy; they were easily involved in the "suction" of the transactional network, and the therapeutic process therefore got stuck. The successful couple therapies of some patients who had been married before their illness were exceptions in this respect.

The favourable effect of long-term individual therapy on the clinical characteristics of typical schizophrenics appears obvious in Figure 5.1. Of the 56 "typical schizophrenia" patients in Cohort III, 14 had individual therapy that met with the aforementioned criteria (at least 2

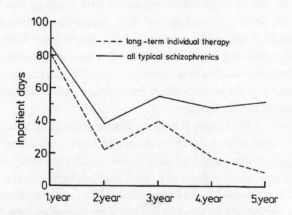

FIGURE 5.1 The Turku Schizophrenia Project Cohort III. Outcome of long-term individual psychotherapy of typical schizophrenic patients, counted as yearly average inpatient days per patient (according to Alanen et al., 1986).

years, at least 80 therapy sessions). The figure shows the better prognosis of these patients with regard to the need for inpatient treatment during the follow-up period. Although it can be assumed that the group of patients given psychotherapy probably included some patients whose original prognosis was better, it is worth noting that the need for inpatient treatment continues to decrease in this sub-group, unlike the whole cohort (Alanen et al., 1986).

Development of family therapy

While confirming the relatively better outcomes of our individual therapies compared with family therapies, the follow-up findings on Cohort III at the same time revealed the significance of the family members' attitudes for the patients' outcome. The fact that the patient had at least one empathic relative at the time of the initial examination turned out to be one of the most important predictors of a good prognosis in the logistic regression analysis five years later (Alanen et al., 1986).

As there was a recognizable need for regular family therapy training in Finland, even in fields other than psychosis therapy, a three-year *multi-professional family therapy training* was established in Finland, through the Finnish Mental Health Association, in accordance with the models available in some other countries. The training was begun in Turku and Helsinki in the autumn of 1979. A majority of the members of the first training team were psychoanalysts. Right from the beginning, however, the training was clearly oriented towards systemic family therapy. I believe that this combination of psychoanalytic and systemic expertise was a great asset both in the training and in the subsequent development of family therapy.

The effects of the family therapy training were quite soon visible in the development of our psychotherapeutic orientation. Two psychiatrists, Klaus Lehtinen and Hilkka Virtanen, and the ward nurse Riitta Rasimus set up a team in the early 1980s and began, under the guidance of Viljo Räkköläinen (a psychiatrist with both psychoanalytic and family therapeutic expertise), to arrange regular joint meetings with the newly admitted patients and their family members, or other people close to the patients, at the very beginning of the treatment (Lehtinen, 1993b, 1994; Lehtinen & Räkköläinen, 1986).

The new way to begin the treatment with regular family meetings soon proved particularly useful. We could give quick support both to the patient and the family members, who often felt extreme anxiety at that time. During the meeting it was possible to obtain further information on the manifestation of the patient's illness and the factors associated with his/her admission. The labelling of the patient as ill was lessened in both the patient's and the family members' minds, when the psychosis was related to their problems. "The situation has been defined as something other than mental illness in the traditional medical and/or mystical and magic sense. What is at hand is a difficult situation which, however, is part of the course of life and involves problems that can be described with ordinary words" (Klaus Lehtinen, in Alanen et al., 1990a, p. 22).

These meetings were often continued even after the initial analysis stage, especially if the patient had been admitted into hospital. As they turned out to have a significant therapeutic effect, we began to call them *therapy meetings* (Alanen et al., 1991; Lehtinen & Räkköläinen, 1986; Räkköläinen, Lehtinen, & Alanen, 1991). They were found to be advantageous not only to the schizophrenia group patients, but also to other patients recommended for inpatient care. Hilkka Virtanen (1991) has reported favourable experiences of family-centred therapy meetings in geriatric psychiatry.

The new orientation was employed systemically in the treatment of patients included in our Cohort IV, collected during 1983–84. The activities were supervised by a team of four psychiatrists (Alanen, Lehtinen, Räkköläinen, & Aaltonen, 1991; Lehtinen, 1993a, 1993b). Lehtinen had the main responsibility for the practical work, and he was assisted by three nurse specialists with family therapy training. They worked in the project alongside their regular jobs. In order to reach developmental goals in general, it is better to incorporate the innovative activities as part of the normal working routine rather than give them a separate status as project work.

The families were quite well motivated for team-work at the time of the first admission of a psychotic family member. A family-centred initial analysis (therapy meeting) was accomplished in 87% of the 32 cases originally included in the series. The initial results were quite encouraging: the psychotic symptoms of many patients disappeared or quickly decreased as a consequence of family-oriented intervention. And, compared with the earlier cohorts, the hospital episodes were significantly shorter.

The supervisory team of the cohort frequently discussed the justifiable duration of the treatment. Lehtinen emphasized that the patients should not be needlessly involved in the therapeutic system, where the treatment may easily become a routine that only maintains the patient role, while I defended the need to continue the psychotherapeutic treatments, pointing out that schizophrenic disorders are serious and frequently recur. By that time, individual therapies had begun to be overshadowed by family therapies; there still were individual therapies, but they were fewer than in the previous cohort and their management was not organized like that of family therapies.

After the follow-ups of Cohort IV (Alanen et al., 1991; Lehtinen, 1993a, 1993b), our views have come closer to each other. Cohort IV included several patients who had become psychotic in an acute crisis, and they were found to cope well after the initial intervention, even without further therapy. On the other hand, however, it turned out that the treatment of many more-seriously ill patients had been terminated much too soon or had suffered from discontinuity, because it had initially not been planned for a sufficient time span.

One consequence of these experiences was the establishment of an *admission clinic* in the hospital. The team working in this clinic meets the patients referred to the hospital together with their families even before the patient is registered as inpatient. Quite often, the patient is not admitted to the hospital ward, but the team continues the treatment as a crisis intervention at the admission clinic.

On the other hand, because of the unsatisfied need for trained individual therapists, a multiprofessional three-year (special level) training in individual therapy, with psychotic patients as one target group, was begun in Turku in 1986, organized in connection with the University's Centre for Extension Studies. Later, advanced special-level training programmes were also established, both in family therapy and in individual psychotherapy, focused on psychotic and borderline patients, comprising six years in all (see pp. 247–248).

The initial family- and milieu-oriented interventions employed with patients recommended for inpatient care are not in themselves a new invention. We remember the work by Langsley's team (Langsley, Machotka, & Flomenhaft, 1971; Langsley, Pittman, & Swank, 1969) in the 1960s, which was described in chapter four, whose favourable results seem to have been regrettably ignored. What is new in our approach, however, is that these interventions are incorporated in an integrated, systemic, and psychodynamically oriented model of treating psychotic patients, where other psychotherapeutic activities such as individual therapy also play a notable role.

The outcome findings

Because the main stress in the Turku Project was on therapeutic development applying action research principles, the interpretation of our follow-up data involved several problems due to our research design. As the data had been collected from different units, they did not specifically represent the effects of our own therapeutic orientation. In particular, the orientation in the Kupittaa Hospital from the late 1960s to the mid-1980s was different from ours, mainly consisting of medication in a conventional hospital environment.

The patients in Cohort I (see Table 5.1) were first admitted to treatment before the Clinic of Psychiatry was founded. In Cohort II, as many as 88% of the patients were admitted into the wards of the newly founded Clinic. In Cohort III, the clinic wards and outpatient activities together were responsible for the primary care of 54% of all the patients, while the Clinic took in 70% of the patients who began as inpatients. In Cohort IV, the corresponding figures were 67% and 83%. In Cohort III, we could compare the effects of different therapeutic environments and orientations. Only in Cohort IV was the same therapeutic orientation, beginning with the family-centred intervention, carried out in the entire Mental Health District.

Another factor that made the comparison of outcome results of the cohorts with each other difficult was the difference in the diagnostic criteria between Cohorts I–III, on the one hand and Cohort IV on the other. While the earlier cohorts included schizophrenia group psychoses in a notably wide sense, the patients for Cohort IV were selected with the distinctly stricter criteria of the DSM–III system. Besides, the follow-up period was seven and a half and eight years in Cohorts I and II and 5 years in Cohorts III and IV.

According to the original criteria used in Cohorts I, II, and III, the patients were subdivided into four diagnostic categories. These were defined as follows:

> The group of *typical schizophrenia* included the patients who, besides a schizophrenic-type thought disorder (in practise, the criterion for inclusion in the whole series), had some other characteristic schizophrenic symptoms which had arisen without any

toxic or organic precipitating factors and indicated a tendency to persistence. We paid particular attention to the presence of eight nuclear symptoms of schizophrenia: autism, schizophrenic thought disorder, hebephrenic affective disorder ("blunting" of affect), schizophrenic auditory hallucinosis, physical delusions of being influenced, massive psychological delusions of being influenced, typical catatonic symptoms (stupor or excitement), and sensations of depersonalization and/or derealization when the patient's consciousness is clear. . . . The group of *schizophreniform psychosis* included short or recurrent psychotic states, where the onset of schizophrenic symptoms had regularly been sudden and the symptoms had been of short duration. . . . *Schizo-affective psychoses* were characterized by a simultaneous occurrence of schizophrenic symptoms and a clearly manic or depressive mental state. . . . The group of *borderline schizophrenia* included the patients whose schizophrenic symptoms were mild, less characteristic and usually short in duration, although they tended to recur in most cases, occasionally even become chronic. (Alanen et al., 1986, pp. 33–34)

The DSM–III criteria for symptoms are the same for both "schizophreniform disorder" and "schizophreniform psychosis". The groups are differentiated by the duration of the characteristic psychotic symptoms (including prodromal and residual symptoms), which is 6 months or more in the schizophrenic disorder and more than 2 weeks but less than 6 months in the schizophreniform disorder. The criteria for schizophrenic disorder further include "deterioration from the previous level of functioning in such areas as work, social relations, and self-care", compared with the prepsychotic period, or, in younger patients, "a failure to achieve the expected level of social development", which attributes are lacking from the criteria of schizophreniform disorder. According to DSM–III, only the group "typical schizophrenia" in our earlier classification clearly fulfilled the criteria of schizophrenic disorder (and even some patients in this group had the DSM–III diagnosis schizophreniform disorder).

To make it possible to compare the outcomes, the patients in Cohort III were retrospectively rediagnosed by using the same criteria derived from the DSM–III-R as were used in the final diagnoses of Cohort IV. The same rediagnostic procedure (see Kendler, Spitzer, & Williams, 1989) was also applied to the schizoaffective psychoses. The rediagnoses were made by Klaus Lehtinen, who used the patient record data and the patient research forms and also consulted the psychiatric researchers who had interviewed the patients at the initial stage. Lehtinen had also been responsible for the final diagnostic characterization of the patients of Cohort IV.

Three different comparisons are made here. In Table 5.2, a comparison of the outcome findings in Cohorts I, II, and III as a whole is presented, following the wide diagnostic criteria originally used by us. In Table 5.3, a comparison of these outcome findings has been restricted to the patients belonging to the typical schizophrenia group only. In Table 5.4, the result of the comparison of five-year follow-up findings of Cohorts III and IV with each other is presented, including the patients who, according to the DSM–III-R system, could be diagnosed as suffering from schizophrenic disorder (38 patients in Cohort III and 18 patients in Cohort IV), schizophreniform disorder (respectively, 12 and 8 patients), or schizoaffective disorder (respectively, 3 and 2 patients). Three prognostic variables are included: one clinical (no psychotic symptoms) and two social (maintenance of working capacity and avoidance of pension). Additionally, in Table 5.4. the average inpatient days per patient during 5 years are included.

There is a tendency towards improvement of the outcome from the earlier cohorts to Cohort III with regard to the presence of psychotic symptoms. However, the social outcome criteria do not confirm the positive prognostic development (which may depend partly on changes in the pension policy).

Table 5.4 indicates that there is a definite improvement of the prognosis observable when the outcome findings of Cohort IV are compared with the findings of Cohort III. An increasingly large proportion of the patients had no psychotic symptoms, and there was a particularly conspicuous change in the ability to maintain working capacity and avoid being pensioned. There was also a significant decrease in the amount of inpatient care needed by the patients, which was 132 days per patient on an average during the whole five-year period in Cohort IV, while the corresponding figure in Cohort III was 272 days. This difference was especially obvious over the first two follow-up years, but it declined slightly during the fourth and fifth year. At the end of the follow-up, 3 patients (9.7%) from Cohort IV and 7 patients from Cohort III (13%) were hospitalized. Every one of our cohorts included a few seriously ill long-term patients, who mostly accounted for the need for hospital care over the later follow-up years.

Lehtinen (1993b) also studied the outcome of these cohorts using the four-dimensional Strauss–Carpenter scales (inpatient care, social con-

TABLE 5.2
The Turku Schizophrenia Project.
Comparison of clinical and social follow-up findings in cohorts
of first-admission patients (original samples of Cohorts I–III)

			Outcome variable		
	Cohort		Percent without	Percent	Percent without
No.	Year of admission	Size of sample	psychotic symptoms	fully able to work	disability pension
I	1965–67 (24 mos.)	100	48	39	67
II	1969 (12 mos.)	75	46	41	54
III	1976–77 (19 mos.)	100	69	43	59

The findings are based on eight-year follow-ups of Cohorts I and II, and on a five-year follow-up of Cohort III.

The percentages are calculated for the patients who attended the follow-up examinations (more than 90% in all series). There were 5 suicides in Cohort I, 2 in Cohort II, and 3 in Cohort III.

tacts, working, symptoms) as prognostic criteria (Strauss & Carpenter, 1972, 1974). The sum of the subscales (range 0–16) was compared, using the two-tailed t-test. The mean for the 1983–84 series was 12.0 ($SD = 4.2$) and that for the 1976–77 series 9.8 ($SD = 4.2$). The difference between the cohorts was significant ($p = 0.03$), being most striking on the working ("usefully employed") variable ($p = 0.002$)

When examining these follow-up findings, it is useful to remember that the influence of our therapeutic orientation in the 1970s did not reach all parts of the mental health district. There were considerable differences in the treatment received by the patients of Cohort III, depending on where they were treated. The treatment of the patients in Cohort IV was notably more uniform, one reason being that the teams of family therapists saw all of the patients and their families in the meetings arranged initially, regardless of the unit responsible for the treatment. However, this fact does not explain the significant difference between the outcome findings of these two patient cohorts.

The follow-up findings on our Cohort IV can be considered quite good, even when compared with the international findings reviewed in chapter two. The major difference between the treatment of Cohort IV and the previous cohorts was the establishment of family-oriented therapy meetings, which were attended jointly by the patient, the family members, and the team responsible for treatment, and which were often continued as family-oriented crisis interventions. The families of the patients in Cohorts II and III were also met at an early stage of the treatment, but mainly for purposes of research and separately from the patients. These meetings were therefore not intended as therapeutic intervention, as were the meetings of Cohort IV.

Actual family therapy was also notably more common in Cohort IV than previously. While 25% of the patients in Cohort III received family therapy, the corresponding figure in Cohort IV was 60%. The family therapies were clearly most common at the beginning of the treatment: only two couple therapies continued after the first follow-up year, and

TABLE 5.3
The Turku Schizophrenia Project.
Comparison of clinical and social follow-up findings in cohorts of first-admission patients. Only patients diagnosed as "typical schizophrenia" included (original samples of Cohorts I–III)

| | Cohort | | Outcome variable | | |
| | | | Percent without psychotic symptoms | Percent fully able to work | Percent without disability pension |
No.	Year of admission	Size of sample			
I	1965–67 (24 mos.)	50	38	29	58
II	1969 (12 mos.)	39	27	24	32
III	1976–77 (19 mos.)	56	49	33	44

The findings are based on eight-year follow-ups of Cohorts I and II, and on five-year follow-up of Cohort III.

The percentages are calculated for those patients who attended the follow-up examinations (more than 90% in all series). In this patient group, there were 2 suicides in Cohort I, 0 in Cohort II, and 2 in Cohort III.

TABLE 5.4
The Turku Schizophrenia Project.
Comparison of clinical and social follow-up findings
of first-admission schizophrenic patients diagnosed according to
DSM–III-R (Cohorts III and IV)

	Cohort		Outcome variable			
			Percent without psychotic symptoms	Percent fully able to work	Percent without disability pension	Hospital days per person during 5 years
No.	Year of admission	Size of sample				
III	1976–77 (19 mos.)	56	38	30	49	272
IV	1983–84 (12 mos.)	30	61	57	82	132

Source: According to Lehtinen, 1993b.
The findings are based on five-year follow-ups of Cohorts III and IV.

The percentages are again calculated for the patients who attended the follow-up examination (53 patients in Cohort III, 28 patients in Cohort IV). There were 2 suicides in Cohort III and 1 in Cohort IV.

new family therapies were rarely begun at later stages of treatment (Lehtinen, 1993b).

About 30% of the patients in Cohort III received satisfactory individual therapy. In Cohort IV, this percentage was 20%, and the number of individual-oriented therapies with relatively infrequent sessions had also decreased, as many of the patients had discontinued treatment quite early (Lehtinen, 1993b). It was probably due to the longer individual therapies that the outcome in Cohort III improved slightly from the two-year follow-up to the five-year follow-up: the number of "typical schizophrenic patients" without psychotic symptoms increased, in accordance with our original estimates, from 41% to 49% (Alanen et al., 1983, 1986), while the outcome of the patients in Cohort IV decreased slightly, the corresponding percentages being 68% and 61% (Alanen et al., 1991; Lehtinen, 1993a).

Most of the psychotherapeutic treatments in these cohorts were conducted by staff members of the public psychiatric organization, including nurses. The therapeutic activities (especially individual therapy) were complemented by psychiatrists and psychologists working in the private sector, either because the patients wanted this or because we intended to provide more intensive therapeutic opportunities for them. I do not believe, however, that this will restrict in any way the conclusions we can draw on the basis of our findings concerning the development of public psychiatric health care. There is everywhere a tendency to increase the cooperation between the public and the private sectors. In Finland it has been legally possible from 1984 onwards for the public health care system to buy psychotherapeutic services from the private sector to supplement inadequate resources.

It can be concluded on the basis of these observations that the emphasis placed on the initial interventions and on the family orientation seems to have been beneficial. In the light of these findings, the recovery from a regressive psychotic state, brought about by early and intensive family-centred treatment, appears to occupy a key role in the further development of the treatment of schizophrenic patients in community psychiatry. However, the follow-up findings of Cohort III also suggest that long-term individual psychotherapy may benefit a number of patients considerably. This standpoint was further supported by the results of the Inter-Scandinavian NIPS Project, described below.

According to the follow-up findings reported by Lehtinen (1993a, 1993b), the outcome of schizophreniform psychoses and paranoid schizophrenias were statistically significantly better in Cohort IV than in Cohort III, while no similar inter-cohort differences were discernible in the outcomes of the patients outside these diagnostic categories, including the hebephrenic ("disorganized") patients. The principle of candour inherent in our therapeutic orientation was probably well suited to the paranoid schizophrenic patients. Our clinical experiences confirmed the effectiveness of early initial interventions in the treatment especially of acute psychotic states: the psychotic symptoms were alleviated sooner than they had been previously, and the inpatient episodes were shorter. The interventions probably also shortened the schizophrenic psychotic state of some patients, preventing sufficient duration of the psychosis compatible with DSM–III-R criteria for "schizophrenic disorder".

The prognostic findings presented here need to be confirmed by further research. The investigators of the Clinic have now begun a new cohort research project (see Table 5.1). It will take place at a time when the activities of the Turku Mental Health District have been sectorized. The family-centred orientation has become well established, but the findings will not be influenced by the kind of special stimuli involved in the initial enthusiasm present in Cohort IV.

Other observations on factors affecting prognosis and treatability

The follow-up study of Cohort III also included an assessment of the clinical, psychosocial, and therapeutic factors that most affected the patients' outcome in the light of a logistic regression analysis. When this was measured on the four-dimensional prognostic scale of Strauss and Carpenter, the good prognosis of "typical schizophrenics" was explained by the following variables in a decreasing order of importance (Alanen et al., 1986):

1. the patient had received less neuroleptic medication than the average during the follow-up;
2. the initial examination had shown the patient to have at least one empathic relative;
3. the patient was female; and
4. the patient had been in long-term individual therapy.

In a larger series, which also included the milder disorders of the schizophrenia group, the first three variables were the same, and the fourth variable was that the patient had been employed at the time of admission.

The amount of neuroleptic medication given to the patients during the follow-up naturally correlated with the clinical severity of their illness. It was, however, interesting that the severity of the patient's illness did not emerge as an explaining variable in the logistic regression analysis but was "covered" in the analysis by the neuroleptic variable. We interpreted this finding as being related to the effects of the therapeutic approach as a whole: the patients treated predominantly psychopharmacologically were not engaged in psychotherapy, whereas the psychotherapeutic treatment, on the other hand, had a diminishing effect on the need of neuroleptics, particularly towards the end of follow-up period. Moreover, treatment including less neuroleptic medication than was the average during the follow-up retained its extremely strong statistical significance ($p = .001$) when we tried to level off in the logistic regression analysis the influence of the background variables that had the most notable effect on the outcome—i.e. Items 2 and 3 above. The favourable effect of the psychotherapy variable on the prognosis of typical schizophrenic patients, on the other hand, was only marginally significant ($p = 0.068$) in that analysis (Alanen et al., 1986).

The better prognosis for women than for men has also been pointed out in many other studies on the prognosis of schizophrenia (Goldstein & Tsuang, 1990; Salokangas, 1983). In our own study, the difference was probably further enhanced by the fact that we were more successful in enrolling female patients than males in psychotherapy. Male gender turned out to be one factor that contributed to the patients' exclusion from all psychotherapeutic activities in Cohort III. Other similar factors included belonging to the paranoid subgroup, absence of depressive symptoms, a tendency to alcohol abuse or other addiction, and low basic education.

The follow-up of Cohort IV did not involve statistical analyses of this kind. It could be concluded, however, that the increase in family therapies reduced the number of patients left outside psychotherapeutic treatment; many of the patients who lacked motivation for individual therapy were now involved in family therapy.

The Finnish National Schizophrenia Project

A national programme for developing the study, treatment, and rehabilitation of schizophrenic patients organized by the National Board of Health, the Association of Mental Hospitals, and the League of Hospitals was carried out in Finland during 1981–87 (Alanen et al., 1990a, 1990b; State Medical Board in Finland, 1988; Tuori et al., 1997). The aim of the programme was to minimize the hospital orientation of treatment, with the special goal of reducing the number of both new and old long-term schizophrenic patients in institutions by half during a period of ten years. I acted as the leader of the programme throughout its implementation.

A more comprehensive description of the results of the programme appears elsewhere (Tuori et al., 1997). From the viewpoint of this book, the NSP (New Schizophrenic Patients) Project—one of the two main subprojects of the national programme—is interesting, because it provided us with an opportunity to apply our treatment orientation in the larger community psychiatric context. The developmental work of this project was coordinated by Viljo Räkköläinen and the research by Raimo Salokangas, with me as a supervisor.

The project was accomplished in six districts (see Figure 5.2). Of these, the Northern Carelia and Northern Savo districts (both located in

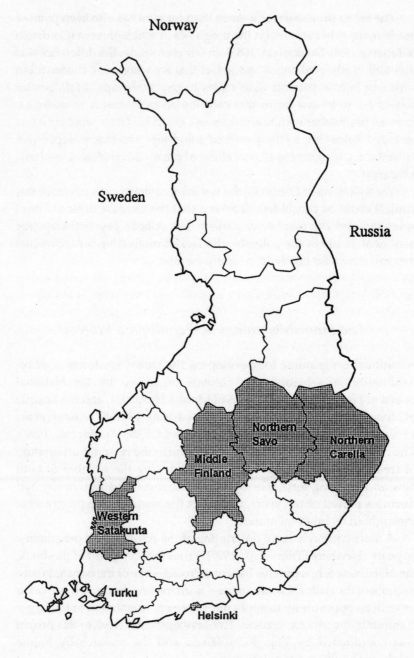

FIGURE 5.2. Districts participating in NSP Project.

eastern Finland) and the Middle Finland district represented the less wealthy parts of the country, as well as the regions with notably high numbers of schizophrenic inpatients. The Western Satakunta district is located in rural western Finland, whereas the Turku and Helsinki districts (the latter represented by one part—the Service District of Eastern Helsinki) constituted the urban environments of southern Finland. The Turku NSP population consisted of Cohort IV described earlier.

The districts that participated account for a population of about 1.1 million, which is more than one fifth of the total population of Finland. They were mainly selected through their own interest, but they were found to represent rather well the whole of Finland as to their population structure, degree of urbanization, occupational structure, degree of unemployment, income level, and availability of public psychiatric services. The availability of private psychiatric services was higher than normal, because Helsinki and Turku were included. Geographically speaking, the sample was inadequate in that it did not include any parts of northern Finland (Salokangas, Stengård, Räkköläinen, et al., 1991).

The *goals* of the treatment activities were defined mainly on the basis of the experiences obtained in Turku:

1. Treatment was to be integrated and case-specifically need-adapted. Its progress was to be followed and the treatment plans revised and altered, if the situation required it.

2. Treatment was to be based on psychotherapeutic and family-oriented principles.

3. At the beginning of the treatment, an interactional analysis of the need for treatment was to be made by arranging therapy meetings attended by the patient, his/her family members or other people close to the patient, and the team responsible for treatment.

4. The treatment was to aim at outpatient care.

5. The role of medication was to be kept small.

6. Rehabilitative activities were to be considered at the initial stage of treatment.

Each of the participating districts set up a project organization with a coordinator and contact persons, who attended the seminar arranged before the beginning of the project and the working meetings arranged during its course. Although the goal of the project was to attain the defined treatment practices, it was simultaneously emphasized that the work towards innovative treatment should not be inflexible but should, rather, proceed from the existing local traditions of care. Accordingly, there were differences of treatment practices in the different districts. The treatment named by the staff as most important for schizophrenic patients was family therapy in Turku, drug treatment in Northern Carelia, and individual therapeutic relationships in the remaining four districts (Salokangas et al., 1987, 1991).

The *patient sample* of the project covered all the patients aged 16–45 years with a psychotic disorder that fulfilled certain diagnostic criteria who were admitted for the first time into any of the public mental health care units in each participating district during 12 months in 1983–84. The diagnostic delineation was according to DSM–III criteria (American Psychiatric Association, 1980) in such a way that schizophrenic disorders and schizophreniform psychoses were included. The schizoaffective psychoses based on RDC criteria (Spitzer, Endicott, & Robins, 1975) were also included, but their number remained small. At the basic study stage, the whole NSP Project covered 227 patients (an annual incidence of 20.2 per 100,000 inhabitants; regional 16–23); 162 patients were diagnosed as suffering from a schizophrenic disorder (incidence 14.4), 58 suffered from schizophreniform psychosis, and 7 from schizoaffective psychosis (Salokangas et al., 1987, 1991).

The regional teams, which were responsible for the basic examination of the patients, managed to carry out a two-year follow-up check on 183 patients (84% of those surviving) and a five-year follow-up on 180 patients (84.5% of those surviving). By that time, 14 patients had died, 9 of them through suicide and 4 in accidents with suicidal implications (Salokangas et al., 1991).

The five-year follow-up findings obtained in the different districts in the NSP Project are presented in Table 5.5. The percentages have been calculated for the patients who attended the follow-up examinations. The loss in the whole population was 15.5%. The GAS (Global Assessment Scale) scores refer to an assessment of the patient's functional status on a scale of 0–9, where a high value implies a good functional status.

The differences between the districts were not very great. When the effect of the background variables that most significantly influenced the outcome was controlled in the statistical analysis, the Turku series differed from the rest of the population in having better GAS scores and fewer patients on pensions in the five-year follow-up. The Helsinki series also differed favourably from the other districts in the social prog-

TABLE 5.5
The NSP Project.
The five-year outcome of the new schizophrenic patients admitted to treatment in different districts

District	N	No psychotic symptoms	GAS score	The outcome variables		Average number of hospital days per patient during 5 years
				Full working capacity	No disability pension	
Turku	31	60	5.9	61	81	123
Western Satakunta	33	61	5.4	27	60	218
Helsinki	24	65	5.3	54	67	175
Middle Finland	34	64	5.1	21	52	199
Northern Carelia	56	47	5.0	20	43	242
Northern Savo	35	53	4.8	23	44	118
total	213	57	5.2	32	59	186

nosis; the difference in maintaining work capacity was significant, which is interesting because relatively many of the Helsinki patients continued with psychotic symptoms. This suggests that an urban environment is more beneficial in this respect than a rural environment. The psychosocial outcome was clearly less favourable in the rural districts (Salokangas et al., 1991).

The percentage of patients not receiving any treatment at the time of the five-year follow-up was highest in Turku (54.8%, while the figures for the other districts ranged from 11.4% to 33.9%). This was related to the relatively good outcome of the Turku patients, but also to the fact that the series included—as already mentioned earlier—a few patients who had dropped out of treatment too early. Generally, the need for treatment not actually given was found to have increased in all the districts over the follow-up period.

The family-oriented initial session, where members of the patient's family were present together with the patient, was arranged in 70% of all cases. This shows that the family members were quite often motivated to meet the therapeutic team at this stage, despite occasional long distances. It was an unexpected finding that 72% of the patients were in need of rehabilitation and sociotherapy at the time admission. This need was most notable in the districts of central and eastern Finland. The modes of rehabilitation and sociotherapy most frequently needed were social interaction practice, vocational guidance, and assistance in finding jobs.

The amount of neuroleptic medication used was clearly smaller in Turku than in the other districts, from early stages onward. At the end of the five-year follow-up, more than 60% of the Turku patients were without neuroleptics, while the corresponding number was 25% in the whole NPS series. It was interesting to note that inpatient treatment was least common during the five-year period in the two districts—Northern Carelia and Turku, see Table 5.5—which differed the most with regard to drug treatment. One reason for the situation prevailing in Northern Carelia was a well-established practice of active home care. Neither this, nor the high-level neuroleptic medication, however, resulted in good outcome in other respects.

In the light of statistical analyses, the good outcome in the NSP study was predicted best by good working capacity and working situation, a good functional status, and a grip on life at the initial examination (see Salokangas et al., 1989), the presence of a heterosexual relationship, and acute onset of the illness (Salokangas et al., 1991). After these predictor variables had been taken into account, the effect of treatments on the outcome was insignificant in the five-year follow-up. The only exception was family therapy with the primary family, which was significantly related to the scarcity of negative symptoms of schizophrenia.

It is difficult to compare the prognostic findings of the NSP Project with those of other studies, because different evaluative criteria have been used in the different studies. The NSP Project—which was carried out as action research—also had its methodological shortcomings, including the fact that the patients' condition was assessed by the same teams that were responsible for their treatment. The findings can, however, be considered relatively favourable when compared with corresponding recent international projects. The NSP Project is best comparable with projects that are similar to it in that they include first-episode schizophrenic patients. There are three recent European studies that, similarly to the NSP Project, dealt with unselected patients treated in community psychiatry over a five-year follow-up, namely those conducted in Mannheim, Germany (Schubart, Krumm, Biehl, & Schwarz, 1986; Biehl et al., 1986), Buckinghamshire, England (Watt, Katz, & Shepherd, 1983; Shepherd et al., 1989), and Scotland (Scottish Schizophrenia Research Group, 1987, 1992). To these, the Turku Cohort III (Alanen et al., 1986) as well as the Inter-Scandinavian NIPS study (Alanen et al., 1994) described below can also be added.

The English and German studies refer to themselves as presenting findings on the "natural course" of first-episode schizophrenics, implying that these patients have been given "usual" treatment and services. The Scottish—and initially also the English—project included a therapeutic trial on the use of two different neuroleptic drugs. None of these projects was psychotherapeutically oriented.

The outcome of psychotic symptoms is relatively good in all of these studies: only about 50% of the patients were symptomatic upon follow-up. With regard to the social prognostic criteria, 57% of the English patients had "minimal or mild" impairment, while 26% of the German patients had "good, sound adjustment", 39% "intermediate", and 35% "poor". Of the Scottish patients, only 19% were in open employment after 5 years. In the light of Table 5.5, the social outcome of the Finnish NSP series as a whole could perhaps be characterized as intermediate compared with the results of these European studies, the Turku and Helsinki patients representing an exception for the better. The mean duration of total stay in hospital during follow-up was 26 weeks (182 days) for the English first-admitted patients—almost exactly the same as that for the NPS patients as a whole (see Table 5.5)—while it was about 9 months (270 days) for the German series and 272 days for the Turku Cohort III.

The NSP findings indicated that the therapeutic orientation developed by us was also applicable elsewhere in Finland and that it seemed to improve the outcome of schizophrenia. The prognostic findings do not, however, justify any further conclusions concerning the influence of the orientation, because the qualitative resources for psychotherapeutic activities were poor and the implementation of family-oriented activities was only beginning in most districts. In addition to this, the active period of treatment was often too short in all districts because of limited resources. Many of the patients would have needed notably more intensive psychotherapy than was offered.

The number of long-stay schizophrenic inpatients in Finnish psychiatric hospitals declined 63% from 1982 to 1992. At the same time the number of staff in outpatient care had risen from 2.7 to 5.1 per 10,000 inhabitants. A summary of the results of the ten-year evaluation of the National Schizophrenia Project is presented in Table 5.6 (Tuori et al., 1997).

TABLE 5.6
The Finnish National Schizophrenia Project.
Achievement of the national goals

Number at end-of-year patient count	Years				Decrease 1982–1992
	1982	1986	1990	1992	
New long-term schizophrenic patients	406	348		161	60%
Old long-term schizophrenic patients	5,687	4,419	3,083	1,822	68%
Psychiatric hospital patients, total	17,368	13,641	10,026	7,401	67%
Psychiatric hospital beds, total	19,692	16,460	12,336	9,730	51%

Source: According to Tuori et al., 1997.
Note: In proportion to population, the number of psychiatric beds decreased from 4.1 per mil in 1982 to 1.9 per mil in 1992. The number of staff working in psychiatric outpatient care increased from 2.7 per 1,000 inhabitants in 1982 to 5.1 per 1,000 inhabitants in 1992.

The Inter-Scandinavian NIPS Project

The Turku district also participated in the Scandinavian project on the development and research of the psychotherapeutic treatment of schizophrenia (Nordic Investigation on Psychotherapy of Schizophrenia, NIPS: Alanen et al., 1994), using Cohort IV in the same way as in the NSP Project. The other regions participating in the project were Uppsala and its environs in Sweden (headed by Rolf Sjöström), part of Oslo in Norway (Endre Ugelstad), and Roskilde and its environs in Denmark (Bent Rosenbaum). All these centres used the same diagnostic criteria to collect an unselected population of first-episode schizophrenia group patients admitted to public mental health units in their catchment area, on whom the initial and follow-up examination were made using standardized research forms.

The therapeutic orientations were notably different, though they were all based on psychodynamic principles. The Danish project was oriented towards individual therapy, focusing on outpatient care. The Swedish project was also individual–therapeutic, but it favoured long-term milieu therapy on a hospital ward. Norway advocated long-term psychodynamic–supportive individual therapy supplemented with family therapy when necessary. Finland used our model of need-adapted treatment emphasizing initial family-oriented interventions, while the number of individual therapies was relatively small.

At the stage of processing the results, the project was joined by Bengt-Åke Armelius (Umeå, Sweden) as an outside researcher, who carried out the statistical analysis of the five-year follow-up findings.

A monograph was recently published on the findings of the project (Alanen et al., 1994). The central prognostic findings are shown in Figure 5.3, where the five-year follow-up findings on the whole population (n originally = 63; at follow-up = 57) have been categorized in accordance with the Strauss and Carpenter scale (Strauss & Carpenter, 1972). The figure shows the number of patients found to fill the demands of the best categories in each item. Furthermore, the number of patients without neuroleptic medication at the end of follow-up is also shown. The shadowed column indicates the findings on the whole population and the black column the findings on the nuclear group of schizophrenics (DSM–III-R diagnosis schizophrenic disorder, n at follow-up = 41).

About half of the patients had no psychotic symptoms (even 39% of those diagnosed as having a schizophrenic disorder), and a similar pro-

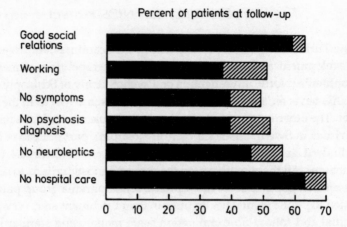

FIGURE 5.3   Five-year follow-up findings of the NIPS Project. Shaded columns indicate findings in the whole patient series (*n* = 57), black columns those of patients with a DSM–III-R diagnosis schizophrenic disorder (*n* = 41). (Alanen et al., 1994.)

portion were able to work. Clearly more than half had retained good or satisfactory social relationships. The proportion of patients who had received hospital treatment during the last follow-up year (see the lowest column in Figure 5.3) was slightly increased by the prolonged institutional care of the Swedish project (then carried out in a treatment home located in an ordinary residential area).

Compared with other studies (Biehl et al., 1986; Scottish Schizophrenia Research Group, 1992; Shepherd et al., 1989) referred to above, it must be remembered that a considerably smaller proportion of the NIPS patients than those in the other studies received neuroleptic treatment during the five-year follow-up phase. At this stage, more than half—that is, 56%—of our patients were without neuroleptic medication (as many as 46% of those with a schizophrenic disorder), and only 8 patients (14% of the whole series) had daily doses of neuroleptics corresponding to more than 250 mg chlorpromazine equivalents per day. As many as 79% of the patients in the Scottish study, for example, were on antipsychotic medication during the last follow-up year. It is well known that these drugs may suppress particularly the positive symptoms of schizophrenia and are often recommended for continuous maintenance treatment. In the NIPS Project, however, the goal was to improve the patients' condition sufficiently to render antipsychotic medication unnecessary.

The regression analysis by Armelius (in Alanen et al., 1994) indicated that almost 70% of the variance in outcome of the NIPS patients was influenced by the effects of the patient's status at intake and the diagnostic subgroup to which he/she belonged. When these variables were taken into account, the differences in treatment represented only an additional 18% of the outcome (which, it should be remembered, was psychotherapeutically oriented in all regions). If we assume that the early and intensive treatment practised especially in Turku prevented some of the patients with an initial diagnosis of schizophreniform psychosis from fulfilling the criteria for schizophrenic disorder later on, the impact of the treatment variable on the outcome should be estimated to be somewhat higher.

At the end of the NIPS Project we concluded that psychotherapeutic modes of treatment in this study did affect the outcome, but that this effect should not be exaggerated, because the effects of the other variables were greater. However, even if we attain only relatively modest changes in the number of the patients who recover fully by early psychotherapeutic treatment—which may be an increase of 10–20%—this will have a considerable economic and quality-of-life impact in the long run.

The follow-up results of the Finnish sub-project in the NIPS were better than those of the others, but a regression analysis showed this to be due to the fact that our population included more patients with a diagnosis of schizophreniform psychosis than did the other sub-populations, resulting—in addition to the probable effects of our intensive initial stage of treatment—from the fact that the diagnostic criteria, despite our attempts at making them uniform, apparently continued to be stricter for them (especially for the Swedish group), in accordance with Scandinavian traditions.

The treatment model as defined in the monograph based on the NIPS Project experiences (Alanen et al., 1994) ascribed crucial significance to intensive family-oriented interventions at the initial stage. It was further emphasized that the results of long-term individual psychotherapy in the NIPS Project were shown by regression analysis to be on the whole gratifying, contradicting adverse opinions based on earlier studies (see chapter four) regarding its usefulness. Psychodynamically oriented supportive psychotherapy with a low frequency of sessions, practised by committed therapists (especially in the Norwegian project), showed results that were as good as more insight-oriented techniques. Outpatient care was recommended as a priority, but patients requiring long-term treatment also seemed to benefit from therapeutic communities. The authors also emphasized the need for psychosocial rehabilitation in first-episode patients addressing problems with social relationships, employment, and lodging, as well as developing daily living skills.

Concept and principles of need-adapted treatment

The term "need-adapted treatment", which denotes our therapeutic orientation, was inspired by the heterogeneity and uniqueness of therapeutic needs of each schizophrenic patient. The term has also been criticized. We have been asked, for example, what we mean by "needs" and how we can define the needs in each case. We do not speak of needs in terms of philosophical or social psychological phenomena, but as a clinical concept that describes what is needed for a particular patient.

Unambiguous definition of therapeutic needs is not easy, nor are tests or check-lists for the assessment of such needs useful. What we are proposing is a hermeneutic approach: a psychological understanding of problems and the therapeutic situation and acting on the basis of this understanding. Aaltonen and Räkköläinen (1994) developed the concept of "shared mental representation guiding the therapeutic process", which they consider a prerequisite for achieving integrated treatment of schizophrenia. By this they mean the understanding shared by the therapeutic team concerning the patient's situation and the significance of his/her symptoms. It may happen in successful therapy meetings that a shared understanding—though often at different levels—is achieved by the team and the patient together with the family members, and this helps to alleviate the psychotic condition.

A significant part of the understanding comes from realizing that the treatment is a process, where the needs may also change. Our wish to emphasize this point was the reason why we gave up the term "need-specific treatment" (Alanen et al., 1986), and replaced it with the more flexible term "need-adapted treatment" (Alanen et al., 1991).

A further justification for the term "need-adapted treatment" is the fact that, as far as I can see, few schizophrenic patients are currently receiving the kind of treatment that they need. Conversely, many are being given treatment that they do not need, such as excessive use of neuroleptic drugs. The concept of "need-adapted treatment" also implies that unnecessary treatments are avoided.

General principles
of need-adapted treatment

The general principles of our therapeutic orientation can be expressed in terms of four maxims (Alanen et al., 1991; Alanen, 1992).

1. *The therapeutic activities are planned and carried out flexibly and individually in each case*, so that they meet the real, changing needs of the patients as well as of the people making up their personal interactional networks; it is therefore important to assess both the patient's subjective clinical, psychological, and social condition and to evaluate the psychological condition of the family or other essential interactional networks to which he/she belongs.

The family-centred investigation of the therapeutic needs is indicated in order to alleviate the strains that the outbreak of a psychosis and the continued psychotic behaviour are likely to arouse in the family members. Furthermore, the interactional approach is of utmost importance in the planning of treatment, because the treatment of schizophrenic patients is, to a great extent, dependent on the quality of the interpersonal relationships prevailing in their close environment. The reason for this is the patient's primary and secondary—illness-induced—dependence on others, and frequently also the dependence of others on the patient through intrafamilial psychodynamic processes, such as mutual symbiotic relationships and related introjective–projective processes.

It is therefore necessary in the initial examination both to search for the possible presence of such psychodynamics and to note the needs of the patient and the other family members (and occasionally of other individuals close to the patient) to get help in a difficult life situation. The positive resources brought out by them should be noted and taken into account while planning the treatment. The subsequent orientation of the treatment in either an individual–therapeutic or a family–therapeutic direction is largely determined by this initial investigation. A systemic evaluation of the situation is best achieved through joint therapy meetings described below.

The patient's social situation and the need for measures to improve it should also be considered upon admission.

2. *Examination and treatment are dominated by a psychotherapeutic attitude.*

"Psychotherapeutic attitude" refers to an attempt to understand what has happened and is happening to patients and the people in their interpersonal network and how we can use this understanding as a basis for approaching and helping them. Sullivan (1954) called investigators and/or therapists with such an attitude participant–observers because they try to approach the patients in an empathic way, but simultaneously retaining an external attitude that allows ego-level observation and helps the observer to keep the necessary separateness.

An attitude of this kind essentially also involves observation of one's own emotional reactions. As Searles (1965), Benedetti (1985), Boyer (1986, 1989), and Herbert Rosenfeld (1987), among others, have repeatedly emphasized, the therapist's countertransference is critically important in the treatment of schizophrenic patients. This attitude serves as the basis in the planning and implementation of all treatments, including psychopharmacological regimes.

3. *Different therapeutic approaches should supplement each other rather than constituting an "either / or" approach.*

Therapeutic activities should be integrated with one another, which is as essential for psychotherapeutic and psychopharmacological modes as it is for the various psychotherapeutic modalities. A further prerequisite for integration is cooperation between different persons and units responsible for the treatment of a patient, including appropriate awareness of the course of therapeutic activities, yet retaining the confidentiality necessary in particularly individual therapies.

4. *The treatment should attain and maintain the quality of a continuous process.*

This means that the treatment must be conceived of as a developmental event, a continuous interactional process, which should not be allowed to decline into a routine sequence of sessions. Optimally, the process activates internal development and new capacity for interpersonal relationships. Naturally, setbacks are possible, but in a continuous process they are generally less serious than the patient's previous crises and may occasionally be a necessary prerequisite for progress (a fact not widely recognized by psychiatrists).

The process quality of treatment can be maintained, if its course and outcomes are monitored and evaluated, with the consequent possibility of changing treatment plans. In hospitals, this is best done by arranging new therapy meetings. They are often also useful in crises encountered in outpatient relationships. In individual therapy, follow-up is best assisted by supervision or—if no supervision is available—discussions with colleagues when necessary.

5.   *Follow-up of the individual patients and of the efficacy of the treatment methods* is also important for the evaluation and development of the functioning of the whole therapeutic system. In his monograph dealing with family therapy and schizophrenia, Klaus Lehtinen (1993b) added this point as the fifth general principle to the four presented above.

These principles are closely related to each other. Need-adapted treatment is not possible unless they are all observed.

Progression of need-adapted treatment and the weighting of different modes of treatment

When therapy meetings became the central starting-point for our activities, as systemic thinking gained ground, our team produced a diagram (Figure 5.4) to represent the usual relative weighting of the psychotherapeutically oriented modes of treatment applied during the course of need-adapted treatment of schizophrenic psychoses. In addition to schizophrenia, the diagram can also be applied to other functional psychoses included in the schizophrenia spectrum (esp. paranoid psychoses and acute psychotic disorders).

In Figure 5.4 the *primary therapeutic concern* is indicated. This does *not* exclude the possibility that other treatment modes should also be used at the same time: on the contrary, it is quite common that the patient has an individual therapeutic relationship along with attending family therapy—in psychotherapeutic communities this is the rule—but the focus of treatment may first be on family therapy and only move over to individual therapy when the basis for successful individual therapeutic relationships has been created through family therapy.

The bottom of the diagram represents the starting-point, the initial analysis upon admission, which is achieved mainly through therapeutic meetings. The shaded vertical arrows indicate how the focus of treatment subsequently shifts, differently for different patients, from one mode of treatment to another, while the light diagonal arrows indicate the termination of treatment, which—as shown by the diagram—is possible at all stages.

Figure 5.4 must not be interpreted too literally. Need adaptation may occasionally require that the therapeutic focus is shifted in a direction opposite to that indicated by the arrows: if, for example, a patient undergoing individual therapy becomes involved in a permanent couple

MODE OF THERAPY   COURSE OF THERAPY

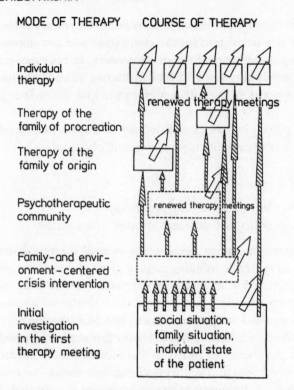

FIGURE 5.4.   The usual weighting of psychotherapeutic modes of treatment during the course of need-adapted treatment.

relationship, it may be indicated that the patient should be met together with his or her partner. Or it may turn out that the decision concerning the mode of treatment was not successful after all—that it may be best to discontinue individual therapy and resume joint meetings. It is certainly not easy in all cases to achieve adequate psychological understanding of the situation in which the patient and the people close to him/her live—this process may take a long time.

In general, the following principle is valid: when several modes of treatment are needed, it is usually expedient to proceed from the less specific family- or environment-oriented modes to the more specific individual-focused ones. This major trend in shifting the focus of treatment is shown in Figure 5.4. This figure was designed based on experience with first-admission patients of the schizophrenia group. It is, however, also applicable when the patient is re-admitted or discharged into outpatient care. In such cases the mode of treatment is quite often chosen on the basis of previous experience—especially if the patient has an existing therapeutic relationship—but a therapy meeting is, nevertheless, indicated in order to re-assess the situation and achieve therapeutic integration.

Initial examination and beginning of treatment: therapy meetings

Examination and treatment always merge into an inseparable whole in psychiatry. The attitudes and definitions that patients face in the initial examination will have a significant impact on their expectations regarding the therapeutic staff and on the attitudes towards them. Martti Siirala (1986) once aptly put this into a few words: the illness and the way it is encountered equals the illness at its next stage.

The *therapy meeting* (Alanen et al., 1991; Räkköläinen et al., 1991) constitutes the most central part of the initial examination, and it is also the part that is therapeutically the most important. Apart from being diagnostically important—with the diagnosis of the therapeutic needs as the core of the procedure—it also begins crisis intervention, which is often continued by arranging new joint meetings over the next few days.

The functions of the therapy meeting can be summarized as follows:

1. Obtaining and sharing information on factors associated with the manifestation and stages of the patient's illness and his/her admission for treatment: *informative function*.

2. A chance to examine the family dynamics *in vivo* and to diagnose therapeutic needs on the basis of an interactional interpretation of the situation: *diagnostic function*.

3. A chance to give support to the patient and the family members right from the beginning: *therapeutic function*.

Depending on case-specific circumstances, the therapeutic significance of the meetings is enhanced by the following additional factors:

4. The meetings make it possible to observe directly the topical problems and controversies in the interactional relationships,

such as reactions to the patient's admission into hospital and the paranoid attitudes that may be involved. A preliminary working-through of this kind of problem is thus made possible.

5. They minimize the experiences of rejection felt by the patient admitted into hospital and make it easier for him/her to maintain the existing interpersonal relationships outside the hospital.

6. They often lessen the tendency to label the patient as ill and the consequent psychological isolation he/she may experience (see "closure", as described by Scott & Ashworth, 1967).

7. According to our experiences, these meetings also often alleviate the patient's psychotic regression; I think that this may be due to two ostensibly opposite factors:

   a. the adult side of the patient is supported through listening and attending to him/her at the same level as the other participants in the meeting;

   b. the meeting is likely to satisfy the symbiotic needs of both patient and parent(s).

8. The meetings motivate family members to attend family-focused treatment at later stages, whenever such treatment is indicated.

If possible, the first therapy meeting should be arranged even before the patient is registered as an inpatient. In the Turku Mental Health District this is carried out by the team working in the admission clinic jointly maintained by the hospitals. In many other districts in Finland, the therapy meetings are arranged by *acute psychosis teams* (see chapter seven), recommended by the Finnish National Schizophrenia Project (Alanen et al., 1990a) and working in the Mental Health Offices. Patients who have been admitted as emergencies during the night are met on the following morning together with a ward staff member. If there are no family members or friends, or if they cannot be contacted, the patient alone is present in the meetings. If the patient is to be registered as an inpatient, the new therapeutic meetings that follow are arranged by the ward staff teams, with a member of the acute psychosis team present for the transmission of information.

In the Finnish NSP Project, 68% of the first-admission schizophrenia group patients were admitted into hospital for observation against their will. Of these, 20% were admitted as voluntary inpatients after an observation period (5 days at that time). According to the experiences of the

Turku Clinic of Psychiatry, the proportion of patients who thus came to realize their need for hospital care increased when the practice of arranging therapy meetings became established and the ward staff made a concentrated effort towards an empathic approach to the patient during the first few inpatient days. By the late 1980s, nearly 50% of the patients admitted for observation continued their inpatient treatment voluntarily after the observation period. This is notably significant for the establishment of therapeutic relationships.

If the joint or individual meetings with the patient are continued over the next few days as an effective crisis intervention, it is often possible to avoid hospital admission altogether. For many patients, being taken into a mental hospital will effect a life-long trauma on their self-esteem. When admission proves to be necessary, it is best to explain the reasons for treatment to the patient in such a way that he/she is able to understand, though not necessarily accept, them.

The arrangement of therapy meetings is facilitated by the fact that the psychotic patient's relatives or friends often come to consult the therapeutic staff or escort the patient for the first visit. If they first come to a basic health care unit, from where the patient is further referred to a psychiatric hospital or outpatient unit, the referring physician should see to it that these relatives or friends accompany the patient. Even if a patient is re-admitted into the hospital, it is useful in most cases to arrange a new therapy meeting to study the situation more extensively, unless the patient refuses this.

I have had some experience of how important the contact with the family may be even at later stages of treatment with psychotic patients. Probably the most memorable experience was with a youngish female patient who had been rejected by her husband and had then, having realized her own lack of balance, given up her child to a children's home and finally regressed into a completely uncommunicative and autistically withdrawn state. Attempts to make the patient's mother and sister attend a therapy meeting failed at first; the mother promised to come, but she always cancelled. The attempts of the ward staff to establish contact with the patient continued to be unsuccessful—she continued mute even with her personal nurse. After a couple of months the mother finally came and attended a meeting. The patient did not speak during the meeting, but a couple of days later she began to speak, though quite psychotically at first. The patient's recovery over the following few weeks was compatible with the developmental processes described in

textbooks on psychoanalysis: having recovered from her autistic condition, she fell in love symbiotically with a male patient, trying to hold his
hand wherever he went. After that she began to be interested in other
relationships around her, she went to see her child in the children's
home, and she was discharged from the ward in a fully organized condition. Throughout, the process of recovery was catalyzed by her personal
nurse relationship.

The patient's individual clinical and psychological condition is also
assessed in the therapy meeting. This assessment, however, often needs
to be supplemented by individual discussions with the patient. This is
quite essential whenever the patient asks for a private interview, or the
team notices that the patient hopes for one, or it turns out that privacy is
necessary for analysing the situation and/or establishing a confidential
relationship with the patient. A patient who is admitted into the hospital
must immediately be provided with a chance to have discussions and to
establish a therapeutic relationship on an individual level.

Some psychotherapeutically oriented American psychiatrists have
suggested that the psychotic symptoms of a schizophrenic patient admitted for treatment must first be suppressed with intensive neuroleptic
medication, after which it becomes possible to approach the patient's
condition psychotherapeutically. I disagree with them. The introduction
of medication—and particularly neuroleptic medication—should, if possible, be postponed at the initial stage, and the main effort should be on
approaching and establishing a psychological contact with the patient
and his/her life situation. This is especially important with first-admis-
sions. Otherwise, we lose the opportunity of seeing the patient's individual and transactional situation *in vivo* and define and label the patient's
condition as an illness in the medical sense, without having tried to
avoid such labelling initially. Also, the psychological approach is often
just as effective in calming down the patient as are neuroleptics.

It is also important at the initial stage to inquire into the patient's
social situation and the rehabilitative needs associated with it—as we
found out particularly clearly in the NSP Project. Matters of this kind
may already come up during the therapy meetings. Later on, rehabilitation is best discussed in cooperation with the patient and the unit's social
worker, and the discussions often involve contacts with the patient's
employer and co-workers or social work officials, for example. The patient should give consent for such contacts and preferably participate in
carrying out the arrangements.

Who needs the hospital?

I have emphasized the significance of outpatient treatment for the self-esteem of many patients in cases where inpatient treatment can justifiably be avoided. This is not, however, always the case and should not be an end in itself. As far as I can see, treatment in a psychotherapeutic community is still necessary for more than half of the first-admission schizophrenia-group patients. It is not always necessary for them to be admitted as inpatients, because psychotherapeutic communities function quite well on day-hospital wards.

Hospital treatment is generally necessary for psychotic patients of three kinds. The first of these—partly overlapping—groups consists of those where the degree of regression or the quality of the disorder (e.g. behaviour imperilling the safety of the patient or other people) requires a safe or constraining environment. In this group, involuntary treatment is usually indicated. The second indication concerns the patient's (and/ or the family members') motivation for adequate psychotherapeutic treatment. Especially for many first-admitted, seriously ill patients, a long-term (usually a few months') treatment in the psychotherapeutic community is a necessary prerequisite for the continuation of treatment on an outpatient basis. The third group consists of patients who find the ward a temporary and necessary social refuge in a difficult life situation—for example, following a divorce or loss of a dwelling.

The duration of the inpatient period needed depends entirely on individual, patient-specific factors. There are, however, a few points I wish to emphasize. First, the time spent in hospital should really benefit the patient. This does not mean that the treatment should be paced so as to hasten the patient's discharge. One colleague of mine once compared the hospital to which he referred his patient to a broken slot-machine, which ejects the coin as soon as it has been inserted. This should not be the case—on the contrary, as soon as the indications for inpatient treatment have been established and the treatment begun, the therapeutic staff should concentrate on the patient's problems without undue haste, aiming at a favourable therapeutic relationship and promoting the developmental process stimulated by it.

This may take time in some cases, but it should clearly be more than mere idle existence. To avoid the risk of institutionalization, we must also continuously support the patient's contacts outside the hospital by arranging leaves, using day-hospital services, and occasionally encouraging the patient to work or to study. This is naturally easier in urban environments than in the country.

We soon learnt in the Turku Clinic to guarantee the *continuity of therapeutic relationships* by avoiding patient transfers from one ward to another while treatment was going on. There are now three kinds of patients on the closed acute ward of the clinic: those who are there following a decision for involuntary treatment, those who are full-time inpatients voluntarily (many of them after a period of involuntary treatment—who now have a right to move about freely, including home leaves), and those who had started their treatment as full-time inpatients but have now become day patients. This arrangement is also expedient for the ward: it is easier to concentrate on the more difficult patients in the evenings, when the ward is relatively empty; also the presence of the day patients, who are generally in a better condition, makes the ward atmosphere less closed and more hopeful even for those patients whose condition is not so good. Transfers from the closed to the open ward or to the special day-hospital ward (and sometimes also in the opposite direction) occur occasionally, depending on patient-specific factors, but they are relatively rare and usually take place during the early stages of the treatment, before a therapeutic relationship with the patient has become established .

Finally, we must remember that one purpose of hospital treatment should always be planning for after-care on an outpatient basis, whenever there is a need for it—and there usually is such a need in the case of schizophrenic patients. For some patients treated in the psychotherapeutic community, the continuation of the treatment with the same therapist should be made possible after discharge. However, this is often not feasible. The preparatory work for the continuation of treatment should be carried out in cooperation with the person or persons responsible for outpatient care, regardless of whether they are members of the hospital staff or outsiders. Therapy meetings with the patient present are the best tool for this planning.

Some psychoanalysts or psychoanalytically oriented therapists (though not all of them) who refer their patients for a temporary hospital treatment and/or resume the therapy of their patient after an inpatient episode are unwilling to attend such meetings, fearing that the transference-based therapeutic relationship may be impaired. In the case of schizophrenic patients, such caution is often unduly excessive, provided that the therapist maintains a consistent therapeutic attitude even during the meetings as well as the confidentiality of the relationship with the patient. The advantages of this procedure outweigh such risks, both to the therapeutic relationship and to the integration of treatment; this is the best way to prevent projective biases possibly present in both staff communities and outside professionals.

On the indications
of different modes of psychotherapy

Internal individuation and external separation are always less adequately developed in schizophrenics than in milder, particularly neurotic disorders. For any assessment of the therapeutic needs of a psychotic patient, it is important to have an idea of the severity of the disorder in this respect—in other words, to find out whether the patient's main psychological problems lie in his/her internalized psychology or whether, and how concretely, they lie in mutual dependency relationships with other people (the degree of *related individuation*, to use Stierlin's term (1983; Stierlin et al., 1977). Although one of the psychotherapeutic goals is always to promote the patient's development towards individuation, it may be impossible to achieve this in individual therapy alone unless some development also takes place in the relationships with others.

The acute or long-term quality of the disorder is also significant for planning the mode and duration of treatment. Hence, for example, a prompt *crisis intervention* following the first therapy meeting may be sufficient for handling psychotic or near-psychotic crises that are obviously related to acute problem situations. A re-assessment of the situation a few weeks later is, however, frequently necessary to ensure that the crisis is genuinely over. It is always useful to advise the different parties in the crisis to contact the therapeutic team, if necessary, which may in itself serve to increase the feeling of security. The need for further treatment at a family or individual level remains to be assessed together with the patient and/or the family.

The crisis intervention is generally family- or milieu-oriented, but it may also take place or continue at an individual level. It would be useful to include in the discussions—with the patient's permission and in his/her presence—people from the patient's studying or working environment more often than has been customary. An attitude of openness may be helpful for both the patient and the environment, lessening mutual mistrust.

The development of family-oriented crisis intervention into *family therapy* often takes place gradually through continued joint meetings. The label "family therapy" may arouse resistance in some cases, nor is its use always indicated even in those cases where the process is being gradually transformed into long-term treatment. Wynne and his co-workers (Wynne et al., 1986), for example, prefer to use the term "consultation". In Finland, we prefer to speak of "family meetings". In practice, these meetings turn into family therapy when it is explicitly agreed that they will be continued and certain goals are defined for them.

Conjoint therapies of families of origin are most often needed by young patients who have become psychotic gradually, whose contacts outside the home are quite limited, and whose differentiation from parents is inadequate. The personalities of many such patients are fragile and have further regressed in the psychotic development, because of which symbiotic relationships with their parents constitute a central part of their internal psychodynamics, or at least of the part accessible to us.

In these cases the problems of the families are always serious, either primarily—as I tend to interpret them in most cases—or at least secondarily, as a consequence of the patient's illness. The goals of therapy are often twofold: on the one hand, support is provided for the whole family, while, on the other hand, the process of differentiation between the patient and his/her parents is encouraged and facilitated. Even when the therapeutic community and individual therapy have succeeded in arousing the patient's symbiotic tendencies—which may also exist hidden in autistic individuals—the further development of the therapeutic relationship may be thwarted without family therapy if a parent finds it difficult to give up his or her symbiotic attachment to the child. In some successful therapeutic processes, the focus of treatment is shifted to individual therapy at the same time as the parents change over to couple therapy, which helps them to differentiate from the patient and makes their relationship more satisfying—factors that are often interrelated.

The most serious cases of schizophrenia also include those where the prerequisites for individual therapy seem permanently poor and both the patient and the family benefit most from long-term family-oriented treatment, which may even go on for decades.

But family therapy of the family of origin may be needed—and frequently is quite successful—even in the treatment of less seriously ill young patients with acute psychosis or classified as having borderline schizophrenia, whenever the core of their problems appears to lie in the ambivalence of growing independent from their families.

Therapy of the family of procreation or *couple therapy* of the patient and his/her spouse or partner is indicated at the initial stages of the treatment of most patients who have established a family or a couple relationship. The manifestation of psychosis in these patients, who have made some progress in both their internal development and their interpersonal relationships—though they still have a notable need for dependence—is often clearly associated with intrafamilial problems, mostly pertaining to the couple relationship. Other aspects of interpersonal relationships are also significant. It may, for example, be important to get the patient's parents or parents-in-law to be present in the first meetings. Psychosis is usually a regressive decompensation, and our experience has shown that the chances of recovery are both quicker and better in family or couple therapy than in individual therapy. If the treatment completely lacks any family orientation, there is the risk that the situation is prolonged in a way that—being compatible with the partner's psychodynamics—results in permanent changes of the family homeostasis that are unfavourable for the patient and solidify his/her role as a patient.

Many psychiatrists may not like the idea of including the children in the family therapy of a psychotic patient, hoping to protect them from traumatic experiences. It is our experience, however, that this argument is justified less often than one might expect, because the psychotic symptoms—which are familiar to the children from the home environment in any case—are frequently alleviated in a therapy situation; the final effect may actually minimize the previous traumas and mystification. Having the children present naturally requires particular sensitivity and control from the therapeutic team, which may have to interfere in the discussion quite firmly, if necessary. The role of the children in family dynamics is often very important, and their inclusion may also be informative. My own way of handling such situations is to have the children present in some of the initial meetings but to leave them out of the following therapy sessions, though questions concerning them will continue to be discussed. It may also be necessary to restrict the treatment to couple therapy because the problems pertain to the spouses' sexual relationship and/or one of them has an extramarital relationship or lover.

Family or couple therapy is not possible in all cases, as the spouse may refuse to attend, which is more common for female than for male patients. In such cases, one has to rely on individual therapy. Individual therapy is necessary as a continuation of family or couple therapy, when the couple relationship ends in a divorce, or the main core of the psychological problems is ultimately located in the patient's own internal development. The quality of the continued treatment is determined by case-specific motivations.

It is hence relatively common that the focus shifts from family therapy to *individual therapy* in advancing treatment (see Figure 5.4). This shift is most natural and most clearly predictive of a good outcome when the initiative to start long-term individual therapy comes from the patient and the matter is also discussed during the family therapy sessions.

Individual therapy right from the beginning (Figure 5.4, right panel) is best suited to patients whose personality development is more differentiated than that of the average schizophrenic. Most will also have moved out of their primary families—although concrete separation as such cannot be considered an indicator of the psychological separation–individuation stage.

A logistic regression analysis in the five-year follow-up of the Turku Cohort III (Alanen et al., 1986) showed that the patients who ultimately underwent long-term psychodynamically oriented individual therapy differed from the rest of the schizophrenic patients on four background variables: (1) an initial insight into the connections between their problems and symptoms, (2) lack of acting-out behaviour, (3) acute onset of symptoms, and (4) the presence of neurotic symptoms along with psychotic ones. Borderline schizophrenias were slightly more common in this group than the other clinical categories, but numerically the largest sub-group consisted of patients with typical schizophrenia who had a tendency to establish symbiotic relationships.

The theories concerning the indications for individual therapy in schizophrenia are unexpectedly confused. Many of the leading therapists—such as Benedetti (1985) and Boyer (1986)—emphasize personal factors associated with the countertransference experienced by the therapist. Volkan (1990) also says that he prefers to start working with the patients whose problems and symptoms appear understandable to him right from the beginning, often at a primary process level. Such understanding may naturally also be achieved at later stages of treatment.

From the viewpoint of public health care, it is important to try to avoid useless attempts at treatment. It is therefore important in individual therapy to underline the difference between supportive therapeutic relationships with relatively infrequent sessions and an empathic attitude—which are notably useful for many patients—and intensive, psychoanalytically oriented relationships aiming at developing the patient's personality. Therapy of the latter kind is most successful when (1) the patient's disorder does not belong in the most serious clinical category, as regards both symptoms (the personality disorganization is not very deep or has not lasted long) and the ability to relate, (2) insightful motivation for long-term work is being or has been aroused in both the patient and the therapist, and (3) the prerequisites for sufficient continuity of the therapeutic relationship exist. Neglect of the latter point may result in disappointments that could be fatal for some patients.

The absence of *group therapy* in Figure 5.4 may seem surprising. As far as I can see, however, its significance in schizophrenia is less primary and less crucial for the pathology of the disorder than the significance of family and individual therapies. Its development has therefore received less attention and fewer resources in our work. The participation of many schizophrenic patients in group therapy has, however, proved beneficial, especially for their social rehabilitation.

Although our own experiences of actual group therapy are relatively scant, various widely defined group activities have gradually become more and more significant in the psychotherapeutic communities of the clinic. They are essentially important both for shaping the overall structure of the activities of the ward community and for improving patients' social skills and contacts. The need for group activities is particularly great in the case of long-term patients, and it can also be felt in the rehabilitation homes, hostels, and other units outside the hospital, as was shown, for example, by the experiences of Anttinen (1983, 1992).

How can modes of psychotherapy with different frames of reference be combined?

How is it possible to combine systemic family therapy and psychodynamic individual therapy? Does not the difference between their frames of reference give rise to problems? The answer is that these modes of treatment should not be perceived as contradictory, but as complementary to each other. Some psychoanalysts and family therapists have tended to exaggerate the differences between these modes of treatment, but this has been due either to prejudice or to ignorance of the real nature of one or the other method. What is needed is a genuinely respectful attitude towards each other's mode of work.

In Turku, the integration has been facilitated by the fact that many of the psychoanalysts have been interested in family therapy and some have even taught it. This probably suffices to show that the two modes of treatment can be combined under one basic conception of the nature of psychotic and other psychic disorders. This is not always the case, however, and problems may therefore arise. But there may equally well be problems between family therapists with different theories of illness, and also between psychoanalysts with different ideas of schizophrenia.

There are more differences in the techniques of these modes of treatment than in their basic conceptions or goals. The technical differences, in turn, are easy to understand as a consequence of what is being done in each kind of therapy: psychoanalytic individual therapy aims at understanding and influencing internal processes, while family therapy works on interactional networks consisting of several individuals. The treatment processes described in the final part of chapter six illustrate how family therapy can be a prerequisite of individual therapy. When the transactional defence mechanisms and external supporting structures become unnecessary, the ability to forego them makes it easier to recognize internal problems and to approach them through individual therapy.

Systemic family therapy—in the form that is practised within our therapeutic orientation—also aims at reaching a psychodynamic understanding, which helps us to formulate the hypotheses and interpretative communications that we present to the families. Apart from achieving this empathic understanding, it is also necessary for both family and individual therapists to observe a neutral distance. This is one important reason for carrying out family therapy as team-work, which may seem strange to psychoanalysts. A family therapist who works alone is notably more prone to losing the observing stance and unwittingly assuming the role of a family member.

The combination of psycho-educative family therapy with individual therapy of a psychodynamic orientation may be more problematic than that of systemic family therapy. With long-term schizophrenic patients, psycho-educative elements can be included more easily in the global treatment plans.

Combining psychopharmacological treatment and psychotherapy is common in the treatment of psychoses, notwithstanding that the therapeutic frames of reference and foci of treatment are clearly different. Despite this, medication can also be integrated as part of the need-adapted therapeutic activities based on psychodynamic understanding.

Conclusions

The term "need-adapted treatment" of schizophrenic psychoses refers to a comprehensive but individualized, psychotherapeutically oriented approach to schizophrenia and related psychoses. It was developed at the Turku Clinic of Psychiatry gradually over a period of two decades and is now also employed elsewhere in Finland and in the other Northern European countries. Treatment is based on a psychodynamic understanding of the case-specific therapeutic needs of the patients. We found this important because of the heterogeneity of schizophrenic disorders, both clinically and with regard to the patients' psychological and social condition. This leads to a diversity of therapeutic challenges. We also found that it is important to evaluate the therapeutic needs of the family and of any other essential interactional network to which the patient belongs and to respond to them, both because of the strains that the patient's psychosis is apt to arouse in the people related to him/her and because the treatment is to a great extent dependent on the quality of the schizophrenic person's interpersonal relationships. Drug treatment is considered an auxiliary measure supporting psychotherapy and is used in small or moderate doses, according to the patients' needs.

The family-oriented approach led us to the establishment of the initial joint meetings (therapy meetings) attended by the therapeutic team, the patient, and family members or other persons close to the patient. Through their informative, diagnostic, and therapeutic functions, these system-oriented meetings proved to be of great importance in planning and carrying out the treatment. The psychotic symptoms of acutely ill patients often disappeared or quickly diminished. With many patients, therapy meetings are continued as crisis intervention, as family therapy, or as renewed diagnostic and integrating means at a later stage of the treatment. However, during the course of therapy it is often expedient to transfer the focus of the therapeutic process from the less specific family- and environmental modes to the more specific ones, including psychodynamically oriented long-term individual psychotherapy.

Both the Turku Schizophrenia Project and the Finnish Multicentre (NSP) Project were based on problem-oriented action research principles, and they were aimed at a development of therapeutic activities within community psychiatry rather than being separate research trials studying the results of specific treatment modes. According to strict scientific principles applied in the controlled psychotherapy trials, it is easy to identify weaknesses of our projects. However, as pointed out earlier, controlled studies can also be criticized because of their rigid methodology. A treatment approach trying to respond to the diversity of therapeutic needs of individual patients cannot be studied following rules that might, for example, prevent any change of treatment practices. The only way of applying controlled methodology to the study of the results of need-adapted treatment would be to compare two or more catchment areas with each other—with one area carrying out its principles as a whole and the other(s) practising treatments based on different premises. Even then, it should be realized that this kind of approach cannot be established all of a sudden in a certain area but is a product of developmental processes of longer duration including, for example, different training and supervision activities.

We have compared our follow-up findings with earlier studies of first-admitted schizophrenic patients, both in Finland and elsewhere, and we found that the need-adapted approach has clearly improved the outcome for first-admitted schizophrenic patients, especially with regard to their psychosocial prognosis. The outcome of Cohort IV of the Turku Project in which the approach was practised in its advanced form was clearly better than that of the earlier Turku cohorts and other earlier follow-up studies made in Finland. The follow-up findings of the NSP Project, in which the approach was initiated within a geographically larger context, were also promising and compared well with the results of other contemporary European studies. Related though different psychotherapeutic approaches included in the Inter-Scandinavian Community Psychiatric NIPS Project were likewise successful. A conspicuous finding both in the Turku cohorts and in the NIPS Project was the considerable decrease in the patients' need for neuroleptic drugs brought about by psychotherapeutic approaches. More than half of the schizophrenic patients of the Turku Cohort IV managed well without neuroleptics five years after their first admission, and the same was true of the NIPS sample as a whole.

One additional factor should be emphasized: the humanizing effect of our orientation. The treatment is based on a psychotherapeutic attitude, which prevails in the treatment milieu as a whole and is characterized by an attempt to approach the patient as a human being rather than as a container of abnormal biological mechanisms to be treated with a pharmacological approach on its own. The problems of family members are also considered, and the positive resources found in the families are taken into account. Not only doctors and psychologists are involved: the members of the nursing staff also have the opportunity to develop their talents through active participation in the therapeutic processes.

Reductionistic attitudes should be abandoned with regard to the use of various psychotherapeutic modes. In the field of community psychiatry, there is no possibility for treating all schizophrenic patients with intensive individual psychotherapy, nor is this indicated.

In summary, four points of our therapeutic experiences may be re-iterated:

1. The systemic (family- and network-centred) orientation including therapy meetings improved the outcome for new schizophrenic patients as a whole. According to Lehtinen's (1993b) analysis, this was connected with a better outcome for acutely ill patients, on the one hand, and for patients included in the group of paranoid schizophrenias, on the other. In the first group, it appeared that the family-centred emphasis clearly accelerated the reintegration of many patients; in the second group, it became possible to reach psychotherapeutically those patients who had no motivation for individual psychotherapy, at least initially. In Finland, these experiences led to the establishment of acute psychosis teams (see chapter seven), now responsible for planning and initiating the treatment of new and recurrent psychotic patients in a large part of the country.

2. The systemic orientation and family therapy cannot replace the need of a large number of the schizophrenic patients for a long-term individual therapeutic relationship aimed at personality development. The experiences of the Turku Cohort III, as well as those of the NIPS Project, indicated the positive effects of individual therapy for many severely ill schizophrenic patients.

3. Psychotherapeutic community treatment, family therapy, and individual therapy should be seen as complementary modes of treatment, used either separately or in combination, as indicated by the case-specific needs. For many patients, community treatment and/or family therapy are important prerequisites for successful individual treatment, both through their increased motivation to study their problems and through a sufficient loosening of inner psychological resources bound into symbiotic intrafamilial relationships.

4. Referring to my view of the therapist functioning as a new and

committed self-object for the schizophrenic patient, I emphasize the importance of the therapist's personality—already indicated by an early study by Whitehorn and Betz (1960)—as well as the "fit" between the therapist and patient, promoting the mutual introjective processes. Both our experiences with nurse therapists in Turku as well as the experiences of psychodynamically oriented supportive individual psychotherapies in the Oslo subproject of the NIPS confirm this theory. It may also explain, for example, the finding by Gunderson et al. (1984) that no difference was found between the results of insight-oriented and supportive psychotherapy in the MacLean Hospital study. A precondition for the extension of the number of therapists is a broad-based organization of psychotherapy supervision and training. In Turku, the findings of our project encouraged us to establish multiprofessional training programmes for both individual and family therapy, emphasizing the treatment of severely ill patients.

CHAPTER SIX

Therapeutic experiences

I begin this chapter by evaluating the application and content of the most common modes of psychotherapy included in the need-adapted treatment of schizophrenic psychoses, based on personal experiences gained while working in public health care in the Turku Clinic and as a private psychiatrist. I also comment on the use of medication in psychotherapeutic treatment. After this, three case vignettes illustrate the integrated need-adapted approach.

Experiences of applying
the different modes of treatment

The psychotherapeutic community

The kind of psychotherapeutic communities best suited to acutely psychotic patients are somewhat different from both the original model proposed by Jones and the communities for primarily border-line patients. Matti Isohanni (1983) in his Finnish study itemized three major ways of influencing patients therapeutically in a hospital ward community: a humane environment, organized interaction, and pre-planned treatment programmes. All of these are needed in a community for psychotic patients, but establishing a humane environment is the priority.

Differences in focus were also clearly observable in the developments of the psychotherapeutic communities of the Turku clinic, between the wards in which a majority of the patients showed less severe disorders, and the wards for psychotic patients. The former relied on organized group activities requiring more conjoint participation, whereas the activities of the psychosis wards were shaped more individually in response to each patient's degree of regression.

I have described the functional structure of our ward of acutely psychotic patients while discussing the development of the Turku Schizophrenia Project (pp. 144–145), but some fundamental psychodynamic viewpoints should be added.

Simo Salonen (1975), who worked in the Turku clinic in the 1970s, pointed out, using Kohut's terms, that for psychotic patients the ward community should be *a re-created early self-object environment*, where empathy, "justifiable optimism" (an expression introduced by Erik Anttinen, 1992), and gratification of some of the patients' symbiotic needs in a humane environment provide for them a starting-point for the processing of their problems and reintegration and growth of their personalities.

As long ago as the 1960s, I wrote to Otto A. Will Jr. (then Director of Psychotherapy at Chestnut Lodge), asking him what he considered the most essential goal in the psychotherapy of schizophrenic patients. Will replied that there is some hope in the patient's future, if he/she gets back something of the condition of children whose life is moderately satisfactory. He pointed out that such children are curious and eager to learn, not constantly on their guard, not torn apart by guilt, relatively open to new interpersonal relationships, and happy with their own growth and development. A psychotherapeutic community has accomplished something if it has aroused some of these qualities in its patients (personal communication, 1963).

Personal nurses play a crucial role in helping the patient in a psychotherapeutic community. Already in the early 1970s, when choosing personal nurses, we considered it important that the contacts that had arisen spontaneously between patients and staff members should be continued. We postulated that therapeutic relationships emerging at the primary-process level would turn out more fruitful in the therapy of schizophrenic patients than patient–therapist selections made at the reality level. As many as 70% of the therapeutic relationships established on the psychosis ward and continued for at least 2 months during 1970–76 were found to have come about in this way (Aaku et al., 1980). It turned out that the nurses who had spontaneously picked out a patient had experienced something that can be called "an immediately involved, caring countertransference" (Orma, 1978) often right after the patient had been admitted to the ward. Such experiences are familiar to people working with psychotic patients fighting to maintain their psychological existence.

It may also happen that the patient spontaneously chooses a personal therapist, being sometimes motivated at a psychotic level. She may, for example, resort to a person whom she considers her sister, because they have the same first name. I think it is important not to ignore such choices: although they may involve transference and/or countertransference problems, the benefits generally outweigh the problems. Sidsel Gilbert and Endre Ugelstad, in the Norwegian part of the NIPS Project (Alanen et al., 1994), also emphasized the importance of the patient's active participation in finding a matching therapist. It is essential, however, that the therapist observes him- or herself at the ego level, to prevent emotional overinvolvement. Help for this comes best from *supervision*, which should be made available to all members of the therapeutic staff working on psychosis wards, regardless of their professional background.

However, spontaneity is not enough for establishing a personal nurse relationship in every case; there are also patients who are not chosen by anybody, and they tend to be therapeutically the most difficult. In these cases the personal nurse is best appointed in a common discussion by the ward staff, preferably with somebody volunteering, rather than being ordered to take on the task.

Although the personal nurse plays a crucial role in the treatment of the patient, the psychotherapeutic team always functions as a whole. Individual therapeutic relationships are doomed to failure unless they are supported by the whole community. The personal nurse or therapist is not the only person whom the patient meets on the ward and who influences him or her. *Joint meetings and negotiations*—both with and without patients—are essential for the promotion and integration of the therapeutic activities, and they should take place frequently. Salonen (1975)—and Schulz (1975)—pointed out how significant it is for the patient's personal integration that the theories of the different staff members concerning him or her are also integrated. A disorganized, psychologically regressed patient may apply to the people around him quite different, even mutually contradictory, transferences, and it is important that they will be understood as parts of a connected whole.

Although responsible for the ward and clinical decisions, the psychiatrist should not assume an omnipotent role and learn from teamwork. While serving as senior psychiatrist, I realized that I could learn a great deal by listening to others and considering their suggestions; this will also help to prevent "passive resistance" on the ward, which may arise if the staff are merely given orders to carry out treatment. It is not infrequent that the nurses who observe the patients at a close range have ideas that are more in keeping with the natural course of the therapeutic process than an order given by a superior. Occasionally the staff tried to use me in an interpersonal power struggle, on, for example, whether or not the dosage of medication for a given patient should be increased. I became particularly wary of hints or suggestions on therapy made to me privately by staff members, and I only promised to take up the matter at the next joint meeting.

Openness, unprejudiced elimination of unnecessary and detrimental hierarchies, and an effort to integrate the therapeutic activities are among the goals of psychotherapeutic communities treating psychotic patients. Considering openness, we also discussed the limits of our own emotional expressions towards the patients. It is not good if the community has an atmosphere where all negative emotions towards the patients are consciously avoided in the same way as in a pseudomutual family; openly expressed irritation at a patient who intentionally breaks a plate is better than suppressed rage, and it certainly also helps the patient to learn the limits to his/her behaviour. But a community with uninhibited emotional expression would be both chaotic and at the mercy of the kind of acting-out that prevents the development of a good and psychotherapeutic working climate. Self-scrutiny of one's emotional reactions and an effort to become conscious of their causes and to utilize them therapeutically are important elements in the therapeutic process.

Different opinions have been put forth concerning the optimal ward community attitude towards the regression of a psychotic patient into a condition that reflects the earliest developmental stages. Many individual therapists, such as Boyer (1986), have emphasized that it is not possible to correct developmental defects without working on the level of regressive psychological phenomena. But it should also be borne in mind that the regression in itself does not help the patient unless there is some insight into its causes. This, in turn, requires that the patient, though tending towards regression, should also be made conscious of these tendencies and enabled to counter them at the ego level. This is best achieved by transference and countertransference relationships during long-term individual therapy, and it does not mean that the therapist would gratify the patient's regressive needs.

It may, however, be useful or even necessary to gratify the needs of some seriously regressive patients on the ward—for example, by feeding them. Even so, excessive babying care—which may also gratify the needs of the care-giver—should not be an end in itself: the goal should always be to help the patient out of the regression. For this purpose, a temporary gratification of regressive needs and a simultaneous attempt to establish an empathic contact with the patient are a better alternative than electroshock treatment or high-dose medication.

But different views concerning the atmosphere on acute psychosis ward communities can also be presented. For example, Ciompi and colleagues (1992), describing the Soteria Berne community and in keeping with his theory of affect logic (Ciompi, 1982), emphasize not only the holding atmosphere, but also a clearly defined structure as a way of promoting the integration of the patient's psychic functions. I agree that the ward communities must have clearly defined rules and that the attitudes of the ward staff and the limits they set for patients' behaviour must not result in double-bind–type situations. Joint meetings of both the staff alone and the staff and patients together are therefore highly important for the functioning of the therapeutic communities. However, the rigid rules characteristic of most medical wards must be avoided. I learnt, for example, to arrange patient rounds in such a way that we met together informally with 6–10 patients and the ward staff on duty in a certain room, and there we discussed the situation of each patient in turn. When there were patients unable or unwilling to attend these meetings, which was quite seldom, I visited them separately.

Family therapy

My experiences with family therapy of schizophrenics cover two periods: the psychodynamic approaches of the 1960s and 1970s and the systemic family therapy approach of the 1980s. I did not abandon my psychoanalytically based ways of thinking even during the latter period but considered them equally essential in systemic–strategic family therapy. Conversely, it can also be said that psychodynamic family therapy will not be successful unless it is based on an interactional approach.

It is therefore important in family therapies of all orientations to see the family field as a whole, with members constantly influencing each other. Equally important is the effort of the therapist or therapists to see the events through empathic understanding of each family member, to "take everybody's part" (*Allparteilichkeit*: Stierlin et al., 1977). If a working atmosphere of this kind has been established and the family members recognize it, the therapist may temporarily align with one family member at a time—usually the one who seems to find it most difficult to make him- or herself understood in the conversation. In systemic–strategic family therapy, "taking everybody's part" often means that the messages given towards the end of the session have been formulated in a way that is significant for everybody.

As a *psychodynamic family therapist*, I was one of the "reactor analysts", who act as catalyzers in developmental processes but prefer to remain in the background, rather than a "conductor", who seems to know in advance what is best for each family. The attitude of the family therapist is, however, always somewhat more active than the attitude of a psychoanalyst working with an individual. At the beginning of the therapy, he/she must try to involve each family member in the therapeutic process by presenting questions to each member and supporting the efforts of the least successful ones, as well as by translating the psychotic expressions of the patient into ordinary language. The therapist should also be ready to intervene and create security and order in the conversation, whenever there is a need for that. When working with two-generation families, the therapist is often assigned the position of an understanding grandparent, whose presence makes it possible to deal with things that would otherwise take the family into a roadless wilderness.

My experiences with psychodynamic family therapy were reasonably satisfactory. Working with relatively seriously ill adolescents and their families during the 1960s and 1970s, my colleagues and I obtained clearly favourable results in about half of the cases (Alanen, 1976). The same was also true of the couple therapies of patients who were married at the time of their illness (Alanen & Kinnunen, 1975). The outcome was best in those families that were genuinely motivated to undertake a therapeutic process. The narcissistically featured self-object relations of parents to their children could, when empathically understood by the therapist, transfer to positive resources important for the developmental progress. Healthy resources were found rather unexpectedly in schismatic families—the family therapy of Paula, which I described in chapter one, is one of the best examples of this—in which the parents' wish, behind their frustrations, to improve their mutual relationship sometimes appeared to be an important factor. One-parent families and skewed families with a strong symbiotic axis, on the other hand, more often showed much resistance towards therapeutic work. In some families the motor for change was the patient, in others the patient's healthier sibling, who showed particular understanding of the patient's problems.

In chaotic families the therapist must support the whole family, especially trying to improve the family's sense of reality. In some cases—which also include families with a symbiotic axis—family-oriented treatment can best be implemented by making a supporting person available to the parent or parents. Rigidly paranoid parents are the most difficult therapeutically; in families dominated by such a parent or parents, it seemed best to concentrate on individual therapy, trying simultaneously to maintain a favourable separate contact with the parents. The outcome of the couple therapy of patients who were already married when their illness became manifest depended more often on the spouse's than the patient's attitude.

Psychodynamic family therapies usually require a relatively long time, preferably 2–4 years, in order to be successful. Even in cases where it is difficult to initiate a dynamic process of development involving the whole family, it is often possible for the therapist to protect the growing space of the young patient, supporting his/her efforts towards independence and allowing the possessive parent to transfer his/her symbiotic needs for dependence from the patient to the therapist, simultaneously helping the parent in the work of mourning that may follow this loss. It is important in all family therapies with schizophrenic patients—regardless of the orientation—to scrutinize the parents' background, for that makes it more possible to understand them and the roots of the problems in their relationships with their parents and children, respectively.

Psychodynamic family therapy was subsequently overshadowed by the use of the systemic–strategic approach. However, it should still be available for families where it is clearly indicated by the motivation of the family or couple for therapeutic work.

The breakthrough of the *systemic–strategic orientation* was partly due—at least in Finland—to the brilliance of the Milan group (Selvini Palazzoli et al., 1978) and the fact that the therapy involved team-work, which is both safer and more pleasant than working alone. There is also the additional advantage that the sessions are infrequent and the therapies relatively short, which makes them easier to carry out in public health care than the psychodynamic family therapy processes, which tend to be longer and require more frequent visits (usually once a week).

Team-work often intensifies family therapy, and the closing of the sessions with jointly prepared interpretative messages may effect changes even in families where the prerequisites for psychodynamic process work are poor. I have found particularly useful the positive connotations engendered by the systemic approach. They often are also useful in individual therapy. I am less familiar with paradoxical interpretations, and the assignments given to families, because I am uncomfortable with their manipulative implications.

Positive connotations refer to the identification of symptoms in family members and their interpretation as positive phenomena, which they actually are from the viewpoint of their role in maintaining family homeostasis and the psychic balance of the other family members. *Paradoxical interpretations* are counterparadoxes for the family's own paradoxical behaviour. They encourage the family members to continue the identified mode of behaviour by saying that any change in it would be risky. This interpretation helps family members to realize the cul-de-sac they are in and does so in a way that—supported by the therapist's emphasis to maintain the homeostasis—often arouses a counter-stimulus in the family to change the situation—that is, it makes them side with the forces aiming at change (Selvini Palazzoli et al., 1978).

An example of such family-therapeutic interventions follows. The relationships of many young—especially male—schizophrenic patients with their mothers are characterized by mutual symbiotic dependence. According to the classical individual–psychological view, this is a sign of the patient's inability to detach himself from his mother because of early fixations. It would not be particularly therapeutic to state this to the patient, however. Approaching the situation from a systemic point of view, we may be better able to perceive another dynamic factor: the loyalty bond of the patient with his mother, who—because of her own separation anxiety—finds it essential to keep her son at home. Using positive connotation, we can recognize and appreciate the way the patient behaviourally shows through his responsibility for his mother. Empathic recognition and interpretation of such psychology tends to improve the patient's self-esteem—unlike the individual–psychological interpretation I referred to—and, simultaneously, similarly to interpretations in general, gives him a stimulus to change his family–psychological position. If the positive connotation is accompanied by a paradoxical interpretation—"You had better continue to stay at home, even giving up the idea of having friends of your own, because this is important for your mother and because changes in life even otherwise tend to provoke anxiety"—the effect may be further strengthened.

It should be emphasized that extensive knowledge of family psychodynamics, combined with skill acquired through training and experience, are necessary prerequisites for applying paradoxical interpretations. According to the experience of some of my colleagues, however, they may be useful stimuli for change within the family, provided that they are based on a careful consideration aroused by a thorough analysis of the family dynamics. Inadequately thought out, however, they may represent therapists' acting out. As senior psychiatrist, I was consulted a couple of times by perplexed parents, whose report of the assignment they had been given by the family therapy team seemed perplexing to me as well.

Exhibit 6.1 presents the central contents of systemically oriented family therapy with schizophrenic patients as I understand it.

Klaus Lehtinen (1993b, 1994) examined the experiences of systemic–strategic family therapy obtained in Turku in the follow-up of Cohort IV patients of our schizophrenia project. He divided the patients into three groups.

The first group consisted of patients whose psychosis was quite obviously related to contemporary problems, and whose prior life course had not been outwardly different from that of their age-mates. In these cases, immediate intervention by the family therapy team and a psychodynamic re-definition of the situation resulted in a disappearance of psychotic behaviour quickly, usually after 2–5 sessions, with a good subsequent prognosis.

The second group did not differ notably from the first as regards the patients' prior life course, though their social adjustment had not been quite so good. There was, however, a greater difference observable during the intervention. Although the connection between the illness and life problems was also recognized in this group, their interpretation or re-definition did not result in an equally good outcome. The team experienced this as a feeling of losing their grip, and different types of further treatment—continuation of family therapy or individual therapy—became necessary. As far as I can see, the families in this second group showed greater resistance towards change; many of them were classifi-

---

Exhibit 6.1

Central contents of the systemic–psychodynamically oriented family therapy of schizophrenia

1. *Therapists form a team*
   - all team members should be presented to the family
   - the team may use a therapy room or an observation room provided with audiovisual and telephone connection between the team members

2. *Empathic contact is established with all family members*
   - an atmosphere of "taking everybody's part"
   - stimulating the discussion through circular questioning and/or confronting the family members with each other

3. *Systemic–psychodynamic approach to the intra-familial relationships*
   - identification of family homeostasis and striving to change it
   - identification of symbiotic interrelationships and of strivings for separation and individuation
   - what do the symptoms mean from a systemic viewpoint?
   - attention to three-generational dynamics (the relationships of the parents with their parents)

4. *Systemic interventions*
   - positive connotations
   - messages thought out together and given to the family at the end of the session
   - the team should analyse each session afterwards and also before the beginning of the next session

5. *Some central goals*
   - the family members should gain better understanding of their thoughts, feelings, and intentions towards each other
   - support for healthy strivings and resources
   - support for establishing boundaries between the family members and respective individuation
   - support for the patient's extrafamilial relationships
   - support for the mourning work resulting from the loosening of symbiotic ties

able as rigid families. Lehtinen also pointed out that many of the female patients in this group later started individual therapy, which often turned out successful after a couple of years. The male patients more frequently withdrew from therapy and developed chronic symptoms. Lehtinen underlines the importance of providing special responsibility or case management teams for patients in this category, to guarantee the continuity of their treatment.

The third group consisted of patients who were already chronically ill at the time of their admission; the psychosis had developed gradually and been preceded by social isolation. Families had often shown increasing isolation from their environment. Short interventions are not sufficient in these cases, which require long-term work, including, according to Lehtinen, methods of psycho-educational family therapy—primarily, re-learning of social skills and learning new ones.

I also conclude that the principles of *psychoeducational family therapy* are best suited to the treatment of chronic patients. In less chronic cases this approach has the notable disadvantage of confirming the patient's role as a sick person, because the disorder is typically presented as being due to biological causes and therefore permanent and in need of continuous medication. I felt this quite poignantly when I asked a representative of this orientation whether he did not consider it harmful that such an idea be conveyed to the patient. He replied: "Well, it gives the patient an explanation for why he has not been able to reach the goals he has set for himself in life."

Even so, particularly when listening to Carol Anderson (1979) in the United States and to Julian Leff (1994) in Turku, I have also realized that the differences in the therapeutic attitude between the different orientations may, in fact, be greater in theory than in practice. Leff, for example, invites attention to the goals, whose psychological contents were partly quite similar to those presented in Exhibit 6.1, including support given to the patient's developing independence and elimination of emotionally overinvolved or unwisely critical parental behaviour.

The kind of internal process of development that optimally takes place in individual therapy is seldom achieved in family therapy, with the exception of some long-term psychodynamic family or couple therapies. Although systemic–strategic family therapy often releases the individual's potential for development and thereby increases his or her readiness to resume spontaneously his/her temporarily arrested growth, I recommend beginning individual therapy after the family

therapy stage, whenever the patient clearly suffers from a more profound disorder of personality development and has developed insight
into his/her problems during the family therapy.

Individual psychotherapy

Below, I discuss individual therapy from a viewpoint that should be
applicable even in public health care. I have excluded therapeutic
relationships requiring visits to a trained psychoanalyst four or five
times a week. This also corresponds to my own experience: most of
the psychotic patients whom I have treated since the 1950s were seen
twice weekly.

However, it needs to be emphasized that the frame of reference in
less intensive psychodynamic psychotherapy of psychotic patients
should be based on psychoanalytic insights. Psychodynamic individual
therapy is often divided quite strictly into psychoanalytically oriented
psychotherapy and supportive psychotherapy. In the treatment of psychotic patients, this dividing line is blurred. Even when a schizophrenic
patient is in psychoanalytically oriented therapy, there are always important supportive elements present. Moreover, a therapeutic process
that is intended to be supportive soon activates processes of identification and projection and feelings of transference and countertransference,
connected with the patient's developmental deficits. Therefore, the experiences that have been described by Searles (1965), Boyer (1983, 1986,
1989), Volkan (1990, 1994, 1995), and Benedetti (1979, 1985), for example,
have been of great importance in Turku, both in our supervision activities and during our individual psychotherapy training, of which an
important part is dedicated to psychotherapy of psychotics. I am not
here referring to the less psychotherapeutic, directive therapeutic relationships combined with drug treatment, which also provide support to
a schizophrenic patient.

In psychosis psychotherapy, the use of the couch is not recommended, and it is often not even possible (even if there are some psychoanalysts who try to approach the classical method as much as possible in
the therapy of these patients). For many schizophrenic patients, the concrete face-to-face contact is a necessary precondition for therapy, because
they need it for the establishment of the therapeutic process and for
remaining reality-oriented.

Searles (1965) defines the central goal of psychoanalytically oriented psychotherapy of schizophrenia to be a beneficial, corrective re-working of the patient's early ego development. The focus is on the relationship that is created between the patient and the therapist. This can also be expressed by stating that the therapist becomes a new self-object for the patient. When psychosis psychotherapy is compared with neurosis psychotherapy, the therapeutic process in the former may, in many respects, correspond to a continuation of half-finished construction, whereas the focus in neurosis therapy is on the reparation and renewal of structures that seem distorted. The patient's identification with the behaviour of the therapist plays a crucial role in the psychotherapy of schizophrenic patients (Volkan, 1994).

Through an empathic attitude—often called *holding*, following Winnicott's (1960) description of the early parent–child relationship—the schizophrenia therapist creates an interactional relationship with the patient, in order to induce integrating developmental processes. Holding must include an ability to tune in on the patient's wavelength and an empathic sensitivity to avoid excessive distance on the one hand and intrusion on the other. A permanent contact with autistic schizophrenic patients in particular becomes possible only when the patient has repeatedly experienced that he/she is able to trust the therapist. Empathic attitude also means that the therapist sets limits whenever the regressive patient needs them. It is important to listen, but it is not good to be too passive and non-committal. The most essential requirements in psychosis therapy are persistence, honesty, and an ability to convey to the patient hope for a better future, even if a distant one. To be able to meet these requirements, the therapist must personally believe in the patient's potential within the limits of justifiable optimism.

By becoming an increasingly important *self-object for the patient* (Kohut, 1971; see also chapter three), the therapist corrects the deficiencies of the earlier self-object relationships, helping the patient to integrate his/her personality. It is important to emphasize, following Volkan (1994), that the therapist should not push him/herself into this function, as such behaviour would threaten the patient. The process of development is rooted in the patient's transference relationship with the therapist and proceeds through transference on the patient's terms. The ego-strengthening process involves both an identification with the therapist and his/her attitudes and a release of the patient's previously constrained resources for personality growth. This process can well be described, in Kohut's term, as "transmuting internalization", as long as we remember that the therapist is not only a passive bystander in the process. As emphasized by Benedetti (1985), the interactional process requires that the therapist also identifies with the patient.

Using his concept of "self-object", Kohut emphasized the significance of the therapist as an idealized internal object for the patient. Rothstein (1980) has therefore labelled the Kohutian therapeutic process as supportive, suggesting that the idealized object relationship is not analysed. This is sometimes—though not with all patients!—the case in psychosis therapy.

Although Kohut's self-object theory is widely recognized as a valuable approach to narcissistic disorders, it has so far not been applied to psychotic conditions to any appreciable extent. I found the term "self-object" especially useful with regard to the understanding of disturbed parent–child relationships leading to vulnerability to schizophrenia. However, it also draws attention to the varying degrees of danger to the individual's sense of self and the need for empathic interaction on the part of the therapist.

As expressed elsewhere in this book, I still think that the term "self-object" should be seen as an umbrella under which a more detailed psychoanalytic approach is needed. Using terms of Kleinian origin, we might also call the therapist a "container" and emphasize the significance of projective identification in the constructive efforts based on the transference process. The term "self-object" may also serve as a conceptual introduction to the exploration of psychodynamically more primitive levels of "part-object" relationships when it is necessary and appropriate.

Connected with the function as the self-object, the *therapist's personality* is more significant in the therapy of psychosis patients than in more technically structured neurosis therapy. I referred to this when I related some of the favourable experiences we had in our clinic with therapists, often nurses, who had less formal training but were otherwise familiar with the problems of psychosis patients. Most of these therapists are women. Holding at a psychological level requires that even male therapists show characteristics that—in the development of us all—have come about through early identification with the mother. Men frequently feel such characteristics to threaten their masculinity and therefore tend to suppress or deny them. Such male persons are also found among psychiatrists, and they make perfectly good managers or rehabilitators, but they are less well suited to become psychosis therapists. The same is naturally also true of other mental health staff. Overemphasized rationality, which is sometimes observable in psychoanalysts, may also be detrimental to one's work as a psychosis therapist, as is overemphasized emotionality.

Barbro Sandin, a well-known Swedish psychosis psychotherapist whose therapies were particularly successful with male patients (see Sjöström, 1985), pointed out in an interview by Levander and Cullberg (1994) that certain "male" characteristics, especially resolute tenacity, may have been useful for the reconstruction of her patients' personalities through identification with the therapist's personality traits. Therapists must be more of a mother and father to psychotic patients than to less seriously disturbed patients—though naturally maintaining the role of a therapist—and they therefore benefit from internal multidimensionality of their own personalities.

Both patient and therapist may undergo deep emotional involvement during the therapy. If the frequency of therapy hours is once or twice weekly, the process generally requires slightly less emotional commitment from the therapist than do more intensive long-term therapies. One of the benefits to a less experienced therapist of a less intensive therapy is that it gives a better facility for maintaining an observing attitude towards his/her own involvement and, accordingly, a sufficient internal distance from the patient.

A less well trained therapist should be especially wary of presenting *interpretations* too early. I agree with Boyer (1986), who pointed out that the time is ripe for interpretations only when the therapeutic relationship has advanced so far that the "good" introjects created through it have begun to replace the patient's fixation to the previously internalized "bad" introjects. In other words, a positive transference relationship has been established, including identification with the therapist, and it has begun to replace the effect of previous negative interpersonal relationships. And the interpretations should usually begin from the surface and only gradually proceed to deeper layers. It is often sufficient in successful therapies to point out the connections between the patient's current experiences of symptoms and anxiety and his/her previous sensations and experiences, particularly those related to past life and parents, as indicated by interpretations of the transferences attributed to the therapist. A special mode of working with schizophrenic patients is represented by "interpretations upwards" (see the case history of Eric, chapter one)—interpretations that not only point out such connections but also translate the patient's concretized expressions into normal language.

Paula (see chapter one) believed delusionally that part of her brain had been removed on the hospital ward. When I said that she might be thinking this because she has a feeling that now that she is ill and in the hospital, she is not able to think as clearly as earlier, the delusion disappeared. When more than two decades later I related this experience to Bryce Boyer, then visiting Turku, he pointed out to me that even if Paula's thinking was influenced by my "interpretation upwards", a precondition for its success was also her instinctual acceptance of my empathic attitude, which helped her to give up her delusion, characterized by an accusing and projectively hostile attitude towards us, the hospital people, "take in" my interpretation, and give up the delusion. I agreed and thought this to be a good example of the significance of projective and introjective processes in the psychology of schizophrenia.

Transference interpretations pointing out connections occasionally have a dramatic effect on the anxiety of a patient whose relationship with the therapist is well-established. One of my patients, who had previously had several psychotic episodes but had now been free from psychotic symptoms for a couple of years, once called me in a sudden panic, saying that this was the end of everything, as the communists were taking over in Finland. She also mentioned in passing that she had written such an angry letter to me that she had not dared to mail it. I said, "The communists will not take over in Finland, even if you mail the letter". The patient understood the connection between her panic and the anger that she had felt towards me and which she dreaded would threaten our good mutual relationship, and she calmed down.

No deeper drive-psychological content interpretations may be needed. Deep interpretations—which have sometimes been given inappropriately to psychotic patients right from the beginning of therapy by representatives of the Kleinian school—may, if used by non-experts, only disintegrate the patient further. Besides, they may underline the omnipotence of the therapist in a way that is not advantageous to the later phases in the therapy.

The core of transference is the emergence of a symbiotic dependent relationship between the patient and the therapist. The mutuality of the process gives rise to nuances that are reminiscent of the parent–child relationship. It is, however, important for the therapist to maintain his/her role, being careful not to show excessive activity, such as making decisions on the patient's behalf, and certainly not to make delegation-like suggestions or demands. The therapist is best able to help the patient come to his/her own decisions by taking up alternatives and discussing the problems they involve and by occasional encouraging questions, but by leaving the decision-making to the patient.

The most critical aspect of long-term psychosis therapies is often the ability of the therapist to handle and control his/her countertransference. Countertransference is a major asset for the therapist, but the problems involved in it constitute the most common obstacles thwarting the therapeutic process. The greatest problem is due to the aggressive psychotic accusations by the most seriously ill patients directed at their therapists, which the latter consider unreasonable. Even so, the therapist should not become involved by venting his/her own internal anger at the patient's distorted emotions or claims. Instead, the foundation of the patient's transference should be analysed and patiently interpreted. It will generally turn out that the patient expects from the therapist the kind of emotions and attitudes that were shown by a parent or other early objects, and trying to induce the therapist to take their role, confusing the therapist with parents. But at the same time the therapist must realize that not all anger is necessarily due to transference; he/she may have given a realistic cause for it by showing a lack of empathy or otherwise offending the patient.

The expression of critical and hostile feelings towards the therapist often evokes anxiety in the patient, but their expression is extremely important, as it helps to integrate the dualistic domain of good and evil mental images. Even at the early stages of therapy, the patients often find it a significant experience that they can feel angry towards the therapist without having the relationship break down. This part of the work is, however, most important towards the end of the therapy, and it is generally manifested as feelings of anger triggered by the therapist's vacations—but also by other unavoidable frustrations. At the same time, the idealization of the therapist begins to level off, and he/she is reduced to the status of ordinary mortals in the patient's mind.

It is gratifying for the therapist to bask in the role of an idealized object, but the therapeutic process should go further, and because of this, the inclusion of the negative transference in the dialogue may be essential. One of my patients gave me a very illustrative experience of this after one of our summer breaks.

The patient, now a married woman in her 40s, had been in my therapy twenty years earlier, because of a transient psychotic episode during her university studies. Now she had visited me anew for a couple of years, because of the reproachful and threatening voices she had begun to hear. Her relationship to me was characterized by an idealized and also erotically tinged positive transference, with the help of which her condition had improved, despite continuing auditory hallucinations.

At her first visit after the break, she told me how much she had longed for me during the long summer without the therapy hours and how difficult this had been for her. Because she had earlier expressed guilt feelings related to her fantasies of me, I said that she should not reproach herself because of this. She became angry, and said that I did not understand her at all—the matter in question was how difficult it was for her not to see me. She wanted to give up her visits altogether— "that's the only solution". I listened to her and confirmed the time of her next visit.

The patient came to her therapy session and apologized for her anger. I said to her that I regarded this an important matter that we should discuss. She then continued to criticize me, expressing rather strong feelings of envy of the "better-off" therapist. It appeared that she experienced me as an authority and even consciously resisted the interpretations given by myself. This had obvious connections with the defiance she had secretly felt for her mother and other persons during her childhood and adolescence, even if she had ostensibly adopted their opinions; it was her way of protecting her inner identity. The discussion of these matters and the interpretation of their connection with transference to the therapist helped the stagnated therapeutic process to get started again, followed by the patient's more active participation in the common therapeutic work. The erotically tinged transference had served as a defence against the aggressive feelings towards myself, including an effort to destroy my interpretations by not introjecting them.

Another important aspect of therapeutic work is *attention to and support for the patient's adult characteristics*, which is often ignored in the literature dealing with psychosis psychotherapy. As emphasized also by Jackson and Williams (1994), the adult—and, more generally, non-psychotic—aspects of the patient's personality are important to recognize and nurture from the first contact onward. And in the process of organization and development that takes place during the therapy, this part of the patient's personality continues to play an indispensable role. The patient's subsequent ability to avoid psychotic regression depends significantly on the strengthening of this adult quality, which involves reflective thinking and interest in trying to understand the nature of his disorder.

I have found it to be especially important in therapy to show interest in the patient's life and personality in general, not concentrating exclusively on symptoms and problems. During therapy sessions, attention is mainly focused on matters related to the patient's current life situation; analysis of any previous interpersonal relationships always starts at the contemporary level, pointing out connections. Although the problems and anxiety associated with the current situation—including the relationship with the therapist—are the main object of attention, it is useful to show interest even in "ordinary" matters, such as the patient's work, studies, or hobbies. The interest should not be artificial, but genuine; and genuineness is generally easy to achieve through the countertransference that the therapist has developed towards the patient and his/her developmental potential. The support given to the patient's adult characteristics also includes acknowledgement of that person's own contribution in the therapeutic process.

I consider it a significant observation that I have achieved my best therapeutic results with psychotic patients whose life course or interests have borne some similarity to my own life experiences. This phenomenon is related to the spontaneous choices of personal nurses and therapists that I mentioned when discussing psychotherapeutic communities.

The development that the patients show in an appropriately progressing therapy is frequently reflected as an attempt also to develop themselves in domains other than psychotherapy. Thus, people who are recovering or have recovered from psychosis may become interested in various kinds of creative work, such as art, writing, or music, or begin a new period of studies. Creative interests may even in themselves be of notable therapeutic value. Artistically talented patients often benefit from a combination of art therapy with their psychotherapy.

Sidsel Gilbert and Endre Ugelstad (1994) described cogently the role of the creative efforts of two of their NIPS Project patients in supporting their process of recovery after long-term psychotherapy. One of the patients, a seriously ill young man, wrote a paper on his experiences during the therapy, where he described how he used self-suggestion in his battle against the fears that had resulted in massive isolation, and also tried to promote clear thinking by studying philosophy. It was important to integrate the different levels of activity by "feeling like a child and thinking maturely".

Separations are especially critical events for schizophrenic patients because of their dependence. One should therefore refrain from starting a therapeutic relationship that is doomed to end quickly because the therapist is going to move or is only temporarily employed in the working community. It is not simple to replace one therapist with another when we are dealing with self-object relations, in which the therapist has become a kind of new parent to the patient through transference. The final stage of therapy is often long: it is advisable to start working towards it 10–12 months before the intended discontinuation of sessions. The patient must also be told of the therapist's vacations early enough, so that the future period of separation and the emotions associated with it can be discussed in advance. The discussion should not be restricted to the patient's ideas of how he/she will manage during the therapist's vacation; it is also necessary to discuss the feelings aroused by the vacation. It is recommended—and sometimes necessary—to arrange for the patient to have a substitute therapist during the vacation.

Even so, separations associated with vacations and other events are difficult for the patient despite the preparatory work, especially during the early stages of long-term therapy, because they always signify a rejection at a deeper level. The patient's psychotic condition may deteriorate or recur during a separation. These situations also involve an increased risk of *suicidal behaviour*. Most of psychotic patients' suicides follow an experience of feeling rejected. I too have a few sad experiences of this.

Although the psychodynamics related to the patient's *family background* is mostly worked through as related by the patient and, as the therapy advances, through transference and countertransference manifestations, I consider it useful even for the individual therapist to meet the parents at the beginning of therapy, especially if the patients still live with their primary families. The patient should be present at these meetings. They are important for two reasons: first, because they give the therapist some idea of the current state of family dynamics, and, second, because a contact with the parents may diminish their distrust towards the therapist. In the need-adapted model such an initial contact comes about naturally during the therapy meetings arranged during the patient's admission, provided that the future individual therapist attends these meetings.

The parents or other relatives may occasionally contact the therapist in crisis situations. If they do, the therapist must respect the confidentiality of the therapeutic relationship and also refuse to keep the patient ignorant of the contact. If the therapist works in a public health care unit, repeated contacts by the parents must be referred to another worker with an assignment to support the parents. In more serious crises, it may be useful to arrange a therapy meeting attended jointly by the patient, the relatives, the therapist, and the other members of the team.

Since the goal of the therapy is to promote the patient's increasing individuation and liberation from his/her internal—and often also external—dependency bonds with the parents, the therapeutic work must continuously focus on questions pertaining to this. Theodore and Ruth Lidz (1982) expressed this pointedly: "Efforts are made to imbue in the patient trust in his own ideas and feelings while questioning those that are essentially the parents' feelings and percepts which the patient offers as his own." The relationship with the therapist fills part of the vacuum that may threaten the patient as a consequence of his/her efforts towards independence and also interferes with these efforts. In the final part of therapy a positive, conciliatory development may occur in the patient's feelings towards parents, which may include attempts at reparation for things felt to have been done to them, in fact or in phantasy. A precondition for this is the patient's individuation and a rebuilding of the mutual relationships at a new level, allowing for more separateness.

In the case of patients with children, the therapist should also give some attention to the relationship between them and the patient, helping the latter to avoid the risk of transmitting the psychopathology from one generation to the next. Many of the patients are aware of this possibility. One female patient of mine, who obviously had an admirably empathic attitude towards her children, said that she was trying to do the good turn of not demanding from her children the kind of "responsibility" and care she had had to assume for her own mother (the mother was not psychotic, but transferred her own problems to her relationship to the daughter, which was both binding and deprecatory).

The recommended frequency of visits for individual therapies, even when carried out within the public health care system, is twice or, if possible, three times a week, and at the initial stages in the hospital ward three times a week or more often. If necessary (though not preferably), the frequency of visits can later be dropped to once a week without notably impairing the intensity of the therapeutic relationship. At times of crisis, however, it should be possible to arrange for more frequent visits. Working with long-term patients who already show advanced development towards independence, I have sometimes used a two-week interval between the sessions at later stages. At the earlier stages, however, such long intervals would transform the therapy into maintenance treatment instead of advancing the process.

Many of the therapeutic relationships last long—usually for 4–10 years. The best signs of the approaching end of a successful therapy are the permanent elimination of psychotic symptoms and, even more importantly, the integration of the patient's internal development in such a way that he/she is able to face problems independently, using internalizations made during therapy and the resources that have been released internally. This stage is often also characterized by an important new interpersonal relationship. The therapist should naturally support such a development but also ascertain that the patient is not merely transferring his/her needs for dependency to a new object. In that case, a possible new rejection on the part of the new object could be disastrous.

Many patients retain a certain constructive internal dependency on the therapist, which may result in occasional contacts even long after therapy.

The longest of my own therapeutic relationships has lasted for 38 years and is still going on. During the early years there were several interruptions: my patient was hospitalized for several years altogether, but afterwards resumed the visits. Now she has not been in a hospital for more than 20 years and is asymptomatic. She visits me only three times a year, discussing both some current problems and problems that date back to earlier times, even her childhood, which still are active in her mind.

Comments on psychopharmacological treatment

In the need-adapted treatment model, drug treatment is considered to be an auxiliary method, used to support the psychotherapeutically oriented treatment.

Neuroleptic medication in small or moderate doses often makes it easier to establish contact with the patient, especially if he/she is restless and dominated by psychotic delusions. In the treatment model report of the Finnish National Schizophrenia Project (Alanen et al., 1990a), we specified that an important goal is to find "the minimal neuroleptic dosage required to keep the patient's ability for contact and communication optimal in the situation". At the same time, we emphasized the need to justify the medication to oneself, the patient, and frequently also the patient's environment, in a way that everybody readily understands.

The illness in itself is not a sufficient reason for medication, but the explanation could be, for example, that the patient is now in need of medication in order to be better able to control anxiety and agitation and to be able to live at home without hospitalization, or—in a little more interpretative sense—in order to be able to control better the occasional feelings of anger and anxiety that may arise.

Psychopharmacologically oriented researchers and clinicians prefer to describe neuroleptic medication as a stimulus barrier, which helps the patient to maintain his/her psychic balance. Leff et al. (1983) have reported findings that suggest that the protective dosage should be higher in family environments with high EE values than in environments with low EE values, in order to help the patient to remain out of hospital.

As a counter-argument, one might claim—referring, for example, to the NIPS outcome results (Alanen et al., 1994; see also Figure 5.3)—that an established therapeutic relationship often gives the patient a sense of security, which makes it possible to lower the dosage and eventually discontinue medication. From the viewpoint of psychotherapy, too, low-dose neuroleptic medication, even when used continuously, is often beneficial, whereas higher doses tend to be detrimental to the therapeutic process and to prevent progress. Few patients undergoing psychotherapy need a daily dose higher than 150–200 mg of thioridazine or 12–16 mg of perazine.

As the patient's condition improves, the dosage should be lowered gradually, preferably aiming at discontinuation. This is not, however, possible in all cases, and I also know of patients who want to keep the small dose they take in the evening, mostly for psychological reasons, as a concrete symbol of their internal dependency on their previous therapist; the pharmacological effect of the dose may be insignificant. We also know that sudden discontinuation after a relatively high dose involves a risk for the patient's psychic stability.

Some of my patients have given interesting descriptions of the changes brought about by the discontinuation of even a small dose of medication, saying, for example, that "both one's own feelings and the feelings of others became more visible", or of trying hard to maintain their current state and prevent the previously felt lack of boundaries between oneself and the others from recurring. It is important to take up such problems during the therapy sessions, and they can usually be worked out successfully.

Referring to these experiences, and naturally also to the side-effects of psychoactive drugs, it seems justifiable to support the efforts of

Räkköläinen and his co-workers (Räkköläinen et al., 1994; Vuorio et al., 1993), which I described in chapter four: they suggest that in particular many first-admission schizophrenics should preferably be treated without neuroleptics. But in order to be able to do so, we must vigorously develop our psychotherapeutic resources in a comprehensive way. Otherwise there will be the danger that prolonged in-patient periods will result in poorer outcomes, especially through the negative effects that institutionalization may have on the patients' social status and social skills. For long-term patients—especially those without a psychotherapeutic relationship—a maintenance medication in low or moderate doses is usually in order.

Neuroleptic medication administered as injections at longer intervals, which is advocated in order to guarantee the regularity of treatment (e.g. Hogarty, 1994), is not compatible with psychotherapeutic approaches and their primary goal of promoting the patient's independence. Forced medication has adverse effects on the therapeutic contacts—I experienced the mental violence associated with it personally when I visited a camp arranged by the Society of Psychiatric Rehabilitees in Finland and was assigned a sociodrama role of a patient who was fed pills by force. Nevertheless, involuntary medication is frequently necessary on an acute psychosis ward; it should, however, always be combined with an effort to establish a different kind of contact with the patient by discussing what made him/her feel so bad.

It is important that the medication and the dosage are discussed with the patient, taking his/her opinion into consideration. Many of the outpatients soon learn to regulate their medication, increasing the dosage at times of crisis.

Need-adapted treatment: case excerpts

Marjorie, single parent with three children

The case of Marjorie, a patient included in the Turku Cohort IV (see chapter five), shows particularly well both the individual "tailoring" of our therapeutic activities and the benefits of family-oriented treatment, both for the patient and for the larger family group.

Marjorie, aged 33, began to hear voices upon her return from Sweden to her hometown of Turku with her 3 children. The voices had started from fits of fear, being partly accusing, and Marjorie had lately begun to respond to them and burst into compulsive laughing fits. She thought this to be caused by some kind of hypnosis, saying that she occasionally heard a whipping sound near her ear, as if she were being hit.

Marjorie had moved to Sweden at the age of 16. There she had been married twice and had had several partners living with her for short periods. Her second marriage ended in divorce a year before she moved back to Finland. Out of her marriages she had 3 children who lived with her, the oldest one 13 years old. She told us that both marriages had been wrecked for the same reason: the husbands were aggressive and addicted to alcohol (as Marjorie's father had been, too).

In Turku, Marjorie had a few short, unsuccessful jobs. She tended to go for help to her mother, although their relationship was liable to conflicts. Having heard voices for more than 6 months, Marjorie consulted the Mental Health Office on her own initiative and thereby became included in our series. She received medication, and a therapeutic relationship with a psychologist was arranged for her. However, after taking an overdose of her drugs, she was hospitalized for 5 weeks. Her medication in the hospital consisted of 8 mg perphenazine and 50 mg thioridazine a day. The dose was later cut by half.

Investigation of the family situation in the initial therapeutic meeting, which was also attended by Marjorie's mother and the children, revealed the anxiety of all. It indicated also that Marjorie had notable problems with her children, especially the eldest daughter, who tyrannized her; she was quite helpless when faced by her anger. The older children had also begun to play a parental role in relation to their mother.

Joint sessions were thereafter arranged by the same therapeutic team four times, at intervals of about month. Through their messages, the family therapy team made efforts to support Marjorie in her maternal role and to liberate the children from parentification. One transactional defence that appeared central from the family-dynamic point of view was the patient's unconscious projective identification with her children. She seemed to profit by their outbursts of anger through projecting onto them her own suppressed aggressions directed at her mother and then, by identifying with them, to "maintain" in them this intrapsychic emotion, which was originally her own.

The family situation seemed to have become easier after the summer, when Marjorie and her eldest daughter had had more distance between them while the daughter spent some weeks in Sweden with her father. The focus of Marjorie's therapy now shifted to individual therapy. It had been going on all the time but only acquired a real significance when the transactional defences were clarified and weakened through the family sessions. She visited the psychologist at the Mental Health Office twice weekly; later, the visits were dropped to once a week.

The family was invited to a new joint session at the time of the two-year follow-up. Marjorie had been continuing her individual therapy. She clearly held the mother's role in relation to her children now. The children's psychological individuation had advanced, and they no longer displayed the kinds of transactionally based problems of aggression to the extent that had coloured the initial therapeutic process. Both Marjorie and the children increasingly directed their attention to new fields of interest and relationships outside the home. A similar developmental process had taken place in Marjorie's relationship with her mother, which had become more distant but thereby also less conflicted. Marjorie's attitude towards life and her mental world were, however, still characterized by timidity and wariness, and she still heard voices from time to time, though she understood them to be her own internal experiences. Socially, she had been supported through vocational counselling.

Family intervention and individual therapy made up a continuum here, which shows the implementation of the need-adapted therapeutic approach from the point of view of both patient and family. The most essential outcome of the family intervention, which was important for all the family members, was the preliminary breakdown of the transactional defence mechanisms as unnecessary. Simultaneously, the family therapy created, both through the external support and through an emancipation of the patient's inner psychological resources, a necessary and sufficient prerequisite for Marjorie's individual treatment. The preventive importance of family therapy for the children's development is also reflected in this case vignette.

Catherine, a young woman in search of her identity
[with Irene Aalto]

Catherine, a 27-year-old unmarried clothing designer, attractive and energetic but lacking persistence, belonged to the series of Räkköläinen et al. (see pp. 117–118), which consisted of first-admission patients of the schizophrenia group treated with comprehensive, need-adapted psychotherapy and, whenever possible, without neuroleptics. She began her treatment in the Kupittaa Hospital in Turku in September 1991.

CLINICAL FEATURES AND STAGES OF TREATMENT

Catherine had been suffering from stress for four years, trying to pay back the loans that remained after she had closed down her small boutique. She held various temporary jobs, alternately working overtime and being unemployed. She had started the boutique with her previous common-law husband, Richard, who now joined his relatives in pressing Catherine for the repayment of loans and guarantees. Richard had even battered Catherine and had tried to drive over her; the matter had been taken to a court.

When Richard and Catherine broke off their relationship, she soon found a new boy-friend, Denis, and she was planning to get married to him. With only a week to go before the wedding, Catherine became restless and sleepless, spoke incoherently, and kept leafing through her papers, repeating "everything's all right, everything's all right". A doctor was called when she was found running naked in the corridor, talking about the end of the world and the countdown. She was admitted into the Kupittaa Hospital on 12 September 1991.

On the closed ward of the hospital, Catherine was at first agitated, confused, and restless, hyperactively organizing things, trying to undress, and finding her environment menacing with radio and television messages of perils threatening herself and Denis. Although *one member of the staff was appointed to be available to Catherine at all times*, she had to be isolated several times during her first few days in the hospital, especially at night. When necessary, she was given *benzodiazepines* (lorazepam) intramuscularly and orally. Neuroleptic drugs were not given at any stage.

Catherine's hospital stay was long and eventful. Involuntary hospitalization was considered necessary at first, because the need for occasional isolation persisted and Catherine did not have a sense of illness. Despite this, she began to view the hospital as a refuge about a week after her admission. She continued her anxious, affectively restless activity, which involved hypomanic and histrionic features, but since she was able, despite her psychotic behaviour, to collect herself in strict realities and interaction and felt that the atmosphere in the closed ward only increased her restlessness, she was moved to an open ward for daytime care as early as 19 September, though she continued to spend the nights on the closed ward. One of the mental nurses on the open ward was appointed her *personal nurse*, and she contributed significantly to Catherine's coping in hospital.

Catherine's agitation gradually calmed down, but her hyperactivity and unrealistic thinking, which expressed both her omnipotent level of functioning and her potential for creative imagination, continued until December, and partly even longer. She now became more depressed, but also willing to deal with her problems at the level of realities. Involuntary treatment was discontinued on 12 December 1991, although she still showed psychotic behaviour at that time. This stage of hospital treatment was characterized by *discussion and clarification of Catherine's interpersonal borderline psychodynamics in repeated therapy meetings* (see pp. 175–177), mostly from a *systemic perspective*; the most essential aspects were her strong and ambivalent dependent relations. Catherine's identity crisis was reflected in her semipsychotic attempt to change both her Christian name and her surname (she wanted to be called Sealand, because, as an infant, she had lived on an island with her maternal grandmother, who still lived there). Since Catherine was still depressed, in need of care, unable to work, and continued to have problems with her interpersonal relationships, her hospital treatment was continued, mostly on a day-patient basis, until 11 June 1992, after which she still kept her day-hospital registration until 16 October 1992, although she came to the hospital only for therapy sessions and art therapy. During the spring, she was also on antidepressive medication (citaloprame 20 mg daily), which did not improve her condition.

Catherine's diagnosis in the patient record was *psychosis schizophreniformis*.

When Catherine was discharged from the hospital, she began *regular individual therapy sessions* with I.A., a specialized nurse educated in both psychodynamic psychotherapy and family therapy. Catherine had come to know her during the therapy meetings. Her individual therapy has since continued. Y.O.A. has been the supervisor of her individual therapy.

Catherine was *readmitted* and remained hospitalized from 4 March to 30 April 1993, after she had taken 100 pills (1 mg) of lorazepam. She was depressed but not psychotic at that time. There was no break in Catherine's individual therapy sessions because of the hospitalization. The clarification of her interpersonal relationships (especially her strained relation with her mother) was continued at renewed therapy meetings.

SYSTEMIC THERAPY PROCESS AND CATHERINE'S FAMILY ANAMNESIS

The therapy process consisted of several integrated aspects. The weekly *therapy meetings*, which are arranged regularly for all patients on the ward, provided the core for systemic work. Catherine attended altogether 73 therapy meetings (some of them after her discharge). Apart from these, she and Denis also attended 8 *couple sessions*, and an unsuccessful attempt was made to involve Catherine's primary family in more regular family therapy. Catherine also participated in *group therapy* and *art therapy*.

The first *therapy meetings* were arranged on the ward on the day of admission and the following day. They were attended by Catherine and her escorts, whose variety illustrated the poor differentiation, controversiality, and tendency to interdependence that characterized her interpersonal relations: the persons present were Catherine's mother, her step-father, her younger step-sister, a female friend, and Denis and his sister. The persons who continued to attend most regularly were her mother and Denis, and therapy meetings were also arranged with Catherine present without her relatives. As far as possible, the basic members of the therapy team were always present. The team consisted of three members of the ward staff—a specialized nurse with family and individual therapy training (I.A.), Catherine's personal nurse, and another mental nurse—less frequently also a doctor and occasionally some other member of the nursing staff.

The *family anamnesis* was taken during the therapy meetings. No one knew of any psychotic disorders in the family. Catherine was the only child of her parents, who had divorced when she was 3 years old. The mother remarried when Catherine was 5, and she had twins (a girl and a boy) two years later. Catherine's father and mother quarrelled over her custodianship. Catherine found out later that her mother had given her up as a 3-month-old baby to her maternal grandparents, who had then handed the 11-month-old baby over to her paternal grandmother (though she had also spent some periods with her mother). The mother only wanted her back when she had divorced her husband, and the father simultaneously wanted to have her custodianship. Catherine was told about all this by her maternal grandmother. The controversial quality of Catherine's parents' relationship is shown by the fact that her mother made sure that she was away when her father came to visit. When the mother remarried, the step-father adopted Catherine, who was thereby given his surname. The team had an impression that Catherine's relatives, including her maternal and paternal grandparents, had been quarrelling over who was the best person to take care of her, and that these quarrels still continued in part, which made Catherine feel that people were interfering with her life and preventing her from being autonomous.

The relatives had considered Catherine a good, cheerful, loveable girl, a "princess" who always put other people's interests before hers. It was quite obvious that Catherine's interpersonal relations were characterized by a deep-rooted need to please others and a desire to have substitute figures ready to step in whenever she was rejected by the others. This tendency was still visible in her interpersonal relations, even in hospital. At the same time, however, she vented her irritation at not being able to take care of her own affairs. For example, both her own family and her in-laws-to-be had been intruding on the arrangements for her wedding, which then had to be cancelled.

The interviews that were conducted during the therapy meetings (and even more significantly Catherine's subsequent individual therapy) revealed a great deal of mutual envy and jealousy in her early environment. Catherine and her younger step-sister competed for their mother's favours, of which Catherine felt deprived, while the mother was jealous of the affection that the step-father—who was probably the least disturbed member of the family—showed towards Catherine as well as of Catherine's affectionate relationship with her maternal grandmother.

Catherine dropped out of high-school—for which she later blamed her mother—and studied clothing manufacture and design in trade school. She received a designer's diploma but gave up the further-education programme she had started. She had her first long-term dating relationship while still a teenager, but she broke it off as a protest to her mother, who liked the boy. When she was 19, she began to see Richard, who was to become her first "open husband", against her mother's will. The man was eight years older than she. When Catherine had to close down the boutique she had been keeping together with Richard, she took various odd jobs as a salesperson, waitress, seamstress, and model, while planning various educational possibilities that she never seriously explored.

Catherine had been meeting Denis for two years, but they only moved in together about six months before her hospitalization. During these months Catherine had come to realize that Denis was inclined to abuse both alcohol and sedatives, which fact he tried to deny from himself and hide from other people. Catherine later said that the onset of her psychosis just before the wedding was a sign of an "unconscious realization that the marriage would never work out". She also faced another serious problem in a diagnosis of *endometriosis*, with the consequent possibility of sterility. This diagnosis came as a blow to her femininity and her dreams of having a baby.

The primary *therapeutic function* of the therapy meetings was to give Catherine a chance to talk about herself in an increasingly organized fashion. She liked this mode of working and was active, occasionally firing a battery of questions at her mother or someone else. In that way, she also began her process of differentiation (though she later needed individual therapy to accomplish this successfully). For Catherine's relatives, the meetings provided a chance to establish contact with the therapeutic community and to develop an enhanced understanding of the connections between Catherine's illness and the problems in her life. The therapy meetings also prevented the quarrels between the relatives, which provoked anxiety in Catherine, from interfering excessively with her therapy. Despite this, the relatives' attitudes showed no major signs of progress during the meetings. The therapy meetings, combined with the meetings of the ward community, also provided a forum for discussing the tendency to split, which was apparent in the ward community and was enhanced by Catherine's fragmentary transference relations. This split was manifested, for example, by a disagreement as to whether Catherine should be "put in a better order" or given space to exercise her semipsychotic creativity.

The *couple sessions* of Catherine and Denis, which were a corollary of the therapy meetings in the spring of 1992, took place at a time when it was discussed whether Catherine should move in with Denis after her discharge. When Catherine began to spend part of her time with Denis, Denis began to drink; Catherine and Denis then began to use benzodiazepine together, and Catherine became depressed. Catherine's prolonged hospital treatment was partly related to these problems. After the couple sessions, Catherine and Denis decided to separate.

Catherine liked *group therapy* (12 sessions) and especially *art therapy*, which was given in small groups. She established a close and favourable relationship with the art therapist. Catherine appreciated most highly her painting of a swan, a southern bird, swimming in an ice-clad landscape and clearly threatened by destruction.

INDIVIDUAL THERAPY PROCESS

Individual therapy was already considered to be indicated for Catherine at the early stages of her hospitalization. The beginning of individual therapy was, however, notably delayed, because Catherine refused to accept the idea (especially when a therapist working outside the hospital was suggested for her), probably because of the confused and binding complexity of her actual and transference relations. She only accepted the idea of individual therapy when she was about to be discharged from the hospital, and she named three "candidates" among the hospital staff (I.A., art therapist, personal nurse)—which she herself associated with the fact that she had had "three mothers" as a baby. I.A. was prepared for the therapy (and was the most competent of the candidates), but considered it important that Catherine should choose the therapist herself. The confidential relationship between Catherine and I.A. had been established gradually during the therapy meetings, where I.A. had been present as a staff member.

The *frequency* of individual therapy sessions was three times a week during the initial stage and at times of crisis, and twice a week later. The *transference relationship* was at first characterized by passively "symbiotic" reliance for omnipotent support and a search for love. Catherine behaved endearingly to "disarm" the therapist, but she soon began to act out and show her unconscious ambivalence. On the one hand, she asked for extra appointments as a sign of the therapist's love, while on the other hand she presented various rationalized reasons for cancelling her regular appointments. The therapist showed caring, motherly *countertransference*: she said that at first she felt Catherine to be a "small, attractive, talented child". Catherine's aggressiveness (initially unconscious, later conscious) did not provoke aggressive irritation in the therapist; she says her patient "confined the aggression within herself" without significantly transferring it through projective identification to the therapist. During vacations and at times when Catherine was in crisis, the therapist allowed her to telephone her at home. Catherine also tried to repeat her previous pattern of "finding substitute people" by contacting her previous art therapist to talk about her problems or "escaping" to her biological father, only to be disappointed even there. The supervisor of the therapy process therefore pointed out the need to increase gradually the regularity of the therapy by making a friendly, but clarifying intervention in Catherine's acting-out tendencies. After interpretations, Catherine did not want a substitute therapist even when I.A. was away on holiday, but she called her at the agreed times. Later on, however, the work at the transference level focused increasingly on the problems deriving from Catherine's early mother relationship, which are discussed in greater detail below.

Catherine was no longer psychotic when she began and continued her individual therapy, although she felt panicky anxiety and fears of becoming psychotic during her frequent crises. Her most important *defence mechanisms* were denial and projection (which soon decreased, however), projective identification (mostly with the therapist), as well as the acting-out of her desire to have other contacts outside the therapeutic relationship. Her moods ranged from creative enthusiasm to depressive sadness. The depressive periods involved fatigue and excessive eating (during late 1993 she put on 20 kg, only to lose it again gradually). Catherine was given no other *medication* during her therapy except 1 mg of lorazepam when necessary. Occasionally, when she felt anxiety and depression, she took 5–6 mg daily, but when her anxiety lessened, she stopped taking pills altogether.

Outwardly, Catherine's life course remained unstable for a long time. She changed jobs and was variably able to work during her therapy: she generally found a job easily, despite the recession, but she was not able to keep it, partly because of her desire to please leading to stressful submissiveness, partly because of her fatigue and depressive tendencies. She had several short sick-leaves for psychiatric reasons or because of the treatment of her endometriosis. At first she lived with her mother and step-father, but after her hospitalization in the spring of 1993 she moved to live in a flat. At about that time she got a dog, Daffy, which was an important transitional object for her. She pampered the dog and identified it with her own desires ("I'm the most important person for Daffy"). Catherine even brought Daffy to the therapy session a few times. Catherine had one of her most intense feelings of hatred ever discussed during the therapy towards her friend, whom she had asked to take care of her dog for a while, and who had done this caring inadequately ("I could have killed her").

Having separated from Denis, Catherine had a few *male friends* over the years, but the relationships involved problems of ambivalent dependence and other difficulties. Quite obviously, Catherine's own problems—both those due to her relationship with her mother and those based on her oedipal need for punishment—contributed to her tendency to make unfortunate choices. In the summer of 1995, almost immediately after the marriage of her therapist, she became "engaged" to an older man she hardly knew, who was just divorcing his wife, and she moved in with him, leaving her own recently re-modelled flat. When the relationship failed due to the man's despotism and inadequate separation from his previous wife, Catherine again had nowhere to live. It was pointed out in the therapy that in becoming engaged she wanted to follow her therapist's example; but feelings of envy were not interpreted at this point. A year later Catherine went to live with a pathologically jealous and clinging man, who even tried to strangle her after she, unconsciously provoking the man, had allowed an innocent dancing partner to see her home in his car, while her friend was suspiciously waiting for her. When this relationship came to an end in late 1996, it became possible in the therapy to discuss Catherine's relationships with men in a way that increased her insight and made her attitudes more solid and realistic. When her attention was drawn to her obsessive pattern of choosing male friends who always failed in their attempt to build a relationship, she said she repeated a pattern related to her mother—trying to "force" the other person to change and to make him understand Catherine better—and projecting murderousness into him when this failed.

Catherine's relationship with her mother was characterized by complex problems of dependence and independence and, especially, a constant *wish that her mother might begin to understand and love her better*, which defied all disappointments. The mother relationship was taken up in the therapy, especially after Catherine's suicide attempt in the spring of 1993. She realized that she had tried "revenge" on her mother, who had caused her intense frustrations. During the therapy session she felt "furiously angry" with her mother. But her hatred was not directed exclusively at her mother. She also became conscious of her hatred towards her therapist, who had had to cancel an extra session despite her patient's anxiety. A year later Catherine had a dream: *the mother was in hospital wearing high-heeled shoes and had had a lump removed from her body. The other patients were nervous. Catherine tried to calm her mother who was also nervous, but when this attempt failed, she attacked her murderously.* In another dream she had at the same time *she quarrelled with her therapist.* There was yet another dream on the same theme: "*It was wartime. I set the house on fire and went out with the dog. Then I came back, woke up the sleeping people, and saved them.*" These dreams seem to portray very vividly both murderous feelings towards her "bad" mother and her therapist and her reparation wishes to protect them.

There were many other events during the course of the therapy that disturbed Catherine, not the least of which was the marriage of her therapist, as mentioned above. However, she was able to work with her therapist on these events, and her problems of envy and jealousy began to resolve themselves. Catherine's own relationships with men broke down, and the attempts to treat her infertility had failed. Her younger step-sister married, and Denis also married and he and his wife had a baby; the step-sister also had a baby. At about this time Catherine and her latest male friend joined an artificial insemination programme recommended by her gynaecologist, despite the problems and the poor prognosis of their relationship and half in secret from her therapist. Having discussed the matter in her therapy, however, Catherine cancelled her participation. According to the therapist's understanding, Catherine's desire for a baby was not only due to the inferiority she felt about her own femininity and her envy of other women—which had been discussed frequently— but was also related to the inadequacy of her relationship with her mother: she wanted to compensate for her own lack of love by having a baby of her own (indication of projective identification).

The insights Catherine developed through transference interpretations included her growing consciousness of her own envy and the pathological aspect of her desire to please her mother: "If I cannot please her, I will lose everything", she said. The growing hatred and bitterness towards her mother was relieved by the insight she had when the therapist (who had seen the mother in the therapy meetings) pointed out that the mother herself was a disturbed person who lived through other people. The therapist pointed out that while Catherine tried to avoid her destructive envy, she also lost part of her creativity. This was particularly true of the depressive phases: Catherine recognized the connections between her depressive feelings and her destructive impulses. The processing of oedipal jealousy proceeded in relation to the divorced wife of her "fiancé"—a situation that was reminiscent of the relationship between her step-father and mother. Catherine also began to become aware of her need for punishment, and she said: "I'm afraid of being punished if things go well." She began to wonder more and more why she had for so long kept up relationships that exposed her to violence.

In the spring of 1996 Catherine faced yet another cause of stress: her maternal grandmother, whom she felt to be very close to her (despite the intrusiveness she showed towards her granddaughter), developed brain cancer, and she died in the early autumn. Catherine grieved for her death and participated actively in the funeral arrangements, despite her mother's jealous reactions, vividly revealed in her reproachful remark to her daughter: "It was me who lost a mother, and it's me who should cry, not you." Catherine told her therapist afterwards that her grandmother's death had eliminated her "compulsion" to please others—she realized that she no longer needed to please others for fear of having something bad happen to her, because her grandmother's death did not result in her own death. "I will not become psychotic any longer", she assured her therapist.

Catherine has become clearly more insightful, especially over the last year of therapy, and she is simultaneously developing more realistic relationships with other people. She is more in contact with her feelings of grief and better able to tolerate them and deal with them in the therapy, and her feelings of depression have become much more manageable. She has no psychoactive medication. Her fragmentary occupational efforts are also being replaced by a more focused educational plan. Her therapy is still incomplete, and she has not yet started the process of separating from the therapist, which will be an important part of the therapy. The situation has, however, stabilized sufficiently to warrant our agreement with Catherine's assurance: she is hardly at risk of becoming psychotic any longer.

Summary

We are dealing with the schizophreniform psychosis of a young woman with borderline features and deeply placed unfulfilled longings for symbiotic love and empathic understanding. During her psychotic state of mind she displayed severe confusion, loss of reality testing, and hypomanic and histrionic features. She was treated without any neuroleptics; her anxiety was relieved with the help of benzodiazepines.

Catherine actually had three mother figures, all of whom both rejected her and competed for the right to "possess" her. She grew up in an atmosphere of envy and jealousy, which was clearly demonstrated to be still active in her family in the present. Since she had not been able to resolve her own envy and jealousy—feelings that may have been intensified by the arrival of twin step-siblings at the age of 7—these coloured the various relationships during the illness and the important transference processes in the therapy. They were one reason that caused her hospital treatment to be prolonged, but it proved possible to expose and clarify these processes in the course of the weekly therapy meetings with Catherine and the members of her family, to an extent that was sufficient to provide the motivation and to improve the preconditions for her embarking on the individual psychotherapy.

After the stage of inpatient treatment, the therapy continued in the form of psychodynamic individual therapy, with 2–3 weekly sessions. Her therapist is a specialist nurse with training in both individual and family therapy. Individual therapy has been going on for four years now, and there have been no recurrences of psychosis. Catherine has no psychoactive medication. Her personality has gradually become consolidated, but the treatment has not yet been completed, and the process of separation remains to be accomplished. The therapist has become a significant new self-object for Catherine. She has provided the empathic understanding that Catherine has always needed. This has made possible Catherine's constructive identification with her "containing" and "thinking" therapist. At the same time, it has been possible to use the transference relationship to interpret Catherine's internal, anxiety-provoking problems, including her feelings of hatred, envy, and guilt. At first the therapist's countertransference mostly consisted of the role of a symbiotic and secure mother, while she has later concentrated increasingly on interpretations that help Catherine to find a more balanced and satisfactory identity.

John, the youngest son in an enmeshed family
[with Jyrki Heikkilä]

John, a 22-year-old carpenter, was living with his parents when he first came to treatment in March 1992. He is the youngest of three brothers and the only one still residing at home. John had been awake over the whole weekend and had eaten almost nothing. He said his thoughts teased him, and he fell to pieces. He thought he could not remember anything. He agreed to see a doctor (a general practitioner), and his brother Jack phoned the resident on duty in the Clinic of Psychiatry. They agreed that John would come to the *admission clinic* (see chapter five) the following day with members of his family. Jack would stay with him until then.

John's treatment history, with the different therapeutic measures included, is depicted in Figure 6.1. The team at the admission clinic (a psychiatrist, a specialized nurse, and a mental nurse) first met John, Jack, and their parents together (*the first therapy meeting*). Their father spoke for all of them, trying to explain the situation. One of his first ideas was that there was no need for John to move away from home. About a year earlier his father had noticed that John had become more withdrawn. A month before the breakdown, John had been in an automobile accident: a girl driver had crashed into John's car, which was a write-off. Both John and the girl were uninjured. Because of the accident, there was a trial, which John later won.

John did not display any marked delusions or hallucinations, but he was very severely confused. He had thought about being mad. He answered after long intervals, and he was suspicious. The situation was not very clear, and the family was given another appointment for the following day.

To the *second therapy meeting* Jack came with John, without the parents. This had been John's wish. He had stayed up for the whole night. He was confused, afraid, but more talkative. It appeared that a man had somehow seduced him as a child. There had been a trial, but John could not speak about it at all. When encouraged to talk, he simply said, "it becomes dark in the attic" and would say no more. Jack had noticed that

A ....ll..ll..ll.............................lll.............................lll..ll.............llllll..ll...l..l..l...l..l..

B .........X.XX.........................XX...

C ....tt t t.......ttt............................
.....iiiii. iii.......f.f.f.f.f.f............fff.. f...........

D ...0.0000..0000000000..........ooooooooooooooooooooooooooooooooooooooo..........ooooooooooooooooo ooo

E ......mm................mmmm.........................mm.......................mmmmmm mmmmmmm

Year ------92--------93--------94--------95--------96----
Month 4 5 6 7 8 9 10 11 12 1 2 3 4 5 6 7 8 9 10 11 12 1 2 3 4 5 6 7 8 9 10 11 12 1 2 3 4 5 6 7 8 9 10 11 12 1 2 3 4 5 6 7

FIGURE 6.1 Summary of John's treatment.

A. Visits at the admission clinic (l)
B. Hospital care (X) and therapy meetings (t)
C. Family meetings (i) and family therapy (f)
D. Own nurse contact (o)
E. Neuroleptic medication (perphenazin 8–16 mg/day) (m)

229

the accident with the car had much too strong an influence on both John and his father. Father himself had been in a car accident at exactly the same crossroads three years earlier, resulting in a back disorder that forced him to retire on a pension. John only kept repeating that it goes round and round in his head, he forgets things and has no grip of time. He said he suspected that a certain girl was actually another girl.

The situation was defined to the family as an individuation crisis concerning both John and the family. It was thought that the accident had quite concretely threatened John's identity and masculinity. Because of his strong confusion, which could not be handled very well by the patient or by the relatives, John was admitted into an open ward at the Clinic of Psychiatry (J.H. being the senior physician of the ward). The situation would be defined more accurately on the ward.

John's first hospitalization. At first John was quite withdrawn and suspicious of everything. His appearance was very stiff—almost catatonic. He answered very slowly or not at all. From the beginning, he had a *personal nurse*, a female mental nurse with no ordinary psychotherapeutic training. She tried to get into an empathic contact with John and succeeded in this within a few days. However, John's attitude was still reserved, and he was not motivated to explore his problems. Because John, too, was included in a research project dealing with first-admitted patients of the schizophrenia group preferably without neuroleptics (see V. Lehtinen et al., 1996), he was given *benzodiazepines* (lorazepam), which was of great help. His confusion gradually disappeared, and he was discharged after 16 days.

At the therapy and family meetings before and during John's hospital stay, *the history of the family* was investigated. The father, a retired book-seller, was the dominating figure in the family, while the mother seemed submissive. The mother was still active as a hairdresser. John's success at school was moderate, and he did well in military service. Trained and pressed by his father, a one-time wrestler himself, John had belonged to the top wrestling team in Finland, but he gave up wrestling when he was 17. He had dated girls only temporarily. But he related proudly that he had had five cars in his possession. With regard to the seduction episode in John's childhood, the family was as reticent as John himself.

John's father dominated these sessions and tried to find somatic explanations for John's condition, referring, for example, to amalgam fillings in his teeth. Again, he opposed the idea of John moving away from home. In that meeting, John was very confused and withdrawn. While listening to the father, the team often thought that the boundary between him and John was blurred. His mother had a more passive attitude, which reflected her submissiveness to her husband.

The parents thought that they had had quite a good relationship with each other. However, John's maternal grandmother, widowed 7 years earlier, had lived in the same house with the family for 24 years, and the relationship between this grandmother and John's father had been very difficult; they wondered whether they could sit together in the same room.

John's EEG was recorded, and it was normal. *Psychological tests* showed delusional and also schizophrenic features, as well as heightened dependency. Cognitively, John managed a little below average. The family was seen as pseudomutual and rated by the Olson circumplex model (Olson, Sprenkle, & Russell, 1979) as being relatively rigid (axis: rigid–chaotic) and enmeshed (axis: enmeshed–disengaged).

At an *integrative meeting of the treating team* at the end of the hospital treatment, John's situation was considered to be an emancipation crisis, as well as a sexuality crisis. There were features of homosexual panic. Symptoms had started after a sauna evening with friends. The automobile accident had obviously endangered John's phallic stability. A big news event, boxer Mike Tyson's rape trial, had a special meaning to John, and he once thought he could foretell his sentence. It looked as though John had identified himself with Tyson and the frightening idea of aggressive sexuality. The automobile accident as such and in the context of the two trials seemed to have the same kind of meanings.

John's official *diagnosis* was *brief reactive psychosis*. He agreed to visit his own nurse once a week after his discharge, and a continuation of a systemically oriented family therapy was planned. John was given no medication after the hospital care.

John had *two further hospitalizations*, the first as soon as a month after his first discharge. A contributing fact may have been that John's visits to his personal nurse had not turned out as planned because the nurse had been ill; they had met only once after the first hospital stay. John was again sleepless during the second hospitalization, had not eaten, was withdrawn and suspicious, asking whether there was a conspiracy against him and whether everything bad was his fault. He did not want to go out, because people might suggest that he was homosexual. He had suicidal thoughts and climbed to a high chimney, threatening to jump. He suspected that the staff accused him of evil acts, and shouted: "Others would have it better if I were dead." However, he came down after a brief discussion. He was then transferred to the closed ward, and a *neuroleptic medication (perphenazine 8 mg daily)* was initiated.

During the third hospitalization in 1993, John had taken an overdose of hypnotics, was depressed, and had suicidal thoughts. Some time earlier, he had moved to live with his girlfriend. He was bitter towards his father and had thoughts of revenge. During these later hospitalizations, the diagnosis of *schizoaffective psychosis* was defined, because of John's depressive features.

After the hospital periods, the team of the admission clinic had the main responsibility for John's treatment. He and his parents were seen regularly in family meetings, and small-dosage neuroleptic medication was continued; however, because of John's reluctance to take medicines, it was repeatedly interrupted. At the same time, the visits to the personal nurse were continued on a more regular basis. During the following years, John had some crisis periods, and rapid therapy meetings were then arranged at the admission clinic.

Family meetings differed from therapy meetings in that they aimed at a longer *systemically oriented family therapy*. The team consisted of a senior psychiatrist, a specialized nurse with family therapy training working on the ward, and a specialized nurse who had met the family at the admission clinic. Sessions were conducted by the nurse with family therapy training, the other members of the team staying behind a one-way mirror.

Methods included circular questioning, reframing, and positive connotations directed especially at promoting more structural flexibility in the family and trying to make a mutual differentiation possible between John and his parents. It was repeatedly found that the father invaded John's privacy and had difficulties in differentiating his own life from that of John's—even more so after he had retired. He saw John as a weak person who could easily be deceived and was afraid that John had used anabolic steroids or narcotics, without any grounds for this suspicion. He also interfered in John's relationship with his girlfriends. During his third hospital period, John had delusions about the meaning of his father shaking hands with his girlfriend and his comments to her; he had doubts about his dating because he thought that his father would not accept her.

The meetings were continued until December 1993. It was then thought, both by the team and the family, that there was now more mutual differentiation between John and his parents and that both parties could manage on their own. As a sign of this the team saw that John now could arrange his treatment issues alone. Father and grandmother had now tried to come to terms with each other. John worked, and he was living with a girlfriend, although there were minor conflicts between them.

During John's second hospital period, his *relationship to his personal nurse* seemed the only thing that was somehow clear in John's mind and free from suspicions. Visits to this nurse were continued after the hospital periods—as a general rule, once weekly—supervised by another nurse therapist with psychotherapeutic training. In 1996, the frequency was diminished to once a fortnight. There were some breaks, however, and John was very sensitive to them—for example, in January 1995 a month after he had stopped visits to the personal nurse as then agreed mutually, he became more anxious and sleepless and was on sick-leave for a week. On the other hand, John was often reluctant to continue the visits, because he wanted to deny his illness. Another reason was that he was now living with a new girlfriend and was afraid about what she would think of the visits.

The contact remained at a supportive level because of the nurse's lack of psychotherapeutic experience. John's actual problems—especially his relationship to his father—were discussed, and gradually he became more capable of criticizing his father and opposing him. It became clear that the mutual relation between mother and John was very close. John never said a bad word about his mother, and he often visited her in her beauty salon. The therapist thought that John had remained at home for so long because he was afraid to leave the mother at home alone with the father. During his first hospital period John had had nightmares about his relatives fighting and killing each other.

It seems obvious that John's relationship to his therapist was an idealized mother transference, and this was also reflected in the countertransference. Also, John only wanted to talk about nice things with the therapist, because "his head would break otherwise". He also avoided the expression of negative feelings in connection with separations. However, he could strongly criticize his girlfriend's mother (sign of a split transference). While he was talking about this girlfriend, he made indistinct hints at "another girl"; only gradually did the therapist understand that this meant herself. The eroticized transference was dealt with with the nurse's remark that she was in the role of John's therapist, not of a girlfriend. No interpretations dealing with John's mother relationship and his aggression problems were given, nor any transference interpretations.

John had his last (until now) mildly psychotic episode in November 1995. There were marks of auditory hallucinations, but afterwards John denied them. It came out that the wife of John's eldest brother was pregnant, and John and his girlfriend also had plans about having children. John and his girlfriend were then repeatedly met at the admission clinic, and the situation calmed down in three weeks. For the first time, John now accepted the idea of taking neuroleptics regularly to prevent relapses. In a follow-up at the admission clinic in October 1996, it was found that there had been no symptoms during the previous ten months. John visits his own nurse regularly, he continues his neuroleptic dosage (perphenazin 8 mg daily), he works normally, and he plans to marry and perhaps to have children.

SUMMARY

This case history can be criticized with regard to the individual therapeutic relationship with an untrained and inexperienced psychotherapist, which was due, on the one hand, to the patient's relative unsuitability for a more exploratory psychotherapy because of his lack of motivation and the fragility of his personality, and to a (relative) lack of more experienced therapists, on the other. Still, the supportive contract with the nurse therapist was important for John.

To the credit side of John's treatment belong the rapid family-centred interventions by the admission clinic team, repeated also after his hospital periods during crisis situations threatening his stability. Despite the diagnosis of schizoaffective psychosis, one could ask whether John's psychotic regression would have been more severe if he had not received treatment very quickly. There were signs of imminent catatonic and paranoid disintegration both at the beginning of his illness and later on. In this respect, the work of the admission clinic team in their care of John offers a good illustration of the usual functions of the *psychosis teams* in Finland (see pp. 244–246). Through their activity, the teams have been able to prevent or alleviate psychotic states of numerous schizophrenic patients as well as their social labelling. John's case—like Catherine's—is also a good example of the support given both through family- and individual-oriented approach to the individuation–separation processes of young patients of the schizophrenia group, which often also requires an increasing separation of the parents from their children.

However, a comparison of Catherine's and John's treatments also illustrates the importance of a psychoanalytically oriented individual psychotherapy for the patient's further development and prognosis. In Catherine's treatment the initial systemic process was continued with a psychodynamically oriented psychotherapy, giving stimulus to an inner developmental process deep enough to bring about a gradual personality growth. This also lessened considerably the danger of new psychotic episodes. This was not the case with John, who is still clearly dependent on the supportive contact with his therapist and neuroleptic medication to avoid the threat of further psychotic breakdown.

John's case might also be considered an illustration of the problems presented by the shortage of therapists with advanced training in the psychotherapy of psychosis. Given the daily problem of using what is available, John's therapy is more "resource-adapted" than "need-adapted". In the frames of community psychiatry, this is often necessarily the case. Nonetheless, we believe that endeavours exemplified by John's treatment, including his individual therapy—preferably backed by competent supervision—should be strongly encouraged. Long-term and regular supportive relationships can help a great many patients to resolve their problems in the framework of open care. The psychotherapeutic orientation offers a human quality that may be missing in a purely biological approach. This kind of relationship with patients is also a part of the educational process in the field, aiming at an increasing interest in the problems of psychosis psychotherapy, as well as at staff members' perception and motivation to acquire further training for it.

CHAPTER SEVEN

Treatment of schizophrenia and society

The last chapter of this book deals with the social dimension in the treatment of schizophrenia. My thoughts are closely connected, as is only natural, with the current developments and contemporary challenges in the public health system for psychiatric treatment in Finland and the other Scandinavian countries. I hope that this background does not unduly restrict the interest of readers in countries in which the development of the treatment of psychiatric disorders has taken a course different from ours. All over the world, an overwhelming majority of schizophrenic patients are being cared for in a community psychiatric framework, because most patients need a variety of services, including both outpatient and inpatient care as well as supportive measures and social welfare services. On the other hand, because of limits to public resources, a growing cooperation between the public and private services has become more and more typical in many countries, the Scandinavian countries included.

Political factors affecting the treatment of schizophrenia

Due to both ideological and economic considerations, political factors have often influenced the fate of schizophrenic patients. Their influence on the attitudes towards schizophrenics and their treatment has been most conspicuous in societies with extreme ideologies. In the twentieth century, such extremist policies prevailed in two totalitarian systems: Nazi Germany of the 1930s and the Soviet Union of the past few decades.

In the Nazi doctrine of eugenics, schizophrenia was considered a degenerative illness that was to be eliminated from society. Support for this view was obtained from heredity research, and further confirmation was provided by some leading German psychiatrists, who later launched an extensive programme for sterilizing schizophrenic patients before and during the Second World War. The number of mentally ill people who died in extermination camps is not known.

In the Soviet Union, the forensic psychiatrists blackened their reputation by agreeing to support the authoritarian power-holders' habit of incarcerating dissidents in mental hospitals by misapplying the diagnosis of schizophrenia (Bloch & Reddaway, 1984). Disagreement with the prevailing regime was said to be a psychiatric symptom common in those with "insidious schizophrenia". Even in this case the malpractice was connected with biomedical theories of the causes and postulated incurability of schizophrenia.

In democratic societies, the influence of social–political ideologies on psychiatry is less obvious, but it is still clearly detectable. During the last decades, psychiatric hospitals have begun to be closed down in many Western countries, mostly for purely financial reasons, despite the protests of psychiatrists (e.g. Borus, 1981; Weller, 1989). As there was insufficient semi-institutional care available, large numbers of patients were left without a place to live; they have made up one of the many marginal groups in a society with hard values.

Svein Haugsgjerd (1971) pointed out that theories tend to be shaped so as to justify existing practice. Would it be going too far to postulate that this may, to some extent, be reflected in the predominance of biomedical theories of schizophrenia prevalent especially in the leading Western nations? The idea that schizophrenia "is now considered chronic and virtually incurable, a belief transmitted to both patients and families, and therapy is directed towards suppressing the symptoms and towards rehabilitation at a low level of social functioning" are quite compatible with the social policies at the 1980s. The quotation is from the abstract of the lightly nostalgic presentation by Ruth W. Lidz (1993) at the International Symposium on the Psychotherapy of Schizophrenia in Turin in 1988. She also emphasized her own opinion that it was wrong, through long-term high-dose drug treatment, to deprive the patients of the opportunity to resolve in psychotherapeutic treatment "the very real problems that have existed between themselves and persons closely related to them" and to be stimulated towards a healthier development.

Stephen Fleck (1995) recently published a critical survey on dehumanizing developments in American psychiatry in recent decades. He pointed out that there has been a regressive development of reductionistic ideas of patient care, leading to a view of patients as containers of neurochemical aberrations, in place of the emphasis placed earlier on interviewing skills and understanding patients in terms of their personal development. Management programmes have displaced psychotherapeutic treatment, and psychiatrists have been reduced to the role of diagnostician and prescription writer. Fleck also criticizes the policy of insurance companies and their managed care agents, which have increasingly balked at payments for "prolonged" psychiatric treatments, interfering with lengthy and intensive psychotherapies or full-time hospitalization. The decisive factor is the cost of treatment—of short duration—and inexpensive choices are preferred.

Until now, the situation in Northern European societies has been better. But the recession and the prevailing economic–political theories have also begun to lend an increasing significance to these issues in our countries. Continuing progress in public psychiatric care system is now being threatened (Pylkkänen, 1994). And it is not only a matter of continued development that will be debated in the near future, but it is also questionable whether we will be able to maintain functioning at a level compatible with our knowledge and required by our shared responsibility for the common good of our citizens.

It is worth while to develop treatment

Connected with the National Schizophrenia Project in Finland, Vinni (1987) presented a summary of the overall costs of schizophrenia in Finland in 1985. According to his calculation, the total financial expenses due to schizophrenia added up to 2,500 million Finnish marks. The costs directly related to treatment (mostly hospital expenses) accounted for 40% of this amount, while the indirect costs (mainly due to the loss of earnings) amounted to 60%. More-or-less parallel findings on the ratio of direct to indirect costs were made by Rice, Kelman, Miller, & Dunmeyer (1990), who calculated the cost of all psychiatric illnesses (except alcohol and drug abuse) in the United States (at the federal, state, and private levels) in 1985: the direct losses were calculated at 42,500 million U.S. dollars, and the indirect ones at 56,700 million dollars.

The well-known British social psychiatrist David Goldberg (1991) reviewed the research on the cost of the treatment of schizophrenia, in the *Schizophrenia Bulletin*. He primarily concentrated on four controlled studies conducted in the United States, Australia, Britain, and Canada. His most central conclusions were as follows:

- Care in the community is generally cheaper than care in a hospital. This is true also of the treatment of acute psychoses. However, it is important to note that these results cannot be generalized to all patients requiring full-time admission to psychiatric beds.
- The more expensive treatment may sometimes be cheaper for society in the long run.
- For patients who require prolonged hospital stays, hostel wards provide a cost-effective alternative that is preferred by the patients themselves.

The financial profitability of the rehabilitation of long-term schizophrenic patients is easy to understand, because the staff expenses per patient are notably smaller in rehabilitative and residential homes than in hospitals. The case with acute patients is more complex. It seems that the work of family-centred teams working in the community can markedly reduce the use of hospitals by promoting the treatment of acute patients, as indicated by the experiences of Langsley et al. (1971) and Falloon (1992) described in chapter four. The most important financial justification for the development of the treatment of new schizophrenic patients, however, is in the amount of indirect losses reported by Vinni (1987) as well as by Rice et al. (1990). If it is possible to increase notably the number of schizophrenic patients who become capable of resuming work, as it is implied by the most recent findings of the Scandinavian projects with a comprehensive psychotherapeutic orientation, there will be opportunities for long-term financial savings in indirect losses (Alanen et al., 1994). A precondition is that short-sighted profitability-based decisions can be avoided, and more possibilities for long-term psychotherapeutic relationships—including longer inpatient periods when necessary—will be provided for schizophrenic patients. This would also reflect a more humane attitude towards the mentally ill.

Development of the treatment organization

In this section, the developmental needs of treatment systems are examined, starting specifically from the premises for carrying out the need-adapted treatment of schizophrenic patients.

The catchment area model

The sectorized model is clearly the best alternative for developing therapeutic systems in psychiatry. There is widespread agreement on this internationally.

In the sectorized model, there is an overall responsibility to provide care and treatment to a given population. The therapeutic systems in each area are responsible for both outpatient and inpatient care: instead of being limited to a given institution or given therapeutic procedure, the system is responsible for all specialized psychiatric treatment. Usually there is a stratified structure: in Finland, for example, the upper stratum consists of major mental health districts with an average population of 220,000, which, in turn, are divided (at least in the sphere of outpatient care) into local mental health districts, each with 25,000–40,000 inhabitants, an important part of their work consisting of cooperation with basic health care system.

The close connections between psychiatric in- and outpatient care outlined in the catchment area model are of vital importance to a guaranteed consistent overall planning of treatment and rehabilitation and a continuity of therapeutic relationships. This need for consistency and continuity is generally felt to be a problem in psychiatric work. Once the administrative dividing-wall between hospital and outpatient care has been removed, it is easier for a member of the outpatient staff to keep up a significant therapeutic relationship, even during the patient's temporary inpatient episodes, or for a relationship first established in a hospital to be continued after the patient's discharge.

An even more important benefit of the sectorized model is the proximity of the services to the users. Decentralization of the functions makes it easier to arrange locally family- and milieu-oriented activities, home visits, and day-hospital services. As a consequence of all this, the therapeutic system becomes more flexible and mobile and at the same time more open, and the hospital orientation subsides. Cooperation with the basic health care and social welfare units also becomes easier. It is hence optimum for the local mental health centres to be located in the same buildings as the basic health care units.

From the viewpoint of psychiatric functions, it is useful to keep the units—that is, the hospital and day-hospital wards and the rehabilitative and residential homes—sufficiently small. The upper limit for therapeutic communities is generally considered to be about 15 patient members; units larger than this should be divided up to keep the group activities effective. It is also easier in a small unit to achieve a peaceful and unhurried atmosphere, which is beneficial for the work of the psychotherapeutic community.

It is possible that the significance of hostel-type units separate from actual hospitals will increase in the care of acutely psychotic patients. The benefits of such units have been demonstrated, for example, by the experiences in "Soteria Berne", described in chapter four (Ciompi et al, 1992). In Sweden, where psychiatric hostels have increased in number over the past few years, a study into their effects has been organized by Armelius (1989). Most of these hostel units have been established by private foundations, but their integration with the public mental health care system is just as feasible as that of rehabilitative and residential homes for long-term patients.

It is important that the knowledge gained would not be lost on the way towards decentralization but would, rather, be transferred to smaller units. This can best be guaranteed by promoting training and education. It is, however, possible that the patients in decentralized hospital units may be so heterogeneous that the units will be unable to develop sufficiently specialized skills required by patients to achieve appropriate differentiation in treatment.

In Turku, with a population of 160,000, the following efforts have been made to avoid this: although the outpatient functions have been divided into four sectors, which coincide with the basic health care districts, the inpatient functions are carried out by two units, each consisting of several wards, which collaborate with the teams of two outpatient sectors. The staff of the wards for acute patients also have after-care activities. The single geropsychiatric ward for acute patients serves the whole town. There is a special rehabilitation team responsible for integrating rehabilitative functions, arranging preparatory meetings on the wards together with the patients and the staff, and for supervision of the rehabilitative homes and supported dwellings.

Qualitative resources are crucially important

Suitably allocated qualitative resources turned out to be clearly the most important factor in promoting the care of patients in our state-wide schizophrenia project. The number of working staff is naturally also important, but we realized that numerical increase is not in itself sufficient to guarantee an increase in efficiency. In several districts where outpatient staff were relatively numerous, no changes took place until the qualitative development of functions was defined as a goal.

The most important *qualitative resources* and their target areas in the treatment and rehabilitation of schizophrenics are:

- providing *effective cooperation* between specialized mental health care services and the basic health care system through consultation and counselling, with an emphasis on earlier detection and admission as one of the main goals;
- establishing *acute psychosis teams* able to carry out the family- and milieu-oriented initial examination of psychotic patients with responsibility for the planning and integration of the treatment of these patients, as well as counselling in family-oriented therapy;
- establishing *case management* to guarantee the continuity of treatment necessary for long-term psychotic patients;
- improving staff competence for *psychotherapeutic work with psychotics* and establishing *supervision* and *training* for individual, group, and family therapists;

- creating an adequate *rehabilitative system* with the necessary units and establishing a rehabilitative team to integrate rehabilitative functions;
- developing the wards, day wards, and rehabilitative homes into effectively goal-oriented *therapeutic communities*.

The commitment of both administrative and medical leadership to the developmental work and its goals is of crucial importance.

Acute psychosis teams

Of these different categories of resources, the acute psychosis teams are particularly important for the development of the treatment of schizophrenia in the frame of community psychiatry. The idea of establishing psychosis teams arose in the project group responsible for the Finnish National Schizophrenia Project. The actual impetus for the establishment of the teams was the practical experience with the joint therapeutic meetings at the initial stages of treatment in Turku. After an integrated trial organized in one of the mental health districts (The Northern Savo Project), the establishment of such teams became one of the central recommendations issued by the state-wide project (Alanen et al., 1990a).

The most essential task of the psychosis team was defined above. The teams are also responsible for most of the collaboration with the health care centres concerning the schizophrenic patients admitted there.

The psychosis team consists of three or four people with different occupational backgrounds (including a psychiatrist), who should be particularly knowledgeable in the treatment of psychoses from an interactional point of view. This usually means that one or two of the members have had family therapy training.

In 1992, three-quarters of the districts responsible for psychiatric health care in Finland had established one or several psychosis teams (Tuori et al., 1997)—a total of about 50 such family-centred teams working in a population of 5 million. The Finnish model has also inspired the development of similar family-oriented methods in Sweden and Norway.

In the spring of 1991, I needed data for a presentation at the tenth International Symposium for the Psychotherapy of Schizophrenia in

Stockholm (Alanen, 1992). At the time I knew of about 20 teams that had already had some experience in this work and in organizing it, and I sent them each a questionnaire. I received replies from 14 teams working in 6 districts. A summary of their replies illustrates the development of such teamwork.

Most of the teams worked part-time, because their members also had other obligations. About half of them had their "home base" in mental health offices, while the other half were stationed in hospitals. Outpatient connections seemed better for providing a good mobility, which is necessary for the team's work. All of the teams were multiprofessional. They generally included a psychiatrist and one or two nurses, frequently a psychologist, but rarely a social worker, although the inclusion of social workers had been recommended. It therefore seemed that the assessment of the patient's social condition and need for rehabilitation were, for practical reasons, outside the sphere of responsibility of the psychosis teams, which seemed to concentrate on treatment. The significance of the social aspects of the overall treatment should not be underestimated and should be accomplished as a separate function.

The teams were responsible for carrying out the family-oriented initial examination that analysed the patient's condition and life situation and assessed the therapeutic needs of patients and of the interactional network to which they belonged. Included were patients recommended for hospital admission and patients in an acute psychotic crisis. The work was not limited to patients with schizophrenia but included other psychoses and often also other crises, such as suicidal patients.

Two aspects of the work were emphasized in particular: (1) the ability to respond quickly to the needs of the patients and their families, and (2) the integration of the different modes of treatment and therapeutic relationships. Consultations and cooperation with the other psychiatric units were considered important. The team members often attended therapeutic meetings in the units—such as hospital wards—that had become responsible for the patient's treatment, and they made home visits as well. Cooperation with the health care centres also increased. Long-term follow-up of the patients and their treatment, however, although recommended, had generally not been pursued further than the planning stage. In the future development of treatment, arranging such follow-up should be a priority. Follow-up could be accomplished by using case management teams, as proposed by K. Lehtinen (1993b) and the NIPS Project (Alanen et al., 1994).

The following consequences were regularly reported following the establishment of teams:

- it was possible to obtain treatment more quickly than previously;
- the number of hospital admissions clearly decreased;
- cooperation with the families increased; and
- (as one team put it) it became more common to assume that a person who has undergone a psychotic crisis will be able to continue normal life and resume work.

Many of the teams described their family-therapeutic orientation as systemic consultation (Wynne et al., 1986) or a combination of systemic–strategic and psychodynamic orientations, while some others said that their approach varied, depending on the case. A few teams also applied psychoeducational or structural techniques in their work. Interestingly, the patients' family members were as often felt to be co-workers as they were felt to be patients; they were frequently also thought to have both roles simultaneously.

The feedback from the families was favourable in a majority of the cases. When I inquired whether the family members' guilt feelings possibly associated with the patient's illness had been a problem in the team's work, the answer was negative. Many of the teams said that they told the families that they wanted to analyse the factors that had led to the crisis, not to find the guilty ones. Some said they would point out—if necessary—that guilt feelings and self-accusations are a normal part of the situation and that it is useful to discuss such matters.

Some teams had had problems in cooperating with other psychiatric units. To prevent this, it would be important to define clearly the division of tasks between the psychosis teams and the teams of the different units. Mutual trust and respect are an important prerequisite for co-operation. It should be underlined, moreover, that the psychosis teams certainly cannot assume overall responsibility for the treatment of the patient, which requires expertise of various kinds. The main responsibility for treatment belongs to the unit where the patient has been registered.

Psychotherapy training
and psychotherapeutic work in practice

It is not possible to learn psychotherapy during the basic training of mental health staff, although aspects of psychotherapy are naturally presented. The capacity for psychotherapeutic work is always acquired through special further training.

In Finland, a basic division of *psychotherapy training* was established during the 1980s. The training programmes were divided into two levels—a special level and an advanced special level, of which the former requires approximately three years and the latter in its entirety five to six years of training, along with regular work. For entrance into advanced special training, a university degree is generally required (though exceptions to this have been made, especially in family therapy), whereas the special training is available to all mental health professionals.

Training programmes are provided by the Centres for Extension Studies of the universities on the one hand, and private associations on the other. During the 1980s the training activities increased notably. At the end of 1994, there were about 1,200 professionals—including psychiatrists, child psychiatrists, psychologists, nurses, social workers, as well as some general practitioners and theologians—who had completed special-level psychotherapy training either in psychodynamic individual therapy, family therapy (the largest group), cognitive therapy, or group therapy.

From the viewpoint of developing the treatment of schizophrenia, many of the individual therapy training programmes have the weakness that they are, in practice, restricted to the treatment of less seriously disturbed patients. This is particularly true of psychoanalytic training, which is the most prestigious type of advanced special-level training as regards both theoretical level and the general quality of content. It consists mainly of presenting the classical psychoanalytic method, which is well suited to the treatment of neuroses and narcissistic disorders but is hardly applicable to the treatment of psychoses. The situation in family therapy training has been different, although the time allotted to the treatment of psychoses in these programmes has varied.

In Turku, the main emphasis of the special-level individual therapy training has for the past year been on the treatment of psychotic disorders—most specifically schizophrenia. We considered this justified because schizophrenic disorders make special demands on public psychiatric health care. Our experiences have been favourable. In order for therapy to be successful, it is important that the therapist have suitable personal characteristics and training. Personal psychotherapy of the trainee is one of the preconditions of training, and it often helps in achieving a good outcome of long-term therapies. The Centre for Extension Studies of the University of Turku has now also initiated advanced special training in psychodynamic individual therapy, with an emphasis on borderline and psychotic-level disorders, to close the gap in systematic training for the treatment of the most serious psychiatric disorders.

The accomplishment of *intensive long-term therapeutic relationships* in public mental health care is problematic, because they consume a great deal of staff time. This is true especially of individual psychotherapy. In this respect, family therapy is better suited to public health care. Though even family therapy may require frequent sessions at times of crisis, the normal interval between sessions in systemic–strategic therapy is several weeks. The teamwork approach is well suited to public health care practices. The same is also true of group therapy, which has the further advantage that several patients can attend therapy at the same time.

Psychodynamic individual therapy of schizophrenic patients requires sessions at least twice weekly at the initial stage to activate a sufficiently intensive developmental process. Later on, it may become possible to space the sessions at weekly intervals. Since therapeutic relationships often last for years, it is, quite understandably, difficult for the mental health offices and hospital wards to provide adequate therapeutic services to meet their patients' needs. Cooperation with therapists working in the private sector increased in Finland especially after 1984, when it was made possible for the public sector to purchase their services.

From the viewpoint of the development of the public health care units, however, it is essential that they are also able to conduct a certain number of sufficiently intensive long-term individual therapeutic relationships. It is also important that *supervision* of the therapeutic work is widely provided, using both each unit's own staff with psychotherapy training and outside experts as supervisors. It has been said, and with good reason, that supervision is just as indispensable for the activities of a psychotherapeutic unit as X-ray and laboratory facilities are for somatic wards. All the staff members participating in therapeutic work should have an opportunity to benefit from it. This improves the outcome of the treatment, promotes the staff members' professional development, and often also alleviates the anxiety evoked by the work and prevents burnout. A non-authoritarian atmosphere based on co-operation is an inseparable part of the therapeutic work: each person should feel that it is possible for him or her to develop and use his or her abilities and skills in a creative and versatile way.

As Endre Ugelstad (1979) emphasized in the late 1970s, the number of individuals who annually become schizophrenic is so small—and the long-term financial losses incurred by society due to their illness so large—that it should be possible in the future to provide much more active and intensive treatment for these patients than is available currently. The qualitative resources for this will come from the increasing numbers of psychosis teams on the one hand and trained psychotherapists on the other. According to the experiences based on the need-adapted model, all schizophrenics do not need long-term individual therapy in order to be treated adequately.

Development of rehabilitative activities

In 1993 Erik Anttinen illustrated the integrated step-wise system of rehabilitation used at the Sopimusvuori r.y. (registered association), as shown in Figure 7.1.

The figure shows the progression of long-term patients, many of whom have been living on hospital wards for years, first into rehabilitative homes and then, along the left branch of the ladder, towards less sheltered and constrained living and, along the right branch, towards new adjustment into working life. The chances to reach the topmost step are better in residential rehabilitation than in occupational rehabilitation.

Sopimusvuori r.y. was founded in Tampere in 1970 without any money, the patients and their relatives being responsible for the costs. Soon afterwards, financial support began to be provided by municipalities and parishes, and later by the state-controlled Finnish Slot Machine Association. The progress that has been made is shown by a summary of the society's resources 21 years later:

- 9 rehabilitative homes for 110 clients
- 7 small homes for 31 clients
- 20 supported dwellings for 31 clients
- 2 day-care homes for 55 clients

- 3 therapeutic sheltered workshops for 128 clients
- a social club for 30–35 clients
- a preventive rehabilitative home for 15 clients

According to Anttinen, the purpose of these therapeutic communities is to provide their members with "a new safe, unconstrained and humane social network, whose purpose is to replace their previous, at least temporarily 'frozen' or lost, human relations with new ones". He also calls the rehabilitative homes "primary schools of a new life",

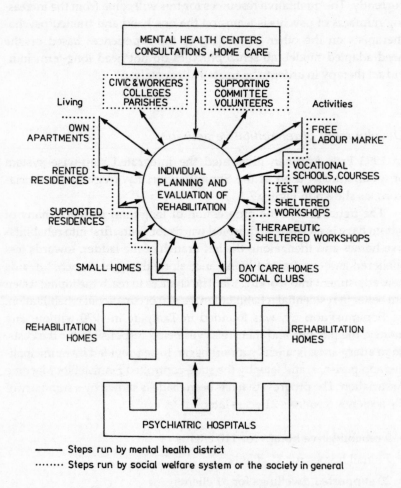

FIGURE 7.1   Integrated step-wise system of rehabilitation for long-term psychiatric patients. [Courtesy of Erik E. Anttinen]

where the plans and decisions are made together and the tasks and duties are shared. The number of paid staff is intentionally kept small, to encourage the clients to take responsibility for their activities and to enhance their own role in their treatment and rehabilitation.

In the 1980s, similar organizations were set up both at the initiative of the state-wide schizophrenia project and outside it. Some of them are following the Sopimusvuori model, others employ learning-theory models with a more strictly defined organization.

The Sopimusvuori model brings to mind the follow-up findings of the WHO multicentre study (World Health Organization, 1979), which suggested that the outcome of schizophrenia seems to be better in developing than in industrialized countries, probably because the atmosphere in the former is in a more "symbiotic" way based on mutual caring. One of the main factors impairing the prognosis of mental health disorders in the Western societies are the weakness of the closest interpersonal relationships and social networks and the therapeutic practice that tends to isolate the patients from their natural environments and communities. In our differentiated culture, individuals whose ability to differentiate is inadequate are easily isolated. The task of the mental health organizations is to create new developmental environments for them through family- and milieu-oriented treatment on the one hand and rehabilitative milieus that provide new interpersonal relationships on the other.

It is not always necessary to use a rehabilitative system with as many steps as in Sopimusvuori: rehabilitative homes and day-centres providing shared activities and hobbies may suffice, if the most advanced clients are assisted in their efforts to find dwellings. Sheltered work is also important for many, especially young clients, despite the poor chances of getting jobs now that there is widespread unemployment in many European countries.

As demonstrated by the Sopimusvuori organization, the need for staff is small. However, a long-term relationship with a person working in a Mental Health Centre or in the framework of the basic health services would be beneficial for many clients of such rehabilitative homes. Family therapy training is often useful in this work, especially when collaborative relationships with the clients' families are to be established.

Advance planning is also needed. The best way to provide for this is to set up a special *rehabilitation team* to integrate the functions. This team is responsible for such matters as arranging patient–staff meetings on rehabilitation, allocating the patients into rehabilitative and residential homes, and supervising the use of residential units.

To achieve successful rehabilitation, it is important to establish collaborative relationships with *private associations*, especially with *patient associations*, which have became more common in Finland during the 1980s in the field of psychiatry. This can be interpreted as a sign of a favourable change in the atmosphere regarding discrimination against the mentally ill. Previous inpatients in particular find in the patient associations an important social network of new interpersonal relationships. It is also important to cooperate with the *relatives' associations*, both to support the relatives and to prevent conflicts that may arise between them and the therapeutic organizations, as such conflicts may obviate the efforts of both patients and relatives as well as of staff.

Is it possible to prevent schizophrenia?

Quite a few psychiatrists and researchers will reply to this question in the negative—or, like some biologically oriented researchers, they may point out that a competent management of deliveries (especially if the mother is psychotic) and vaccinations preventing viral influenzas during the second trimester of pregnancy may have a limited effect.

These matters should naturally be considered. But even so, I am not pessimistic about the significance of even other kinds of preventive work to reduce the risk for schizophrenia. The Finnish National Schizophrenia Project included a special group to discuss matters pertaining to prevention. Most of the following points are based on their report.

The group started from the assumption that human life—including the lives of schizophrenic individuals—involves a process between the individual and his/her environment. They also referred to the adoption study findings reported by Tienari (1992; Tienari et al., 1987, 1993, 1994; see also chapter three), which showed that a psychically healthy family environment may protect even children with a hereditary predisposition from becoming schizophrenic.

If we accept this starting-point, we should conclude that the prevention of schizophrenia is part of a large-scale development of constructive and prophylactic mental health work at the level of families, communities, and societies.

One of the most important aspects of this effort is to support families through maternity and child welfare clinics, starting during the pregnancy and continuing afterwards, not forgetting the fathers and the totality of the intrafamilial relationships. It is also extremely important to provide support for families during crises. In families where the parents divorce, special attention should be given to the children's welfare. Many families also need support in other situations of crisis, of which the problems and conflicts faced by children and adolescents in their individuation are particularly important for the liability for schizophrenia. Even before adolescents leave home, it is important to observe children's adjustment in day-care and at school. A thorough survey of family-centred psychiatric prevention throughout the personal and familial life cycles was published in the United States by the Group for the Advancement of Psychiatry (1989).

All these issues are especially critical in families known to be at high risk for psychosis. When the parent of a family is admitted because of psychosis, it is essential to carry out a family-oriented examination and to analyse the condition and situation of the children. When necessary, each child should also be given an opportunity to have a child-psychiatric consultation and treatment.

Both day-care and school staff as well as school health care personnel should make an effort to support children who do not adjust easily or are shy and tend to withdraw and isolate themselves from others. The supporters should have the professional skill to act in such a way that the children will not be picked on by others. Supervision for teachers might be a good part of preventive mental health work on a large scale.

Within the psychiatric care organization, it is important to develop youth-psychiatric function services on the one hand and to promote consulting and counselling cooperation with the basic health care workers, particularly public health nurses, on the other. The experiences of Falloon (1992) in Buckinghamshire indicated that the ability of these workers to detect early signs of psychic disorders may contribute to the prevention of psychotic developments. Early case-finding projects have also been initiated elsewhere—in Finland, the pioneering activities of the family- and network-centred Western Lapland Project (Aaltonen et al., 1997) should be followed by acute psychosis teams working in other districts.

Other opportunities that may require more active attention than is customary at present exist in social welfare procedures, conscription check-ups, and student health care services, among others. But a word of warning is also in order at this point: looking for signs of disorder and interfering inexpertly may lead to unnecessary anxiety and bring about

harm and damage. Preventive mental health work requires both professional skill and empathy; coercion has no place in it.

In chapter two I mentioned the as yet unverified findings that seem
to suggest that schizophrenia appears to be decreasing in the Western
countries. I am inclined to agree that such a development may be slowly
taking place—based on my observations in Finland during the past forty
years—and that the decline is particularly notable in the most severe
forms of schizophrenia. I consider it possible that one of the factors
contributing to this favourable development has been the increasing
contacts of children with their environment from the day-care stage
onwards, as well as the decrease of rigid families that embrace their
children too tightly. On the other side of the coin, however, living
milieus have become less stable, with an increasing number of separations, whose effects may be seen in the increase of borderline disorders,
drug abuse, depressions, and psychosomatic illnesses rather than a liability for schizophrenia.

What does the future look like?

The future of psychiatric treatment and research is difficult to predict,
as indeed is the future in general. As indicated by the history of
psychiatry, development has been carried forward—or occasionally
backward—by unexpected observations and influences. There are
some points I wish to emphasize here.

In chapter four, when discussing the factors that have prevented the
development of psychodynamic psychiatry and psychotherapy, I mentioned the attitudes frequently prevailing in faculties of medicine and
medical training. When a majority of the professors view science as
exclusively natural science—such as a respected colleague of mine in
Turku, who once said that he only appreciates matters that have been
established at the molecular level—it is often questionable whether
psychodynamic or other qualitative research can gain any ground at all.
This, however, is mostly up to the representatives of psychiatry themselves and their ability and willingness to defend the special characteristics of their field. The attitudes of leading psychiatrists have a notable
influence on how the next generation of psychiatrists will perceive their
duties of research and treatment. Nor is their significance restricted to
psychiatry; it is also felt more widely in medical training. Psychiatrists

have a chance to emphasize the human aspects of doctor–patient relationships in contrast to the alienating dehumanization frequently felt by the students attending biologically oriented medical courses. Being cured of an illness is not merely a molecular process.

In chapter two, I referred to the German philosopher Habermas (1968) with regard to the hermeneutic interest of knowledge differing from the natural-scientific ways of thinking. The Finnish psychiatrist and author Oscar Parland (1991) recently touched upon these questions in an interesting manner, using the thoughts of the philosopher V. Sesemann (1927) as his starting-point. Sesemann differentiated between objective knowledge [*Gegenständliche Erkenntnis*] and non-objective knowing [*Ungegenständliches Wissen*]. The act of knowledge is "rational and observant and isolates, objectifies and conceptualizes its object", while the act of knowing is based on "intuitive insight, interpretation and empathic understanding of the object". The latter definition comes close to the epistemological theories of several psychoanalysts concerning their research (e.g., Bion, 1967; Killingmo, 1989; Kohut, 1977; Matte-Blanco, 1988). Psychiatric research and work, if any, need both knowledge and knowing. Without knowing based on empathy, we cannot understand a schizophrenic person, or indeed any other person.

I hope that the position of the more liberal epistemological theories will gradually be strengthened in future faculties and psychiatric practices. This would also make it possible to integrate the research and treatment of schizophrenia in a better and more versatile way than is possible at present.

As biomedical schizophrenia research advances, new findings will be made to elucidate in greater detail both the cellular structures of different parts of the brain and the functional effects of and links among transmitter substances, including differences in psychotic states. Genetic researchers will continue their as yet not very successful efforts to find chromosomal loci specific for schizophrenia. Psychopharmacological research and the pharmaceutical industry are working hard to find neuroleptics and other psychoactive drugs that would act more selectively than those currently in use and permit differentiation of antipsychotic effects from side-effects. It should be hoped that possible attempts at new kinds of discriminating practice against schizophrenic patients, based on reductionistic ideas, will be avoided.

I do not consider it possible that the fundamental problems in the treatment of schizophrenia will be solved pharmacologically, because this disorder has such obvious connections to human personality development. Follow-up findings such as described in this book suggest that comprehensive, psychotherapeutically oriented approaches improve the patients' prognosis as compared with exclusively biopsychiatric treatment. It may therefore be hoped—as is also to be expected on the basis of the general pendular movement of research—that psychotherapeutic and psychosocial orientations will soon make a comeback, which will probably also bring more conclusive evidence on the significance of the interactionally oriented treatment approaches.

Thanks to the increasing integration of the various research orientations, the indications for need-adapted treatment of schizophrenia will in the future probably not be defined on the basis of psychological criteria alone. They will be supported by biopsychiatric and neuropsychological assessments, which will also be useful in estimating the indications for psychotherapeutic treatment. Such a development, which has been anticipated by the ideas of Cullberg (1993a, 1993b), among others, will not diminish the need for psychotherapeutic and psychosocial measures, but it will probably affect the ways of setting treatment goals for different patients. I would, however, caution against interpreting biopsychiatric findings too exclusively—it is always beneficial to shape a therapeutic relationship specifically in each case and to study the prospects for psychotherapeutic treatment in the light of this assessment.

Psychodynamic psychotherapy of schizophrenia is still far from reaching the goals that will clarify its place in the future. This is not only because of a lack of qualitative and quantitative resources, but also because of a lack of adequate differentiation from methods that are primarily applicable in the treatment of milder disorders. As far as I can see, such differentiation can be achieved by combining the interactional and individual psychological treatment orientations and by promoting therapeutic measures that support the rebuilding of personality. We cannot ignore the obviously favourable effects of family-oriented treatment, especially at the onset of the illness, any more than the fact that many patients also urgently need long-term psychodynamic individual therapy to reach a more stable and permanent balance. Both the experiences of the Finnish psychosis teams and the observations by Sidsel Gilbert and Endre Ugelstad (1994) suggest that the active participation of the patient and his/her relatives in making therapeutic plans should be routine, which is not the case at present.

The need-adapted treatment of schizophrenia, based on a comprehensive psychotherapeutic orientation that focuses both on the individual and the context, has been developed in order to advance these types of views and to oppose reductionistic and dehumanizing views of schizophrenia and its treatment. We have found our follow-up results encouraging and hope that they will stimulate others to carry out similar developmental approaches.

REFERENCES AND BIBLIOGRAPHY

Aaku, T., Rasimus, R., & Alanen, Y. O. (1980). Nursing staff as individual therapists in the psychotherapeutic community. *Psychiatria Fennica. Yearbook*: 9–31. Helsinki: The Foundation for Psychiatric Research in Finland.

Aaltonen, J. (1982). *Basis for Family-Centred Treatment Process in Psychiatric Outpatient Care* [in Finnish, with English summary]. *Annales Universitatis Turkuensis, Ser. C*, Vol. 35 (Turku, Finland).

Räkköläinen, V., & Aaltonen, J. (1994). The shared image guiding the treatment process. A precondition for integration of the treatment of schizophrenia. *British Journal of Psychiatry, 164* (Suppl. 23): 97–102.

Aaltonen, J., Seikkula, J., Alakare, B., et al. (1997). "Western Lapland Project: a comprehensive family- and network-centred community psychiatric project. Abstract with preliminary results." Presented at the Twelfth International Symposium for the Psychotherapy of Schizophrenia, London.

Abraham, K. (1916). The first pregenital stage of the libido. In: *Selected Papers of Karl Abraham, M.D.* (pp. 248–279). London: Hogarth Press, 1949 [reprinted London: Karnac Books, 1988].

Achté, K. A. (1961). *Der Verlauf der Schizophrenien und der schizophreniformen Psychosen. Acta Psychiatrica Scandinavica, 36* (Suppl. 155).

Achté, K. A. (1967). *On Prognosis and Rehabilitation in Schizophrenic and Paranoid Psychoses. Acta Psychiatrica Scandinavica*, 43 (Suppl. 196).

Achté, K. A., Lönnqvist, J., Piirtola, O., & Niskanen, P. (1979). Course and prognosis of schizophrenic psychoses in Helsinki. *Psychiatric Journal of the University of Ottawa*, 4: 344–348.

Alanen, Y. O. (1958). *The Mothers of Schizophrenic Patients. A Study of the Personality and the Mother–Child Relationship of 100 Mothers and the Significance of These Factors in the Pathogenesis of Schizophrenia, in Comparison with Heredity. Acta Psychiatrica et Neurologica Scandinavica*, 33 (Suppl. 124).

Alanen, Y. O. (1962). Erfarenheter av supportiv psykoterapi med schizofrenipatienter [in Swedish, with English summary]. *Nordisk Psykiatrisk Tidsskrift*, 16: 443–456.

Alanen, Y. O. (1968). From the mothers of schizophrenic patients to interactional family dynamics. In: D. Rosenthal & S. S. Kety (Eds.), *The Transmission of Schizophrenia* (pp. 201–212). New York: Pergamon Press.

Alanen, Y. O. (1975). The psychotherapeutic care of schizophrenic patients in a community psychiatric setting. In: M. H. Lader (Ed.), *Studies of Schizophrenia* (pp. 86–93). *British Journal of Psychiatry* (Special Publication No 10).

Alanen, Y. O. (1976). On background factors and goals in the family therapy of young schizophrenic patients. In: J. Jorstad & E. Ugelstad (Eds.), *Schizophrenia, 75. Psychotherapy, Family Studies, Research* (pp. 173–186). Oslo: Universitetsforlaget.

Alanen, Y. O. (1980). In search of the interactional origin of schizophrenia. The Stanley R. Dean Award Lecture. In: C. K. Hofling & J. M. Lewis (Eds.), *The Family, Evaluation and Treatment* (pp. 285–313). New York: Brunner/Mazel.

Alanen, Y. O. (1992). Psychotherapy of schizophrenia in community psychiatry. In: A. Werbart & J. Cullberg (Eds.), *Psychotherapy of Schizophrenia: Facilitating and Obstructive Factors* (pp. 237–253). Oslo: Scandinavian University Press.

Alanen, Y. O. (1994). An attempt to integrate the individual–psychological and interactional concepts of the origins of schizophrenia. *British Journal of Psychiatry*, 164 (Suppl. 23): 56–61.

Alanen, Y. O. (1997). Vulnerability to schizophrenia and psychotherapeutic treatment of schizophrenic patients: towards an integrated view. *Psychiatry*, 60: 142–157.

Alanen, Y. O., Anttinen, E. E., Kokkola, A., Lehtinen, K., Ojanen, M.,

Pylkkänen, K., & Räkköläinen, V. (1990). *Treatment and Rehabilitation of Schizophrenic Psychoses. The Finnish Treatment Model. Nordic Journal of Psychiatry, 44* (Suppl. 22).

Alanen, Y. O., & Kinnunen, P. (1975). Marriage and the development of schizophrenia. *Psychiatry, 38*: 346–355.

Alanen, Y. O., Lehtinen, K., Räkköläinen, V., & Aaltonen, J. (1991). Need-adapted treatment of new schizophrenic patients: experiences and results of the Turku project. *Acta Psychiatrica Scandinavica, 83*: 363–372.

Alanen, Y. O., Räkköläinen, V., Laakso, J., & Rasimus, R. (1980). Problems inherent in the study of psychotherapy of psychoses: conclusions from a community psychiatric action research study. In: J. R. Strauss, M. Bowers, T. W. Downey, S. Fleck, S. Jackson, & I. Levine (Eds.), *The Psychotherapy of Schizophrenia* (pp. 115–129). New York: Plenum Medical.

Alanen, Y. O., Räkköläinen, V., Laakso, J., Rasimus, R., & Järvi, R. (1983). Psychotherapy of schizophrenia in community psychiatry: two-year follow-up findings and the influence of selective processes on psychotherapeutic treatments. In: H. Stierlin, L. C. Wynne, & M. Wirsching (Eds.), *Psychosocial Intervention in Schizophrenia. An International View* (pp. 67–82). Berlin & Heidelberg: Springer-Verlag.

Alanen, Y. O., Räkköläinen, V., Laakso, J., Rasimus, R., & Kaljonen, A. (1986). *Towards Need-specific Treatment of Schizophrenic Psychoses.* Heidelberg: Springer-Verlag.

Alanen, Y. O., Rekola, J. K., Stewen, A., Takala, K., & Tuovinen, M. (1966). *The Family in the Pathogenesis of Schizophrenic and Neurotic Disorders. Acta Psychiatrica Scandinavica, 42* (Suppl. 189).

Alanen, Y. O., Salokangas, R. K. R., Ojanen, M., Räkköläinen, V., & Pylkkänen, K. (1990b). Tertiary prevention: treatment and rehabilitation of schizophrenic patients. Results of the Finnish national programme. In: D. Goldberg & D. Tantam (Eds.), *The Public Health Impact of Mental Disorders* (pp. 176–191). Toronto, Ontario: Hogrefe & Huber.

Alanen, Y. O., Ugelstad, E., Armelius, B.-Å., Lehtinen, K., Rosenbaum, B., & Sjöström, R. (Eds.) (1994). *Early Treatment for Schizophrenic Patients. Scandinavian Psychotherapeutic Approaches.* Oslo: Scandinavian University Press.

Allebeck, P., Adamsson, C., Engström, A., & Rydberg, U. (1993). Cannabis and schizophrenia: a longitudinal study of cases treated in Stockholm County. *Acta Psychiatrica Scandinavica, 88*: 21–24.

Alvir, J. M. J., Lieberman, J. A., Safferman, A. Z., et al. (1993). Clozapine-induced agranulocytosis: incidence and risk factors in the United States. *New England Journal of Medicine, 329*: 162–167.

American Psychiatric Association (1980). *Diagnostic and Statistical Manual for Mental Disorders, DSM–III*. Washington, DC.

American Psychiatric Association (1994). *Diagnostic and Statistical Manual of Mental Disorders, DSM–IV*. Washington, DC.

Anderson, C. M. (1979). Family therapy session, presented at symposium, New Haven, CT.

Anderson, C. M., Reiss, D. J., & Hogarty, G. E. (1986). *Schizophrenia and the Family*. New York: Guilford Press.

André, G. (1995). Oral report on the Falun project (Sweden).

Andreasen, N. C., Arndt, S., Swayze, V. II, et al. (1994).Thalamic abnormalities in schizophrenia visualized through magnetic resonance image averaging. *Science, 266*: 294–298.

Andreasen, N. C., Ehrhardt, J. C., Swayze, V. W. II, et al. (1990). Magnetic resonance imaging of the brain in schizophrenia. *Archives of General Psychiatry, 47*: 35–44.

Andreasen, N. C., & Olsen, S. A. (1982). Negative vs. positive schizophrenia: definition and validation. *Archives of General Psychiatry, 39*: 789–794.

Anthony, E. J. (1968). The developmental precursors of adult schizophrenia. In D. Rosenthal & S. S. Kety (Eds.), *The Transmission of Schizophrenia* (pp. 293–316). New York: Pergamon Press.

Anthony, E. J. (1969). Clinical evaluation of children with psychotic parents. *American Journal of Psychiatry, 126*: 177–184.

Anttinen, E. E. (1983). Can the vicious circle of chronicity and institutionalization be broken? *Psychiatria Fennica. Yearbook:* pp. 21–31. Helsinki: The Foundation for Psychiatric Research in Finland.

Anttinen, E. E. (1992). Flexiblare och kombinerade insatser ger bättre resultat. In: M. Thorslund (Ed.), *Fler vårdbehövande, Familjens roll och samhällets ansvar* (pp. 121–130) [in Swedish]. Helsingfors, Finland: Social- och hälsovårds-ministeriet.

Anttinen, E. E., Eloranta, K. J., & Stenij, P. (1971). *The Care and Rehabilitation of Schizophrenic Out-Patients with Home Care* [in Finnish, with English summary]. *Kansaneläkelaitoksen julkaisuja A: 8*. Helsinki: National Pension Institute.

Arieti, S. (1955). *Interpretation of Schizophrenia*. New York: Brunner.

Arlow, J., & Brenner, C. (1969). Psychopathology of the psychoses: a proposed revision. *International Journal of Psycho-Analysis, 50*: 5–14.

Armelius, B.-Å. (1989). *Samordnadsforskning kring behandlingshem för psykotiska patienter*. Research project [in Swedish, mimeographed]. Umeå, Sweden.

Armelius, B.-Å., Armelius, K., Fogelstam, H., et al. (1989). *Effekter av psykoterapi för psykotiska patienter: En översikt om forskningslitteraturen* [in Swedish]. Stockholm: Socialstyrelsen, Rapport 4.

Baldessarini, R., Cohen, B. M., & Teicher, M. H. (1988). Significance of neuroleptic dose and plasma level in the pharmacological treatment of psychoses. *Archives of General Psychiatry, 45*: 79–91.

Barnes, T. R. E. (Ed.) (1989). Negative symptoms in schizophrenia. *British Journal of Psychiatry, 155* (Suppl. 7).

Barr, C. L., Kennedy, J. L., Pakstis, A. J., et al. (1994). Progress in a genome scan for linkage in schizophrenia in a large Swedish kindred. *American Journal of Medical Genetics, 54*: 51–58.

Bateson, G. (1973). Double bind, 1969. In: *Steps to an Ecology of Mind* (pp. 242–249). Frogmore, St. Albans, U.K.: Paladin.

Bateson, G., Jackson, D. D., Haley, J., & Weakland, J. H. (1956). Towards a theory of schizophrenia. *Behavioural Science, 1*: 251–264.

Benedetti, G. (1975). *Ausgewählte Aufsätze zur Schizophrenielehre*. Göttingen: Vandenhoeck.

Benedetti, G. (1979). The structure of psychotherapeutic relationship in the individual treatment of schizophrenia. In: C. Müller (Ed.), *Psychotherapy of Schizophrenia* (pp. 31–37). Amsterdam: Excerpta Medica.

Benedetti, G. (1985). Persönliche Entwicklung in der Psychotherapie der Schizophrenen. *Schweizer Archiw für Neurologie und Psychiatrie, 136*: 23–28.

Benedetti, G. (1992). From the First to the Tenth International Symposium for the Psychotherapy of Schizophrenia. In: A. Werbart & J. Cullberg (Eds.), *Psychotherapy of Schizophrenia: Facilitating and Obstructive Factors* (pp. 15–27). Oslo: Scandinavian University Press.

Beres, D., & Obers, S. J. (1950). The effects of extreme deprivation in infancy on psychic structure in adolescence. *The Psychoanalytic Study of the Child, 5*: 212–235.

Bertalanffy, L. von (1956). General systems theory. *General Systems, 1*: 1–10.

Biehl, H., Maurer, K., Schubart, C., et al. (1986). Prediction of outcome and utilization of medical services in a prospective study of first onset schizophrenics: results of a prospective 5-year follow-up study. *European Archives of Psychiatry and Neurological Sciences, 236*: 139–147.

Bion, W. R. (1967). *Second Thoughts. Selected Papers on Psycho-Analysis.* London: William Heinemann [reprinted London: Karnac Books, 1990].

Birchwood, M., & Macmillan, F. (1993). Early intervention in schizophrenia. *Australian and New Zealand Journal of Psychiatry, 27:* 374–378.

Birchwood, M., & Preston, M. (1991). Schizophrenia. In: W. Dryden & R. Rentoul (Eds.), *Adult Clinical Problems. A Cognitive–Behavioural Approach* (pp. 171–202). London: Routledge.

Bland, H. C., Parker, J. H., & Orn, H. (1976). Prognosis in schizophrenia: a ten-year follow-up of first admissions. *Archives of General Psychiatry, 33:* 949–954.

Bleuler, E. (1911). *Dementia Praecox oder die Gruppe der Schizophrenien. Handbuch der Psychiatrie, herausgegeben von Prof. G. Aschaffenberg. Special Section 4:* 1. Leipzig, Vienna: Deuticke.

Bleuler, M. (1972). *Die schizophrenen Geistesstörungen im Lichte langjährigen Kranken- und Familiengeschichten.* Stuttgart: Georg Thieme.

Bloch, S., & Reddaway, P. (1984). *Soviet Psychiatric Abuse—The Shadow over World Psychiatry.* London: Gollancz.

Borri, P., & Quartesan, R. (Eds.) (1990). *USA–Europe Joint Meeting on Therapies and Psychotherapy of Schizophrenia.* Perugia: Assoziane per la Ricerca in Psichiatria.

Borus, J. F. (1981). Deinstitutionalization of the chronically mentally ill. *New England Journal of Medicine, 305:* 339–342.

Boszormenyi-Nagy, I., & Framo, J. L. (Eds.) (1965). *Intensive Family Therapy. Theoretical and Practical Aspects.* New York: Hoeber Medical Division, Harper & Row.

Bowen, M. (1960). A family concept of schizophrenia. In: D. D. Jackson (Ed.), *The Aetiology of Schizophrenia* (pp. 346–372). New York: Basic Books.

Bowen, M., Dysinger, R. H., Brodey, W. M., & Basamania, B. W. (1961). The family as the unit of study and treatment. *American Journal of Orthopsychiatry, 31:* 40–86.

Bowlby, J. (1969). *Attachment and Loss,* Vol. 1: *Attachment.* London: Hogarth Press.

Boyer, L. B. (1983). *The Regressed Patient.* New York: Jason Aronson.

Boyer, L. B. (1986). Technical aspects in treating the regressed patient. *Contemporary Psychoanalysis, 22:* 25–44.

Boyer, L. B. (1989). Countertransference and technique in working with the regressed patient: further remarks. *International Journal of Psycho-Analysis, 70:* 701–714.

Bremner, J. D., Randall, P., Scott, T. M., et al. (1995). MRI-based measurement of hippocampal volume in patients with combat-related post-traumatic stress disorder. *American Journal of Psychiatry, 152*: 973–981.

Brown, G. W., Birley, J. L. T, &. Wing, J. K. (1972). Influence of the family life on the course of schizophrenic disorders: a replication. *British Journal of Psychiatry, 121*: 241–258.

Brown, G. W., Bone, M., Dalison, B, & Wing, J. K. (1966). *Schizophrenia and Social Care*. London: Institute of Psychiatry, The Maudsley Hospital.

Burnham, D. L., Gladstone, A. I., & Gibson, R. W. (1969). *Schizophrenia and the Need–Fear Dilemma*. New York: International Universities Press.

Caldwell, C. B., & Gottesman, I. I. (1990). Schizophrenics kill themselves too: a review of risk factors for suicide. *Schizophrenia Bulletin, 16*: 571–589.

Cameron, N. (1938). Reasoning, regression and communication in schizophrenics. *Psychological Monographs, 50*, No 1.

Cannon, T. D., Mednick, S. A., Parnas, J., et al. (1993). Developmental brain abnormalities in the offspring of schizophrenic mothers. I. Contributions of genetic and perinatal factors. *Archives of General Psychiatry, 50*: 551–564.

Carlsson, A., & Lindqvist, M. (1963). Effect of chlorpromazine and haloperidol on formation of methoxytyramine and normetanephrine in mouse brain. *Acta Pharmacology and Toxicology, 20*: 140–144.

Carlsson, M., & Carlsson, A. (1990). Schizophrenia: a subcortical neurotransmitter syndrome? *Schizophrenia Bulletin, 16*: 425–432.

Carpenter, W. T., Heinrichs, D. W., & Hanlon, T. E. (1987). A comparative trial of pharmacological strategies in schizophrenia. *American Journal of Psychiatry, 144*: 1466–1470.

Carpenter, W. T., McGlashan, T. H., & Strauss, J. S (1977). Treatment of acute schizophrenia without drugs: an investigation of some current assumptions. *American Journal of Psychiatry, 134*: 14–21.

Ciompi, L. (1980). The natural history of schizophrenia in the long term. *British Journal of Psychiatry, 136*: 413–420.

Ciompi, L. (1982). *Affektlogik*. Stuttgart: Klett-Cotta [English edition: *The Psyche and Schizophrenia. The Bond Between Affect and Logic*. Cambridge, MA: Harvard University Press, 1988.]

Ciompi, L. (1991). Affects as central organizing and integrating factors. A new psychosocial/biological model of the psyche. *British Journal of Psychiatry, 159*: 97–105.

Ciompi, L. (1994). Affect logic: an integrative model of psyche and its relations to schizophrenia. *British Journal of Psychiatry*, *164* (Suppl. 23): 51–55.

Ciompi, L., Dauwalder, H.-P., Aebi, E., et al. (1992). A new approach of acute schizophrenia. Further results of the pilot project "Soteria Berne". In: A. Werbart & J. Cullberg (Eds.), *Psychotherapy of Schizophrenia: Facilitating and Obstructive Factors* (pp. 95–109). Oslo: Scandinavian University Press.

Ciompi, L., & Müller, C. (1976). *Lebensweg und Alter der Schizophrenen. Eine katamnestische Langzeitstudie bis ins Senium.* Berlin & Heidelberg: Springer Verlag.

Claghorn, J. L., Johnstone, E. E., Cook, T. H., et al. (1974). Group therapy and maintenance treatment of schizophrenics. *Archives of General Psychiatry*, *31*: 361–365.

Cleghorn, J. M., Zipursky, R. B., & List, S. J. (1991). Structural and functional brain imaging in schizophrenia. *Journal of Psychiatry & Neuroscience*, *1*: 53–74.

Cole, J. O., & Davis, J. M. (1969). Antipsychotic drugs. In: L. Bellak & L. Loeb (Eds.), *The Schizophrenic Syndrome* (pp. 478–568). New York: Grune & Stratton.

Conran, M. B. (1972). The relationship between blame and hope. In: D. Rubinstein & Y. O. Alanen (Eds.), *Psychotherapy of Schizophrenia* (pp. 207–210). Amsterdam: Excerpta Medica.

Coon, H., Jensen, S., Holik, J., et al. (1994). Genomic scan for genes predisposing to schizophrenia. *American Journal of Medical Genetics*, *54*: 59–71.

Cooper, J. E., Kendell, R. E., Gurland, B. J., et al. (1972). *Psychiatric Diagnosis in New York and London. Maudsley Monograph No 20*. London: Oxford University Press.

Crow, T. J. (1985). The two-syndrome concept: origins and current status. *Schizophrenia Bulletin*, *11*: 471–485.

Crow, T. J. (1994). Prenatal exposure to influenza as a cause of schizophrenia. There are inconsistencies and contradictions in the evidence. *British Journal of Psychiatry*, *164*: 588–592.

Cullberg, J. (1993a). A proposal for a three-dimensional aetiologic view of the schizophrenias. I. *Nordic Journal of Psychiatry*, *47*: 355–359.

Cullberg, J. (1993b). A three dimensional aetiologic view of the schizophrenias. II. Hypothetical clinical consequences. *Nordic Journal of Psychiatry*, *47*: 421–424.

Davis, A. E., Dinitz, S., & Pasamanick, B. (1972). The prevention of hospitalization in schizophrenia. *American Journal of Orthopsychiatry, 42*: 1375–1388.

Davis, O. R., Breier, A., Buchanan, R. W., & Holstein, C. (1991). Obstetric complications in schizophrenia. *Schizophrenia Research, 4*: 254.

Dean, C., Phillips, J., Gadd, E. M., et al. (1993). Comparison of community based service with hospital based service for people with acute severe psychiatric illness. *British Medical Journal, 307*: 473–476.

Dein, E. (1964). Personlighedstyper ved skizofreni og skizofreniforme psykoset [in Danish]. *Nordisk Psykiatrisk Tidskrift, 18*: 87–105.

Delay, J., Deniker, P., & Green, A. (1957). Essai de description et de définition psycho-pathologique des parents des schizophrènes. *Congress Report of the Second International Congress for Psychiatry, IV*: 49–56. Zurich: Orell Füssli.

Delay, J., Deniker, P., & Green, A. (1962). Le milieu familial des schizophrènes. *L'encëphal, 51*: 1–73.

Delay, J., Deniker, P., & Harl, J. M. (1952). Traitment des états d'excitation et d'agitation par une méthode medicamenteuse derivée de l'hibernotherapie. *Annales Médico-psychologique, 110*: 267–273.

DeLisi, L. E., Goldin, L. R., Hamovit, J. R., et al. (1986). A family study of the association of increased ventricular size with schizophrenia. *Archives of General Psychiatry, 43*: 148–153.

Dell, P. (1980). Researching the family theories of schizophrenia: an exercise in epistemological confusion. *Family Process, 19*: 321–335.

De Sisto, M. J., Harding, C. M., McCormick, R. V., et al. (1995). The Maine and Vermont three-decade studies of serious mental illness. I. Matched comparison and cross-sectional outcome. II. Longitudinal course comparisons. *British Journal of Psychiatry, 167*: 331–342.

Der, G., Gupta, S., & Murray, R. M. N. (1990). Is schizophrenia disappearing? *Lancet, 335*: 409–413.

Doane, J. A. (1978). Family interaction and communication deviance in disturbed and normal families. A review of research. *Family Process, 17*: 357–376.

Doane, J. A., Falloon, I. R. H., Goldstein, M. J., & Mintz, J. (1985). Parental affective style and the treatment of schizophrenia. Predicting course of illness and social functioning. *Archives of General Psychiatry, 42*: 34–42.

Doane, J. A., Goldstein, M. J., Miklowitz, D. J., & Falloon, I. R. H. (1986). The impact of individual and family treatment on the affective climate of families of schizophrenics. *British Journal of Psychiatry, 148*: 279–287.

Domarus, E. von (1944). The specific laws of logic in schizophrenia. In J. S. Kasanin (Ed.), *Language and Thought in Schizophrenia* (pp. 104–113). Berkeley, CA: University of California Press.

Donaldson, S. R., Gelenberg, A. J., & Baldessarini, R. J. (1983). The pharmacological treatment of schizophrenia: a progress report. *Schizophrenia Bulletin, 9*: 504–527.

Done, D. J., Johnstone, E. C., & Frith, C. D. (1991). Complications of pregnancy and delivery in relation to psychosis in adult life: data from the British perinatal mortality survey sample. *British Medical Journal, 302*: 1576–1580.

Early, D. C. (1960). The industrial therapy organization (Bristol). *Lancet, 2*: 754–757.

Eaton, W. W. (1985). Epidemiology of schizophrenia. *Epidemiological Review, 7*: 105–126.

Emde, R. (1988). Development terminable and interminable. I. Innate and motivational factors from infancy. *International Journal of Psycho-Analysis, 69*: 23–42.

Ernst, K. (1956). "Geordnete Familienverhältnisse" späterer Schizophrener im Lichte einer Nachuntersuchung. *Archiv für Psychiatrie* (Berlin), *194*: 355–367.

Falloon, I. R. H. (1992). Early intervention for first episodes of schizophrenia: a preliminary exploration. *Psychiatry, 55*: 4–15.

Falloon, I. R. H., Boyd, J. L., McGill, C. W., et al. (1982). Family management in the prevention of exacerbations of schizophrenia. *New England Journal of Medicine, 306*: 1437–1440.

Falloon, I. R. H., Boyd, J. L., McGill, C. W., et al. (1985). Family management in the prevention of morbidity of schizophrenia. Clinical outcome of a two-year longitudinal study. *Archives of General Psychiatry, 42*: 887–896.

Farde, L., Wiesel, F.-A., Halldin, C., & Sedvall, G. (1988). Central D2-dopamine receptor occupancy in schizophrenic patients treated with antipsychotic drugs. *Archives of General Psychiatry, 45*: 71–76.

Farde, L., Wiesel, F.-A., Stone-Elander, S., et al. (1990). D2 dopamine receptors in neuroleptic–naive schizophrenic patients. A positron emission tomography study with (11C) Raclopride. *Archives of General Psychiatry, 47*: 213–219.

Federn, P. (1943). Psychoanalysis of psychoses. *Psychiatric Quarterly, 17*: 3–19, 246–257, 470–487. [Also in: E. Weiss (Ed.), *Ego Psychology and the Psychoses*. New York: Basic Books, 1952; reprinted London: Karnac Books, 1977.]

Federn, P. (1952). *Ego Psychology and the Psychoses*. (Ed. E. Weiss). New York: Basic Books [reprinted London: Karnac Books, 1977].

Fenichel, O. (1945). *The Psychoanalytic Theory of Neurosis*. New York: W. W. Norton.

Fenton, F. R., Tessier, L., & Struening, E. L. (1979). A comparative trial of home and hospital psychiatric care. One-year follow-up. *Archives of General Psychiatry, 36*: 1073–1079.

Fischer, M. (1973). Genetic and Environmental Factors in Schizophrenia. *Acta Psychiatrica Scandinavica, 49* (Suppl. 238).

Fleck, S. (1992). The development of schizophrenia: a psychosocial and biological approach. In: A. Werbart & J. Cullberg (Eds.), *Psychotherapy of Schizophrenia: Facilitating and Obstructive Factors* (pp. 179–192). Oslo: Scandinavian University Press.

Fleck S. (1995). Dehumanizing developments in American psychiatry in recent decades. *Journal of Nervous and Mental Diseases, 183*: 195–203.

Forssen, A. (1979). *Roots of Traditional Personality Development among the Zaramo in Coastal Tanzania*. Publication 54. Helsinki: Lastensuojelun Keskusliitto.

Freud, S. (1911c). Psychoanalytic notes on an autobiographical account of a case of paranoia (Dementia paranoides). *Standard Edition, 12*: 3–79. London: Hogarth Press, 1958.

Freud, S. (1914c). On narcissism: an introduction. *Standard Edition, 14*: 121–144. London: Hogarth Press, 1958.

Freud, S (1915e). The unconscious. *Standard Edition, 14*: 161–215. London, Hogarth Press, 1958.

Freud, S. (1917e). Mourning and melancholia. *Standard Edition, 14*: 237–259. London: Hogarth Press, 1958.

Freud S. (1924b). Neurosis and psychosis. *Standard Edition, 19*: 149–170. London: Hogarth Press, 1961.

Freud S. (1924e). The loss of reality in neurosis and psychosis. *Standard Edition, 19*: 183–187. London: Hogarth Press, 1961.

Fromm-Reichmann, F. (1950). *Principles of Intensive Psychotherapy*. Chicago, IL: University of Chicago Press.

Fromm-Reichmann, F. (1952). Some aspects of psychoanalytic psychotherapy with schizophrenics. In: E. B. Brody & F. C. Redlich (Eds.), *Psychotherapy with Schizophrenics* (pp. 89–111). New York: International Universities Press. [Reprinted in: D. M. Bullard (Ed.), *Psychoanalysis and Psychotherapy. Collected Papers of Frieda Fromm-Reichmann* (pp. 176–193). Chicago: University of Chicago Press, 1959.]

Furlan, P. M. (1993). Psychotherapeutic factors in different settings of individual treatment of psychoses. In: C. Benedetti & P. M. Furlan (Eds.), *The Psychotherapy of Schizophrenia. Effective Clinical Approaches—Controversies, Critiques, & Recommendations* (pp. 115–123). Toronto, Ontario: Hogrefe & Huber.

Gelder M., Gath D., & Mayou, R. (1984). *Oxford Textbook of Psychiatry.* Oxford: Oxford University Press.

Gilbert, S., & Ugelstad, E. (1994). The patients' own contributions to long-term supportive psychotherapy of schizophrenic disorder. *British Journal of Psychiatry, 164* (Suppl. 23): 84–88.

Glass, L. L., Katz, H. M., Schnitzer, R. D., et al. (1989). Psychotherapy of schizophrenia: an empirical investigation of the relationship of process to outcome. *American Journal of Psychiatry, 146*: 603–608.

Goethe, J. W. (1808). *Sämtliche Werke*, Vol. 32 (p. 44). Stuttgart & Berlin: Cotta'sche Buchhandlung.

Goffman, E. (1961). *On the Characteristics of Total Institutions.* New York: Garden City.

Goldberg, D. (1991). Cost-effectiveness studies in the treatment of schizophrenia. *Schizophrenia Bulletin, 17*: 453–459.

Goldstein, J. M., & Tsuang, M. T. (1990). Gender and schizophrenia: an introduction and synthesis of the findings. *Schizophrenia Bulletin, 16*: 179–184.

Goldstein, K. (1948). *Language and Language Disturbances.* New York: Grune & Stratton.

Goldstein, M. J. (1985). Family factors that antedate the onset of schizophrenia and related disorders: the results of a fifteen year prospective longitudinal study. *Acta Psychiatrica Scandinavica, 71* (Suppl. 319): 7–18.

Goldstein, M. J. (1987). The UCLA high risk project. *Schizophrenia Bulletin, 13*: 505–514.

Goldstein, M. J., & Kopeikin, H. S. (1981). Short and long time effects on a program combining drug and family therapy. Unpublished manuscript. [Cited in: J. G. Gunderson & A. Carroll, "Clinical considerations from empirical research". In: H. Stierlin, L. C. Wynne, & M. Wirsching (Eds.), *Psychosocial Intervention in Schizophrenia* (pp. 125–142). Berlin & Heidelberg: Springer-Verlag.]

Goldstein, M. J., Rodnick, E. H., Evans, J. R., et al. (1978). Drug and family therapy in the aftercare of acute schizophrenics. *Archives of General Psychiatry, 35*: 1169–1677.

González de Chaves Menéndez, M., & Garcia-Ordás Alvarez, A. (1992). Group therapy as a facilitating factor in the combined treatment approach to schizophrenia. In: A. Werbart & J. Cullberg (Eds.), *Psychotherapy of Schizophrenia—Facilitating and Obstructive Factors* (pp. 120–130). Oslo: Scandinavian University Press.

Gottesman, I. I., & Bertelsen, A. (1989). Confirming unexpressed genotypes for schizophrenia. Risks in the offspring of Fischer's Danish identical and fraternal discordant twins. *Archives of General Psychiatry, 46*: 867–872.

Gottesman, I. I., & Shields, J. (1966). Schizophrenia in twins: 16 years' consecutive admissions to a psychiatric clinic. *British Journal of Psychiatry, 112*: 809–818.

Greenspan, S. I. (1989). The development of the ego: biological and environmental specificity in the psychopathological developmental process and the selection and construction of ego defences. *Journal of American Psychoanalytic Association, 37*: 608–638.

Grigsby, J., & Schneider, J. L. (1991). Neuroscience, modularity and personality theory: conceptual foundation of a model complex human functioning. *Psychiatry, 54*: 21–38.

Grinspoon, L., Ewalt, J., & Shader, R. (1972). *Schizophrenia: Pharmacotherapy and Psychotherapy*. Baltimore, MD: Williams & Wilkins.

Grotstein, J. S. (1977). The psychoanalytic concept of schizophrenia. I. The dilemma. II. Reconciliation. *International Journal of Psycho-Analysis, 58*: 403–452.

Group for the Advancement of Psychiatry (1989). *Psychiatric Prevention and the Family Life Cycle. Risk Reduction by Frontier Practitioners.* Report No 127. New York: Brunner/Mazel.

Gunderson, J. G., Frank, A. F., Katz, H. M., et al. (1984). Effects of psychotherapy in schizophrenia: comparative outcome of two forms of treatment. *Schizophrenia Bulletin, 10*: 564–598.

Guntern, G. (1979). *Social Change, Stress and Mental Health in the Pearl of the Alps. A Systemic Study of a Village Process*. Berlin & Heidelberg: Springer-Verlag.

Haakenaasen, K., & Ugelstad, E. (1986). What is effective in the psychosocial treatment of younger schizophrenic inpatients? A 10-year follow-up study. *Nordic Journal of Psychiatry, 40*: 255–265.

Habermas, J. (1968). *Erkenntnis und Intresse*. Frankfurt: Suhrkamp.

Häfner, H., Maurer, K., Löffler, W., et al. (1994). The epidemiology of early schizophrenia: influence of age and gender on onset and early course. *British Journal of Psychiatry, 164* (Suppl. 23): 29–38.

Harding, C. M., Brooks, G. W., Ashikaga, T., et al. (1987). The Vermont longitudinal study of persons with severe mental illness. II. Long-term outcomes of subjects who retrospectively met DSM–III criteria for schizophrenia. *American Journal of Psychiatry, 144*: 727–735.

Harlow, H. F., Harlow, M. K. (1966). Learning to love. *American Science, 54*: 244–272.

Harris, A., Linker, I., & Norris, V. (1956). Schizophrenia: a social and prognostic study. *British Journal of Preventive and Social Medicine, 10*: 107–114.

Hartmann, H. (1953). Contribution to the metapsychology of schizophrenia. *The Psychoanalytic Study of the Child, 8*: 177–198.

Hartmann, H. (1958). *Ego Psychology and the Problem of Adaptation*. New York: International Universities Press.

Hartmann, H., Kris, E., & Loewenstein, R. M. (1946). Comments on the formation of psychic structure. *The Psychoanalytic Study of the Child, 2*: 11–38.

Haug, J. O. (1962). *Pneumoencephalographic Studies in Mental Disease*. *Acta Psychiatrica Scandinavica, 38* (Suppl. 165).

Haugsgjerd, S. (1971). *Nytt perspektiv på psykiatrin* [in Swedish]. Stockholm: Prisma.

Hauser P., Altshuler, L. L., Berritini, W., et al. (1989). Temporal lobe measurements in primary affective disorder by magnetic resonance imaging. *Journal of Neuropsychiatry & Clinical Neuroscience, 1*: 128–134.

Hegarty, J. D., Baldessarini, R. J., Tohen, M., et al. (1994). One hundred years of schizophrenia: a meta-analysis of the outcome literature. *American Journal of Psychiatry, 151*: 1409–1411.

Heston, L. L. (1966). Psychiatric disorders in foster-home-reared children of schizophrenic mothers. *British Journal of Psychiatry, 112*: 819–825.

Hietala, J., Syvälahti, E., Vuorio, K., et al. (1994). Striatal D2 dopamine receptor characteristics in neuroleptic-naive schizophrenics studied with positron emission tomography. *Archives of General Psychiatry, 51*: 116–123.

Hietala, J., Syvälahti, E., Vuorio, K., et al. (1995). Presynaptic dopamine function in striatum of neuroleptic-naive schizophrenic patients. *Lancet, 346*: 1130–1131.

Hirsch, S. R., & Leff, J. P. (1971). Parental abnormalities of verbal communication in the transmission of schizophrenia. *Psychological Medicine, 1*: 118–127.

Hirsch, S. R., & Leff, J. (1975). *Abnormalities in Parents of Schizophrenics*. Institute of Psychiatry, Maudsley Monographs, No 22. London: Oxford University Press.

Hjort, H., & Ugelstad, E. (1994). Dually diagnosed patients in the Norwegian sample—schizophrenia and drug abuse. Appendix to: Y. O. Alanen, E. Ugelstad, B.-Å. Armelius, et al., *Early Treatment for Schizophrenic Patients: Scandinavian Psychotherapeutic Approaches* (pp. 155–162). Oslo: Scandinavian University Press.

Hogarty, G. E. (1994). "Integration of psychopharmacologic and psychosocial therapies in schizophrenia." Paper read at the Eleventh International Symposium for Psychotherapy of Schizophrenia, Washington, DC.

Hogarty, G. E., Anderson, C. M., Reiss, D. J., et al. (1986). Family psychoeducation, social skills training, and maintenance chemotherapy in the aftercare treatment of schizophrenia. I. One-year effects of a controlled study on relapse and expressed emotion. *Archives of General Psychiatry, 43*: 633–642.

Hogarty, G. E., Anderson, C. M., Reiss, D. J., et al. (1991). Family psychoeducation, social skills training and chemotherapy in the aftercare treatment of schizophrenia. II. Two-year effects of a controlled study on relapse and adjustment. *Archives of General Psychiatry, 48*: 340–347.

Hoult, J., Reynolds, I., Charbonneau-Powis, J., et al. (1983). Psychiatric hospital versus community treatment: the results of a randomized trial. *Australian and New Zealand Journal of Psychiatry, 17*: 160–167.

Hsia, C. Y., & Chang, M. Y. (1978). Long term follow-up study of schizophrenia. *Chinese Medical Journal, 4*: 266–270.

Huber, G. (1961). *Chronische Schizophrenie. Synopsis klinischer und neuroradiologischer Untersuchungen an defektschizophrenen Anstaltpatienten. Einzeldarstellungen aus der theoretischer und klinischer Medizin, Band 13.* Heidelberg: Dr. A Huthig Verlag.

Huber, G., Gross, G., Schüttler, R., & Linz, M. (1980). Longitudinal studies of schizophrenic patients. *Schizophrenia Bulletin, 6*: 592–605.

Huttunen, M. O., Machon, R. A., & Mednick, S. A. (1994). Pre-natal factors in the pathogenesis of schizophrenia. *British Journal of Psychiatry, 164* (Suppl. 23): 15–19.

Idänpään-Heikkilä, J., Alhava, E., Olkinuora, M., et al. (1977). Agranulocytosis during treatment with clozapine. *European Journal of Clinical Pharmacology, 11*: 193–198.

Illowsky, B., Juliano, D. M., Bigelow, L. B., & Weinberger, D. R. (1988). Stability of CT scan findings in schizophrenia: results of an 8-year follow-up study. *Journal of Neurology, Neurosurgery & Psychiatry, 51*: 209–213.

Inoye, E. (1961). Similarity and dissimilarity of schizophrenia in twins.

Proceedings of the Third World Congress of Psychiatry, 1: 524–530. Montreal: University of Toronto Press.

Isohanni, M. (1983). *The Psychiatric Ward as a Therapeutic Community. Acta Universitatis Ouluensis*, Series D Medica, No 111. (Oulu, Finland).

Jablensky, A., Sartorius, N., Ernberg, G., et al. (1992). *Schizophrenia: Manifestation, Incidence and Course in Different Cultures.* Psychological Medicine Monographs (Suppl. 20). Cambridge: Cambridge University Press.

Jackson, D. D. (1957). The question of family homeostasis. *Psychiatric Quarterly* (Suppl. 31): 79–90.

Jackson, D. D., & Weakland, J. H. (1961). Conjoint family therapy: some considerations on theory, technique, and results. *Psychiatry, 24* (Suppl. 2): 30–45.

Jackson, M., & Cawley, R. (1992). Psychodynamics and psychotherapy on an acute ward. The story of an experimental unit. *British Journal of Psychiatry, 160*: 41–50.

Jackson, M., & Williams, P. (1994). *Unimaginable Storms: A Search for Meaning in Psychosis.* London: Karnac Books.

Jacob, T. (1975). Family interaction in disturbed and normal families: a methodological and substantive review. *Psychological Bulletin, 82*: 33–65.

Jenkins, J. H., & Karno, M. (1992). The meaning of expressed emotion: theoretical issues raised by cross-cultural research. *American Journal of Psychiatry, 149*: 9–21.

Johansson, A. (1956). Psychotherapeutische Behandlung eines Falles von Schizophrenie. *Psyche, 10*: 568–587.

Johansson, A. (1985). *Skitsofrenian analyyttisen psykoterapian ongelma.* [The problem of the psychoanalytic psychotherapy of schizophrenia; in Finnish]. *Annales Universitatis Turkuensis, Ser. C*, Vol. 53 (Turku, Finland).

Johnstone, E. C., Crow, T. J., Frith, C. D., et al. (1976). Cerebral ventricular size and cognitive impairment in chronic schizophrenia. *Lancet, 1*: 924–926.

Jones, M. (1953). *The Therapeutic Community.* New York: Basic Books.

Jones, P., Rodgers, B., Murray, R., & Marmot, M. (1994). Child development risk factors for adult schizophrenia in the British 1946 birth cohort. *Lancet, 344*: 1398–1402.

Kallmann, F. J. (1946). The genetic theory of schizophrenia. An analysis of 691 schizophrenic twin index families. *American Journal of Psychiatry, 103*: 309–322.

Kanas, N. (1986). Group therapy with schizophrenics: a review of controlled studies. *International Journal of Group Psychotherapy, 36*: 339–351.

Karon, B. P., & VandenBos, G. R. (1972). The consequences of psychotherapy for schizophrenic patients. *Psychotherapy: Theory, Research and Practice, 9*: 111–119.

Karon, B. P., & VandenBos, G. R. (1981). *Psychotherapy of Schizophrenia— Treatment of Choice.* New York: Jason Aronson.

Kasanin, J. (1933). The acute schizoaffective psychosis. *American Journal of Psychiatry, 13*: 97–126.

Kasanin, J., Knight, E., & Sage, P. (1934). The parent–child relationship in schizophrenia: I. Over-protection—rejection. *Journal of Nervous and Mental Diseases, 79*: 249–263.

Kaufmann, L. (1976). Long-term family therapy with schizophrenics. In. J. Jorstad & E. Ugelstad (Eds.), *Schizophrenia, 75, Psychotherapy, Family Studies, Research* (pp. 229–242). Oslo: Universitetsforlaget.

Kavanagh, D. J. (1992). Expressed emotion and schizophrenia. *British Journal of Psychiatry, 160*: 601–169.

Kendler, K. S., & Robinette, C. D. (1983). Schizophrenia in the National Academy of Sciences—National Research Council Twin Registry: a 16-year update. *American Journal of Psychiatry, 140*: 1551–1563.

Kendler, K. S., Spitzer, R. L., & Williams, J. B. W. (1989). Psychotic disorders in DSM–III R. *American Journal of Psychiatry, 146*: 953–962.

Kernberg, O. F. (1975). *Borderline Conditions and Pathological Narcissism.* New York: Jason Aronson.

Kernberg, O. F. (1984). *Object Relations Theory and Clinical Psychoanalysis.* New York: Jason Aronson.

Keränen, J. (1992). *The Choice between Outpatient and Inpatient Treatment in a Family Centred Psychiatric Treatment System* [in Finnish, with English summary]. *Jyväskylä Studies in Education, Psychology and Social Research, 93* (Jyväskylä, Finland).

Kety, S. S., Rosenthal, D., Wender, P. H., et al. (1968). The types and prevalence of mental illness in the biological and adptive families of adopted schizophrenics. In: D. Rosenthal & S. S. Kety (Eds.), *The Transmission of Schizophrenia* (pp. 345–362). New York: Pergamon .

Kety, S. S., Wender P. H., Jacobsen, J., et al. (1994). Mental illness in the biological and adoptive relatives of schizophrenic adoptees. *Archives of General Psychiatry, 51*: 442–455.

Killingmo, B. (1989). Conflict and deficit: implications for technique. *International Journal of Psycho-Analysis, 70*: 65–79.

Klein, M. (1946). Notes on some schizoid mechanisms. *International Journal of Psycho-Analysis, 27*: 99–110. [Also in: *The Writings of Melanie Klein.* Vol. 3: *Envy and Gratitude and Other Works.* London: Hogarth Press and the Institute of Psychoanalysis [reprinted London: Karnac Books, 1993.]

Klein, M. (1975). *Envy and Gratitude and Other Works, 1946–63.* London: Hogarth Press and the Institute of Psychoanalysis [reprinted London: Karnac Books, 1993].

Kohut, H. (1971). *The Analysis of the Self. A Systematic Approach to the Psychoanalysis of Narcissistic Personality Disorders.* New York: International Universities Press.

Kohut, H. (1977). *The Restoration of the Self.* New York: International Universities Press.

Kringlen, E. (1967). *Heredity and Environment in Functional Psychoses,* Vols. I–II. Oslo: Universitetsforlaget.

Kringlen, E. (1978). Adult offspring of two psychotic parents with special reference to schizophrenia. In: L. C. Wynne, R. L. Cromwell, & S. Matthysse (Eds.), *The Nature of Schizophrenia* (pp. 9–24). New York: John Wiley & Sons.

Kringlen, E. (1994). Is the concept of schizophrenia useful from an aetiological point of view? A selective review of findings and paradoxes. *Acta Psychiatrica Scandinavica, 90* (Suppl. 384): 17–25.

Kringlen, E., & Cramer, G. (1989). Offsprings of monozygotic twins discordant for schizophrenia. *Archives of General Psychiatry, 46*: 770–779.

Kuipers, L. (1993). Family burden in schizophrenia: implications for services. *Social Psychiatry & Psychiatric Epidemiology, 28*: 207–210.

Kuusi, K. (1986). *Prognosis of Schizophrenic Psychoses in Helsinki in 1975–1983* [in Finnish, with English summary]. *Monographs of Psychiatria Fennica,* No 13. Helsinki.

Laing, R. D., & Esterson, A. (1964). *Sanity, Madness and the Family.* Vol. I: *Families of Schizophrenics.* London: Tavistock Publications.

Lambo, T. A. (1955). The role of cultural factors in paranoid psychoses among the Yoruba tribe. *Journal of Mental Science, 101*: 239–266.

Langfeldt, G. (1939). *The Schizophreniform States.* Copenhagen: Munksgaard.

Langfeldt, G. (1953). Some points regarding the symptomatology and diagnosis of schizophrenia. *Acta Psychiatrica et Neurologica Scandinavica, 28* (Suppl. 80): 7–26.

Langsley D. G., Machotka, P., & Flomenhaft, K. (1971). Avoiding mental hospital admission: a follow-up study. *American Journal of Psychiatry*, 127: 1391–1394.

Langsley, D. G., Pittman, F. S., & Swank, G. E. (1969). Family crises in schizophrenics and other patients. *Journal of Nervous and Mental Diseases*, 149: 270–276.

Larmo, A. (1992). *The Parent's Psychosis, Impact on Family and Children. Annales Universitatis Turkuensis, Ser. D*, Vol. 84 (Turku, Finland).

Larsen, T. K. (1994). "Early detection of first-episode schizophrenia." Paper read at the Eleventh International Symposium for the Psychotherapy of Schizophrenia, Washington, DC.

Lazell, E. (1921). The group treatment of dementia praecox. *Psychoanalytical Review*, 8: 168–179.

Leff, J. (1994). Working with the families of schizophrenic patients. *British Journal of Psychiatry*, 164 (Suppl. 23): 71–76.

Leff, J., Kuipers, L., Berkowitz, R., et al. (1982). A controlled trial of social intervention in the families of schizophrenic patients. *British Journal of Psychiatry*, 141: 121–134.

Leff, J., Kuipers, L., Berkowitz, R., et al. (1983). Life events, relatives' expressed emotions and maintenance neuroleptics in schizophrenic relapse. *Psychological Medicine*, 13: 799–807.

Leff, J., Kuipers, L., Berkowitz, R., & Sturgeon, D. (1985). A controlled trial of social intervention in the families of schizophrenic patients: two-year follow-up. *British Journal of Psychiatry*, 146: 594–600.

Lehtinen, K. (1993a). Need-adapted treatment of schizophrenia: a five-year follow-up study from the Turku project. *Acta Psychiatrica Scandinavica*, 87: 96–101.

Lehtinen, K. (1993b). *Family Therapy and Schizophrenia in Public Mental Health. Annales Universitatis Turkuensis, Ser. D*, Vol. 106 (Turku, Finland).

Lehtinen, K. (1994). Need-adapted treatment of schizophrenia: family interventions. *British Journal of Psychiatry*, 164 (Suppl. 23): 89–96.

Lehtinen, K., & Räkköläinen, V. (1986). System-analytic treatment of acute psychosis [in Finnish]. In: V.-P. Avento (Ed.), Suomen Psykiatriyhdistyksen syksyn koulutuspäivien luentojulkaisu. Skitsofrenian hoidon kehittäminen. *Psychiatria Fennica. Reports*, No. 71: 79–91. Helsinki: Foundation for Psychiatric Research in Finland.

Lehtinen, V., Aaltonen, J., Koffert, T., et al. (1996). Integrated treatment model for first-contact patients with schizophrenia-type psychosis. The Finnish API-project. *Nordic Journal of Psychiatry*, 50: 281–287.

Lehtinen, V., & Joukamaa, M. (1987). Mental disorders in the sample representative of the whole Finnish adult population, In: B. Cooper (Ed.), *Psychiatric Epidemiology: Progress and Prospects* (pp. 43–54). London: Croon Helm.

Levander, S., & Cullberg, J. (1994). Psychotherapy in retrospect. Accounts of experiences in psychotherapy obtained from five former schizophrenic patients. *Nordic Journal of Psychiatry, 48*: 263–269.

Levene, J. E., Newman, F., & Jefferies, J. J. (1989). Focal family therapy outcome study. I. Patient and family functioning. *Canadian Journal of Psychiatry, 14*: 641–647.

Lewis, S. (1990). Computerised tomography in schizophrenia 15 years on. *British Journal of Psychiatry, 157*: 16–24.

Lidz, R. W. (1993). The effect of neurotropic drugs on the psychotherapy of schizophrenic patients. In: G. Benedetti & P. M. Furlan (Eds.), *The Psychotherapy of Schizophrenia* (pp. 311–317). Toronto, Ontario: Hogrefe & Huber.

Lidz, R. W., & Lidz, T. (1949). The family environment of schizophrenic patients. *American Journal of Psychiatry, 106*: 332–345.

Lidz, T. (1964). *The Family and Human Adaptation*. London: Hogarth Press and the Institute of Psycho-Analysis.

Lidz, T. (1992). *The Relevance of the Family to Psychoanalytic Theory*. Madison, CT: International Universities Press.

Lidz, T., & Blatt, S. (1983). Critic of the Danish–American studies of the biological and adoptive relatives of adoptees who became schizophrenic. *American Journal of Psychiatry, 140*: 426–434.

Lidz, T., Cornelison, A. R., Fleck, S., & Terry, D. (1957a). The intrafamilial environment of the schizophrenic patient: I. The fathers. *Psychiatry, 20*: 329–342.

Lidz, T., Cornelison, A. R., Fleck, S., & Terry, D. (1957b). The intrafamilial environment of schizophrenic patients: II. Marital schism and marital skew. *American Journal of Psychiatry, 114*: 241–248.

Lidz, T., Cornelison, A. R., Fleck, S., & Terry, D. (1958). Intrafamilial environment of the schizophrenic patient: VI. The transmission of irrationality. *A.M.A. Archives of Neurology and Psychiatry, 79*: 305–316.

Lidz, T., Fleck, S., & Cornelison, A. R. (1965). *Schizophrenia and the Family*. New York: International Universities Press.

Lidz, T., & Lidz, R. W. (1982). The curative factors in psychotherapy of schizophrenic disorders. In: S. Slipp (Ed.), *Curative Factors in Dynamic Psychiatry*. New York: McGraw-Hill.

Lieberman, J. A. (1993). Understanding the mechanism of action of atypical antipsychotic drugs. A review of compounds in use and development. *British Journal of Psychiatry, 163* (Suppl. 22): 7–18.

Lin, K.-M., & Kleinman, A. M. (1988). Psychopathology and clinical course of schizophrenia: a cross-cultural perspective. *Schizophrenia Bulletin, 14:* 555–574.

Lindberg, D. (1981). *Management of Schizophrenia. Acta Psychiatrica Scandinavica* (Suppl. 283).

Linszen, D. H., Dingemans, P. M., & Lenior, M. E. (1994). Cannabis abuse and the course of recent-onset schizophrenic disorders. *Acta Psychiatrica Scandinavica, 51:* 273–279.

London, N. J. (1973). An essay on psychoanalytic theory: two theories of schizophrenia. Parts I and II. *International Journal of Psycho-Analysis, 54:* 169–193.

MacFarlane, J. (1975). Olfaction in the development of social references in the human neonate. In: M. Hofer (Ed.), *Parent–Infant Interaction.* Amsterdam: Elsevier. [Cited in Stern, 1985.]

Mahler, M. S. (1968). *On Human Symbiosis and the Vicissitudes of Individuation.* Vol. 1: *Infantile Psychosis.* New York: International Universities Press.

Mahler, M. S., Pine, F., & Bergman, A. (1975). *The Psychological Birth of the Infant.* New York: Basic Books.

Main, T. F. (1946). The hospital as a therapeutic institution. *Bulletin of the Menninger Clinic, 10:* 66.

Malkiewicz-Borkowska, M., & Namyslowska, I. (1991). Results of family therapy of hospitalized adolescents. *Abstracts: Third World Family Therapy Congress,* 2–6 June, Jyväskylä, Finland (p. 234). Jyväskylä: University of Jyväskylä.

Malm, U. (1982). *The Influence of Group Therapy on Schizophrenia. Acta Psychiatrica Scandinavica* (Suppl. 297).

Malmivaara, K., Keinänen, E., & Saarelma, M. (1975). Factors affecting child psychiatric hospital care and its immediate results. *Psychiatria Fennica. Yearbook:* 225–238. Helsinki: The Foundation for Psychiatric Research in Finland.

Malson, L. (1972). *Wolf Children and the Problem of Human Nature.* New York: Monthly Review Press. [Includes two papers by J. Itard, on the "wild boy of Aveyron", 1799 and 1806.]

Marder, R. S., Van Putten, T., Mintz, J., et al. (1987). Low- and conventional-dose maintenance therapy with fluphenazine decanoate. Two-year outcome. *Archives of General Psychiatry, 44:* 518–521.

Marsh, L. C. (1933). Experiments in group treatment of patients at Worcester State Hospital. *Mental Hygiene, 17*: 396–416.

Martinot, J.-L., Peron-Magnan, P., Huret, D.-C., et al. (1990). Striatal D2 dopaminergic receptors assessed with positron emission tomography and (76Br) Bromospiperone in untreated schizophrenic patients. *American Journal of Psychiatry, 147*: 44–50.

Matte Blanco, I. (1988). *Thinking, Feeling and Being.* London: Routledge.

Mattila, V. (1984). *Onset of Functional Psychoses in Later Middle Age: A Social Psychiatric, Psychodynamic and Family-Dynamic Study. Annales Universitatis Turkuensis, Ser. D,* Vol. 16 (Turku, Finland).

May, P. R. A. (1968). *Treatment of Schizophrenia. A Comparative Study of Five Treatment Methods.* New York: Science House.

May, P. R. A., Tuma, A. H., & Dixon, W. J. (1981). Schizophrenia: a follow-up study of the results of the five forms of treatment. *Archives of General Psychiatry, 38*: 776–784.

May, P. R. A., Tuma, A. H., Yale, C., et al. (1976). Schizophrenia: follow-up study of results of treatment. *Archives of General Psychiatry, 33*: 474–486.

McGhie, A. (1961). A comparative study of mother–child relationship in schizophrenia. *British Journal of Medical Psychology, 34*: 195–221.

McGlashan, T. H. (1984). The Chestnut Lodge follow-up study. I. Follow-up methodology and study sample. II. Long-term outcome of schizophrenia and the affective disorders. *Archives of General Psychiatry, 41*: 573–601.

McGorry, P. D., McFarlane, C., Patton, G. C., et al. (1995). The prevalence of prodromal features in adolescence: a preliminary survey. *Acta Psychiatrica Scandinavica, 92*: 241–249.

McNeil, T. F., Cantor-Graae, E., Torrey, E. F., et al. (1994). Obstetric complications in histories of monozygotic twins discordant and concordant for schizophrenia. *Acta Psychiatrica Scandinavica, 89*: 196–204.

Mednick, S. A., Machon, R., Huttunen, M. O., & Bonett, D. (1988). Adult schizophrenia following prenatal infection to an influenza epidemic. *Archives of General Psychiatry, 45*: 189–192.

Mednick, S. A., Parnas, J., & Schulsinger, F. (1987). The Copenhagen high-risk project. *Schizophrenia Bulletin, 13*: 485–495.

Mednick, S., & Schulsinger, F. (1968). Some pre-morbic characteristics related to breakdown in children with schizophrenic mothers. In: D. Rosenthal & S. S. Kety (Eds.), *The Transmission of Schizophrenia* (pp. 267–291). New York: Pergamon Press.

Meyer, A. (1906). Fundamental conceptions of dementia praecox. *British*

Medical Journal, 2: 755–759. [Also in: E. E. Winters (Ed.), *The Collected Papers of Adolph Meyer*. Baltimore, MD: The Johns Hopkins University Press, 1950–1952.]

Meyer, A. (1910). The dynamic interpretation of dementia praecox. *American Journal of Psychology, 21*: 385. [Also in: E. E. Winters (Ed.), *The Collected Papers of Adolph Meyer*. Baltimore, MD: The Johns Hopkins University Press, 1950–1952.]

Miles, C. (1977). Conditions predisposing to suicide: a review. *Journal of Nervous and Mental Diseases, 164*: 231–246.

Mishler, E. G., & Waxler, N. (1968). Family interaction and schizophrenia. Alternative frameworks of interpretation. *Journal of Psychiatric Research, 6*: 213–222.

Moises, H. W., Yang, L., Kristbjarnarson, H., et al. (1995). An international two-stage genome-wide search for schizophrenia susceptibility genes. *Nature Genetics, 11*: 321–324.

Mosher, L. R., & Keith, S. J. (1979). Research on the psychosocial treatment of schizophrenia: a summary report. *American Journal of Psychiatry, 136*: 623–631.

Mosher, L. R., & Menn, A. Z. (1978). Community residential treatment for schizophrenia: two-year follow-up data. *Hospital & Community Psychiatry, 29*: 715–723.

Mosher, L. R., & Menn, A. Z. (1983). Scientific evidence and system change: the Soteria experience. In: H. Stierlin, L. C. Wynne, & M. Wirsching (Eds.), *Psychosocial Intervention in Schizophrenia* (pp. 93–108). Berlin & Heidelberg: Springer-Verlag.

Muijen, M., Marks, I. M., Connolly, J., et al. (1992). The daily living programme. Preliminary comparison of community versus hospital-based treatment for the seriously mentally ill facing emergency admission. *British Journal of Psychiatry, 160*: 379–384.

Müller, C. (1961). Die Psychotherapie Schizophrener an der Zürcher Klinik. Versuch einer vorläufigen katamnestischen Übersicht. *Nervenarzt, 32*: 354–368.

Munk-Jorgensen, P., & Mortensen, P. B. (1992). Incidence and other aspects of the epidemiology of schizophrenia in Denmark 1971–87. *British Journal of Psychiatry, 161*: 489–495.

Murphy, H. B. (1973). Current trends in transcultural psychiatry. *Proceedings of the Royal Society of Medicine, 66*: 711–716.

Myers, J. K., Weissman, M. M., Tischler, G. L., et al. (1984). Six-month prevalence of psychiatric disorders in three communities. *Archives of General Psychiatry, 41*: 959–967.

Nasrallah, H. A., McCalley-Whitters, M., & Jacoby, C. G. (1982). Cortical atrophy in schizophrenia and mania: a comparative CT study. *Journal of Clinical Psychiatry*, 43: 439–442.

Nasrallah, H. A., Olson, S. C., McCalley-Whitters, M., et al. (1986). Cerebral ventricular enlargement in schizophrenia: a preliminary follow-up study. *Archives of General Psychiatry*, 43: 157–159.

National Pension Institute (1989). *Yearbook*. Helsinki: National Pension Institute.

Niederland, W. G. (1984). *The Schreber Case* (expanded edition). Hillsdale, NJ: The Analytic Press.

Nybäck, H., Wiesel, F.-A, Berggren, B.-M., & Hindmarsh, T. (1982). Computed tomography of the brain in patients with acute psychosis and in healthy volunteers. *Acta Psychiatrica Scandinavica*, 65: 403–414.

O'Brien, C. B., Hamm, K. B., Ray, B. A., et al. (1972). Group vs. individual psychotherapy with schizophrenics: a controlled outcome study. *Archives of General Psychiatry*, 27: 474–478.

O'Callaghan, E., Gibson, T., Colohan, H. A., et al. (1991). Season of birth in schizophrenia: evidence for confinement of an excess of winter births to patients without a family history of mental disorder. *British Journal of Psychiatry*, 158: 764–769.

Ogden, T. H. (1979). On projective identification. *International Journal of Psycho-Analysis*, 60: 357–373.

Ojanen, M. (1984). The Sopimusvuori Society: an integrated system of rehabilitation. *International Journal of Therapeutic Communities*, 5: 193–207.

Olson, D. H., Sprenkle, D. H., & Russell, C. S. (1979). Circumplex model of marital and family systems: I. Cohesion and adaptability dimensions, family types, and clinical applications. *Family Process*, 18: 3–28.

Onstad, S., Skre, I., Torgersen, S., & Kringlen, E. (1991). Twin concordance for DSM–III R schizophrenia. *Acta Psychiatrica Scandinavica*, 83: 395–440.

Onstad, S., Skre, I., Torgersen, S., & Kringlen, E. (1994). Family interaction: parental representation in schizophrenic patients. *Acta Psychiatrica Scandinavica*, 90 (Suppl. 384): 67–70.

Orma, E. (1978). Unpublished presentation delivered at the meeting of the Turku Psychotherapy Society, Turku.

Pao, P.-N. (1979). *Schizophrenic Disorders. Theory and Treatment from a Psychodynamic Point of View*. New York: International Universities Press.

Parland, O. (1991). *Tieto ja eläytyminen. Esseitä ja muistelmia* [Knowledge and Empathy. Essays and Memoirs; in Finnish]. Juva: WSOY.

Parloff, M. B., & Dies, R. R. (1977). Group psychotherapy outcome research 1965–1975. *International Journal of Group Psychotherapy, 27*: 281–319.

Paul, G. L., & Lentz, R. J. (1977). *Psychosocial Treatment of Chronic Mental Patients: Milieu vs. Social-learning Programs.* Cambridge MA: Harvard University Press.

Perris, C. (1992). Some aspects of the use of cognitive psychotherapy with patients suffering from a schizophrenic disorder. In: A. Werbart & J. Cullberg (Eds.), *Psychotherapy of Schizophrenia. Facilitating and Obstructive Factors* (pp. 131–144). Oslo: Scandinavian University Press.

Pietruszewski, K. (1991). Psychotic versus non-psychotic family dynamics during adolescents' in-patient treatment. In: *Abstracts: Third World Family Therapy Congress*, 2–6 June, Jyväskylä, Finland (p. 314). Jyväskylä: University of Jyväskylä.

Pines, M. (1992). "The world according to Kohut." Lecture delivered at the meeting of the Finnish Psychoanalytical Society, Helsinki.

Pollin, W., Allen, M. G., Hoffer, A., et al. (1969). Psychopathology in 15,909 pairs of veteran twins: evidence for a genetic factor in the pathogenesis of schizophrenia and its relative absence in psychoneurosis. *American Journal of Psychiatry, 126*: 597–610.

Portin, P., & Alanen, Y. O. (1997). A critical review of genetical studies of schizophrenia. I. Epidemiological and brain studies. II. Molecular genetic studies. *Acta Psychiatrica Scandinavica, 95*: 1–5, 73–80.

Pylkkänen, K. (1994). The Finnish National Schizophrenia Project 1982–1992: is a balanced and controlled deinstitutionalisation process possible? *Psychiatria Fennica. Yearbook*: 169–183. Helsinki: Foundation for Psychiatric Research in Finland.

Pylkkänen, K., & Eskola, J. (1984). Kokemuksia mielisairaanhoidon uudistuksesta Italiassa [Experiences from the innovation of psychiatric care in Italy; in Finnish]. *Suomen Lääkärilehti, 39*: 1520–1522.

Räkköläinen, V. (1977). *Onset of Psychosis: A Clinical Study of 68 Cases. Annales Universitatis Turkuensis*, Ser. D, Vol. 7 (Turku, Finland).

Räkköläinen, V., & Alanen, Y. O. (1982). On the transactionality of defensive processes. *International Review of Psycho-Analysis, 9*: 263–272.

Räkköläinen, V., Lehtinen, K., & Alanen, Y. O. (1991). Need-adapted treatment of schizophrenic processes: the essential role of family-centred therapy meetings. *Contemporary Family Therapy, 13*: 573–582.

Räkköläinen, V., Salokangas, R., & Lehtinen, P. (1979). Protective constructions in the course of psychosis. In: C. Müller (Ed.), *Psychotherapy of Schizophrenia* (pp. 233–243). Amsterdam: Excerpta Medica.

Räkköläinen, V., Vuorio, K. A., Syvälahti, E., et al. (1994). "Observations of comprehensive psychotherapeutic treatment of new schizophrenic patients without neuroleptic drugs in Kupittaa hospital in 1989–92." Paper read at the Eleventh International Symposium for Psychotherapy of Schizophrenia, Washington, DC.

Raman, A. C., & Murphy, H. B. (1972). Failure of traditional prognostic indications in Afro–Asian psychotics: results of a long-term follow-up survey. *Journal of Nervous and Mental Diseases, 154*: 238–247.

Rang, B. (1987). Wolfskinderen en de ontwikkeling van de menswetenschappen [When the social environment of a child approaches zero; in Dutch]. *Comenius, 27*: 316–342.

Rapaport, M., Hopkins, H. K., Hall, K., et al. (1978). Are there schizophrenics for whom drugs may be unnecessary or contraindicated? *International Journal of Pharmacopsychiatry, 13*: 100–111.

Rechardt, E. (1971). Skitsofreniapotilaan kieli [The language of the schizophrenic patient; in Finnish]. *Duodecim, 87*: 1591–1599.

Reiss, D. (1971). Varieties of consensual experience. III. Contrast between families of normals, delinquents, and schizophrenics. *Journal of Nervous and Mental Diseases, 152*: 73–96.

Retzer, A., Simon, F. B., Weber, G., et al. (1991). A follow-up study of manic–depressive and schizo–affective psychoses after systemic family therapy. *Family Process, 30*: 139–153.

Reveley, A. M., Reveley, M. A., Clifford, C. A., & Murray, R. M. (1982). Cerebral ventricular size in twins discordant for schizophrenia. *Lancet, 1*: 540–541.

Reveley, A. M., Reveley, M. A., & Murray, R. M. (1984). Cerebral ventricular enlargement in non-genetic schizophrenia: a controlled twin study. *British Journal of Psychiatry, 144*: 89–93.

Rice, D. P., Kelman, S., Miller, L. S., & Dunmeyer, S. (1990). *The Economic Costs of Alcohol and Drug Abuse and Mental Illness: 1985*. Rockville MD: National Institutes of Mental Health, DHHS Pub. No (ADM), 90-1694.

Rieder, R. O., Mann, L. S., Weinberger, D. R., et al. (1983). Computed tomographic scans in patients with schizophrenic, schizo–affective and bipolar affective disorder. *Archives of General Psychiatry, 40*: 735–739.

Riskin, J. R., & Faunce, E. E. (1972). An evaluative review of family interaction research. *Family Process, 11*: 365–455.

Robbins, M. (1993). *Experiences of Schizophrenia: An Integration of the Personal, Scientific, and Therapeutic.* New York: Guilford Press.

Roberts, G. W. (1990). Schizophrenia: the cellular biology of a functional psychosis. *Trends of Neuroscience, 13*: 207–211.

Robins, J. N., Helzer, J. F., Weissman, M. M., et al. (1984). Lifetime prevalence of specific psychiatric disorders in three sites. *Archives of General Psychiatry, 41*: 949–958.

Rosenfeld, H. A. (1987). *Impasse and Interpretation.* London: Tavistock.

Rosenthal, D. (1970). *Genetic Theory and Abnormal Behaviour.* New York: McGraw-Hill.

Rosenthal, D., Wender, P. H., Kety, S. S., et al. (1968). Schizophrenic's offspring reared in adoptive homes. In D. Rosenthal & S. S. Kety (Eds.), *The Transmission of Schizophrenia* (pp. 377–391). New York: Pergamon Press.

Rosenthal, D., Wender, P. H., Kety, S. S., et al. (1971). The adopted-away offspring of schizophrenics. *American Journal of Psychiatry, 128*: 307–311.

Rothstein, A. (1980). Towards a critique of the psychology of the self. *Psychoanalytic Quarterly, 49*: 423–455.

Rund, B. R. (1986). Communication deviances in parents of schizophrenics. *Family Process, 25*: 133–147.

Salokangas, R. K. R. (1977). *The Psychosocial Prognosis of Schizophrenia* [in Finnish, with English summary]. Publications of the National Pension Institute, Series AL: 7. Turku, Finland: National Pension Institute.

Salokangas, R. K. R. (1983). Prognostic implication of the sex of schizophrenic patients. *British Journal of Psychiatry, 142*: 145–151.

Salokangas, R. K. R. (1986). Psychosocial outcome in schizophrenia and psychotherapeutic orientation. *Acta Psychiatrica Scandinavica, 74*: 497–506.

Salokangas, R. K. R., Räkköläinen, V., & Alanen, Y.O. (1989). Maintenance of grip on life and goals of life: a valuable criterion for evaluating outcome in schizophrenia. *Acta Psychiatrica Scandinavica, 80*: 187–193.

Salokangas R. K. R., Stengård, E., Räkköläinen, V., et al. (1987). Uudet skitsofreniapotilaat ja heidän perheensä. USP-projekti III [New schizophrenic patients and their families: NSP-Project III; in Finnish, with English summary]. *Psychiatria Fennica. Reports*, No. 78. Helsinki: The Foundation for Psychiatric Research in Finland.

Salokangas, R. K. R., Stengård, E., Räkköläinen et al., V. (1991). Uusien skitsofreniapotilaiden hoito ja ennuste. Viiden vuoden seuranta. USP-projekti V [Treatment and prognosis of new schizophrenic patients: a five-year follow-up. NSP-Project V; in Finnish, with English summary]. *Psychiatria Fennica. Reports*, No. 95. Helsinki: The Foundation for Psychiatric Research in Finland.

Salonen, S. (1975). The hospital ward from the standpoint of the patient's self-esteem. *Psychiatria Fennica. Yearbook*: 325–331. Helsinki: The Foundation for Psychiatric Research in Finland. [Reprinted in: S. Salonen, *Psychotherapeutic Studies in Schizophrenia. Annales Universitatis Turkuensis, Ser. D*, Vol. 12 (Turku, Finland).

Salonen, S. (1979). On the metapsychology of schizophrenia. *International Journal of Psycho-Analysis*, 60: 73–81. [Reprinted in: S. Salonen, *Psychotherapeutic Studies in Schizophrenia. Annales Universitatis Turkuensis, Ser. D*, Vol. 12 (Turku, Finland).

Sandin, B. (1992). Schizophrenic strategies for survival. In: A. Werbart, & J. Cullberg (Eds.), *Psychotherapy of Schizophrenia: Facilitating and Obstructive Factors* (pp. 50–57). Oslo: Scandinavian University Press.

Schubart, C., Krumm, B., Biehl, H., & Schwarz, R. (1986). Measurement of social disability in a schizophrenic patients group: definition, assessment, and outcome over 2 years in a cohort of schizophrenic patients of recent onset. *Social Psychiatry*, 21: 1–19.

Schulz, C. G. (1975). An individualized psychotherapeutic approach with the schizophrenic patient. *Schizophrenia Bulletin* (Issue 13): 44–69.

Schulz, C. G., & Kilgalen, R. K. (1969). *Case Studies in Schizophrenia*. New York: Basic Books.

Schwarz, F. (1982). Group analysis with schizophrenics. In: M. Pines & L. Rafaelsen (Eds.), *The Individual and the Group*, Vol. 2 (pp. 239–249). New York: Plenum Publications.

Scott, R. D., & Alwyn, S. (1978). Patient–parent relationships and the course and outcome of schizophrenia. *British Journal of Medical Psychology*, 51: 343–355.

Scott, R. D., & Ashworth, P. L. (1967). "Closure" at the first schizophrenic breakdown: a family study. *British Journal of Medical Psychology*, 40: 109–145.

Scott, R. D., & Ashworth, P. L. (1969). The shadow of the ancestor: a historical factor in the transmission of schizophrenia. *British Journal of Medical Psychology*, 42: 13–31.

Scottish Schizophrenia Research Group (1987). The Scottish first episode schizophrenia study. I. Patient identification and categorization. II. Treatment: Pimozide versus flupenthixol. *British Journal of Psychiatry*, 150: 331–338.

Scottish Schizophrenia Research Group (1992). The Scottish first episode schizophrenia study. VIII. Five-year follow-up: clinical and psychosocial findings. *British Journal of Psychiatry*, 161: 496–500.

Searles, H. F. (1955). Dependency processes in the psychotherapy of schizophrenia. *Journal of American Psychoanalytic Association*, 3: 19–66. [Also in: *Collected Papers on Schizophrenia and Related Subjects* (pp. 114–156). Madison, CT: International Universities Press, 1965; reprinted London: Karnac Books, 1986.]

Searles, H. F. (1958). Positive feelings in the relationship between the schizophrenic and his mother. *International Journal of Psycho-Analysis*, 39: 569–586. [Also in: *Collected Papers on Schizophrenia and Related Subjects* (pp. 216–253). Madison, CT: International Universities Press, 1965; reprinted London: Karnac Books, 1986.]

Searles, H. F. (1961). Phases of patient–therapist interaction in the psychotherapy of chronic schizophrenia. *British Journal of Medical Psychology*, 34: 169–193. [Also in: *Collected Papers on Schizophrenia and Related Subjects* (pp. 521–559). Madison, CT: International Universities Press, 1965; reprinted London: Karnac Books, 1986.]

Searles H. F. (1965). *Collected Papers on Schizophrenia and Related Subjects*. Madison, CT: International Universities Press [reprinted London: Karnac Books, 1986].

Sechehaye, M.-A. (1955). *Die symbolische Wunscherfüllung* [Symbolic realization]. *Darstellung einer neuen psychotherapeutischen Methode und Tagebuch der Kranken*. Bern: Hans Huber.

Sedvall, G., & Farde, L. (1995). Chemical brain anatomy in schizophrenia. *Lancet*, 346: 743–749.

Sedvall, G. C., & Wode-Helgodt, B. (1980). Aberrant monoamine metabolite levels in CSF and family history of schizophrenia. *Archives of General Psychiatry*, 37: 1113–1116.

Seeman, P. (1993). Schizophrenia as a brain disease. The dopamine receptor story. *Archives of Neurology*, 50: 1093–1095.

Seeman, P., Guan, H.-C., & Van Tol, H. H. M. (1993). Dopamine D4 receptors elevated in schizophrenia. *Nature*, 365: 441–445.

Segal, H. (1973). *Introduction to the Work of Melanie Klein*. London: The Hogarth Press, and the Institute of Psychoanalysis [reprinted London: Karnac Books, 1988].

Seikkula, J. (1991). *The Family–Hospital Boundary System in the Social Network* [in Finnish, with English summary]. *Jyväskylä Studies in Education, Psychology and Social Research, 80*. Jyväskylä, Finland.

Selvini Palazzoli, M., Boscolo, L., Cecchin, G., & Prata, G. (1978). *Paradox and Counterparadox. A New Model in the Therapy of Schizophrenic Transaction*. New York: Jason Aronson.

Selvini Palazzoli, M., Boscolo, L., Cecchin, G., & Prata, G. (1980). Hypothesizing–circularity–neutrality: three guidelines for the conductor of the session. *Family Process, 19*: 3–12.

Sesemann, V. (1927). *Beiträge zur Erkenntnisproblem: über gegenständliches und ungegenständliches Wissen*. Kaunas: Lietuvos Universito Humanitarniu Mokslu Fakulteto.

Shakow, D. (1962). Segmental set: a theory of the formal psychological deficit in schizophrenia. *Archives of General Psychiatry, 6*: 1–17.

Sham, P. C., O'Callaghan, E., Takei, N., et al. (1992). Schizophrenia following pre-natal exposure to influenza epidemic between 1939 and 1960. *British Journal of Psychiatry, 160*: 461–466.

Shepherd, M., Watt, D., Falloon, I., & Smeeton, N. (1989). The natural history of schizophrenia: a five-year follow-up study of outcome and prediction in a representative sample of schizophrenics. *Psychological Medicine Monographs* (Suppl. 15). Cambridge, U.K.: Cambridge University Press.

Siirala, M. (1986). Unpublished presentation delivered at Kupittaa Hospital, Turku.

Simon, W., & Wirt, R. D. (1961). Prognostic factors in schizophrenia. *American Journal of Psychiatry, 117*: 887–890.

Singer, M. T., & Wynne, L. C. (1963). Differentiation characteristics of the parents of childhood schizophrenics, childhood neurotics, and young adult schizophrenics. *American Journal of Psychiatry, 120*: 234–243.

Singer, M. T., & Wynne, L. C. (1965). Thought disorders and family relations of schizophrenics. III–IV. *Archives of General Psychiatry, 12*: 187–212.

Singer, M. T., Wynne, L. C., & Toohey, M. L. (1978). Communication disorders and the families of schizophrenics. In: L. C. Wynne, R. L. Cromwell, & S. Matthysse (Eds.), *The Nature of Schizophrenia: New Approaches to Research and Treatment* (pp. 499–511). New York: John Wiley & Sons.

Sjöström, R. (1985). Effects of psychotherapy in schizophrenia. *Acta Psychiatrica Scandinavica, 71*: 513–522.

Sjöström, R. (1990). Psykoterapi vid schizofreni—en prospektiv studie [in Swedish]. *Svenska Läkartidningen, 87*: 3279–3282.

Slater, E. (1953). *Psychotic and Neurotic Illnesses in Twins.* Medical Research Council, Special Report Series No. 278. London: Her Majesty's Stationery Office.

Sledge, W. H., Tebes, J., Rakfeldt, J., et al. (1996). Day hospital/crisis respite care versus inpatient care. Part I. Clinical outcomes. Part II. Service utilization and costs. *American Journal of Psychiatry, 153*: 1065–1083.

Snyder, S. H. (1981). Dopamine receptors, neuroleptics, and schizophrenias. *American Journal of Psychiatry, 138*: 460–464.

Speijer, N. (1961). *The Mentally Handicapped in the Sheltered Workshops.* The Hague: Ministry of Social Affairs and Public Health.

Spitzer, R. L., Endicott, J., & Robins, E. (1975). *Research Diagnostic Criteria.* New York: Biometric Research Division, New York State Psychiatric Institute.

Stabenau, J. R., Tupin, J., Werner, M., & Pollin, W. (1965). A comparative study of the families of schizophrenics, delinquents, and normals. *Psychiatry, 28*: 45–59.

Stanton, A. H., Gunderson, J. G., Knapp, P. H., et al. (1984). Effects of psychotherapy in schizophrenia: I. Design and implementation of a controlled study. *Schizophrenia Bulletin, 10*: 520–563.

Stanton, A., & Schwarz, M. (1954). *The Mental Hospital.* New York: Basic Books.

State Medical Board in Finland (1988). *The Schizophrenia Project 1981–87. Final Report of the National Programme of the Study, Treatment and Rehabilitation of Schizophrenic Patients in Finland* [in Finnish, with English summary]. Series Handbooks No 4. Helsinki: Valtion painatuskeskus.

Stein, L. I. (1993). A system approach to reducing relapse in schizophrenia. *Journal of Clinical Psychiatry, 54* (Suppl. 3): 7–12.

Stein, L. I., & Test, M. A. (1980). Alternative to mental hospital treatment. I. Conceptual model, treatment program, and clinical evaluation. *Archives of General Psychiatry, 37*: 392–397.

Steinglass, P. (1987). Psychoeducational family therapy in schizophrenia. A review essay. *Psychiatry, 50*: 14–23.

Stern, D. N. (1985). *The Interpersonal World of the Infant. A View from Psychoanalysis and Developmental Psychology.* New York: Basic Books.

Stierlin, H. (1972). Family dynamics and separation patterns of potential schizophrenics. In: D. Rubinstein & Y. O. Alanen (Eds.), *Psychotherapy of Schizophrenia* (pp. 169–179). Amsterdam: Excerpta Medica.

Stierlin, H. (1974). *Separating Parents and Adolescents. A Perspective on Running Away, Schizophrenia, and Waywardness.* New York: Quadrangle & The New York Times Book Co.

Stierlin, H. (1976). The dynamics of owning and disowning. Psychoanalytic and family perspectives. *Family Process, 15*: 277–288.

Stierlin, H. (1983). Reflections on the family therapy of schizo-present families. In: H. Stierlin, L. C. Wynne, & M. Wirsching (Eds.), *Psychosocial Intervention in Schizophrenia* (pp. 191–198). Berlin & Heidelberg: Springer-Verlag.

Stierlin, H., Rücker-Embden, I., Wetzel, N., & Wirsching, M. (1977). *Das erste Familiengespräch*. Stuttgart: Ernst Klett.

Strauss, J. S., & Carpenter, W. T. (1972). The prediction of outcome of schizophrenia: I. Characteristics of outcome. *Archives of General Psychiatry, 27*: 739–746.

Strauss, J .S., & Carpenter, W. T. (1974). The prediction of outcome in schizophrenia, II. Relationships between predictor and outcome variables. A report from the WHO International Pilot Study of Schizophrenia. *Archives of General Psychiatry, 31*: 37–42.

Strauss, J. S., Rakfeldt, J., Harding, C. M., & Lieberman, L. (1989). Psychological and social aspects of negative symptoms. *British Journal of Psychiatry, 155* (Suppl. 7): 128–132.

Suddath, R. L., Christison, G. W., Goldberg, T. E., et al. (1989). Temporal lobe pathology in schizophrenia. *American Journal of Psychiatry, 146*: 464–472.

Suddath, R. L., Christison, C. W., & Torrey, E. F. (1990). Anatomical abnormalities in the brains of monozygotic twins discordant for schizophrenia. *New England Journal of Medicine, 322*: 789–794.

Sullivan, H. S. (1924). Schizophrenia: its conservative and malignant features. *American Journal of Psychiatry, 81*: 77–91. [Also in: *Schizophrenia as a Human Process*. New York: W. W. Norton, 1962.]

Sullivan, H. S. (1930). Socio-psychiatric research. Its implications for the schizophrenia problem and for mental hygiene. *American Journal of Psychiatry, 87*: 977–991. [Also in: *Schizophrenia as a Human Process*. New York: W. W. Norton, 1962.]

Sullivan, H. S. (1931). The modified psychoanalytic treatment of schizophrenia. *American Journal of Psychiatry, 88*: 519–540. [Also in: *Schizophrenia as a Human Process*. New York: W. W. Norton, 1962.]

Sullivan, H. S. (1954). *The Psychiatric Interview.* New York: W. W. Norton.

Sullivan, H. S. (1956). *Clinical Studies in Psychiatry.* New York: W. W. Norton.

Sullivan, H. S. (1962). *Schizophrenia as a Human Process.* New York: W. W. Norton.

Syvälahti, E. K. G. (1994). Biological factors in schizophrenia. Structural and functional aspects. *British Journal of Psychiatry, 164* (Suppl. 23): 9–14.

Szasz, T. (1961). *The Myth of Mental Illness.* New York: Random House.

Tähkä, V. (1984). Psychoanalytic treatment as a developmental continuum: considerations of disturbed structuralization and its phase-specific encounter. *Scandinavian Psychoanalytic Review, 7:* 133–160.

Tähkä, V. (1993). *Mind and Its Treatment: Psychoanalytic Approach.* New York: International Universities Press.

Tarrier, N., Barrowclough, C., Vaughn, C., et al. (1989). Community management of schizophrenia: a two-year follow-up of behavioural intervention with families. *British Journal of Psychiatry, 154:* 625–628.

Tienari, P. (1963). *Psychiatric Illnesses in Identical Twins. Acta Psychiatrica Scandinavica, 39* (Suppl. 171).

Tienari, P. (1975). Schizophrenia in Finnish male twins. In: M. H. Lader (Ed.), *Studies of Schizophrenia. British Journal of Psychiatry Special Publication No 10* (pp. 29–35).

Tienari, P. (1992). Interaction between genetic vulnerability and rearing environment. In: A. Werbart & J. Cullberg (Eds.), *Psychotherapy of Schizophrenia: Facilitating and Obstructive Factors* (pp. 154–172). Oslo: Scandinavian University Press.

Tienari, P., Sorri, A., Lahti, I., et al. (1987). Genetic and psychosocial factors in schizophrenia: the Finnish adoptive family study. *Schizophrenia Bulletin, 13:* 477–484.

Tienari, P., Wynne, L. C., Moring, J., et al. (1993). Genetic vulnerability or family environment? Implications from the Finnish adoptive family study of schizophrenia. *Psychiatria Fennica. Yearbook:* 23–41. Helsinki: The Foundation for Psychiatric Research in Finland.

Tienari, P., Wynne, L. C., Moring, J., et al. (1994). The Finnish adoptive family study of schizophrenia. Implications for family research. *British Journal of Psychiatry, 164* (Suppl. 23): 20–26.

Torrey, E. F. (1983). *Surviving Schizophrenia. A Family Manual.* New York: Harper & Row.

Torrey, E. F., McGuire, M., O'Hare, A., et al. (1984). Endemic psychosis in western Ireland. *American Journal of Psychiatry, 141:* 966–970.

Torrey, E. F., Taylor, E. H., Bracha, H. S., et al. (1994). Prenatal origin of schizophrenia in a subgroup of discordant monozygotic twins. *Schizophrenia Bulletin, 20*: 423–432.

Tsuang, M. T., Woolson, R. F., & Fleming, J. A. (1979). Long-term outcome of major psychoses: I. Schizophrenia and affective disorders compared with psychiatrically symptom-free surgical conditions. *Archives of General Psychiatry, 39*: 1295–1301.

Tuori, T. (1987). *The Systemic Family Therapy of Married Schizophrenic Patients* [in Finnish, with English summary]. *Annales Universitatus Turkuensis, Ser. C*, Vol. 62 (Turku, Finland).

Tuori, T., Lehtinen, V., Hakkarainen, A., et al. (1997). The Finnish National Schizophrenia Project 1981–1987: 10-year evaluation of its results. *Acta Psychiatrica Scandinavica*.

Ugelstad, E. (1978). *Psykotiske langtidspasienter i psykiatriske sykehus—Nye behandlingsforsok* [in Norwegian]. Oslo: Universitetsforlaget.

Ugelstad, E. (1979). Possibilities of organizing psychotherapeutically oriented treatment programs for schizophrenia within sectorized psychiatric service. In: C. Müller (Ed.), *Psychotherapy of Schizophrenia* (pp. 253–258). Amsterdam: Excerpta Medica.

Uttal, W. R. (1997). Do theoretical bridges exist between perceptual experience and neurophysiology? *Perspectives in Biology and Medicine, 40*: 280–301.

Van Putten, T., Marshall, B. D., Liberman, R., et al. (1993). Systematic dosage reduction in treatment-resistant schizophrenic patients. *Psychopharmacological Bulletin, 29*: 315–320.

Van Tol, H. H. M., Bunzow, J. R., Guan, H. C., et al. (1991). Cloning of a human dopamine D4 receptor gene with high affinity for the antipsychotic clozapine. *Nature, 350*: 614–619.

Varvin, S. (1991). A retrospective follow-up investigation of a group of schizophrenic patients treated in a psychotherapeutic unit: the Kastanjebakken study. *Psychopathology, 24*: 335–344.

Vaughn, C. E., & Leff, J. P. (1976). The influence of family and social factors on the course of psychiatric illness. *British Journal of Psychiatry, 129*: 125–137.

Vinni, K. (1987). The costs of schizophrenia to the society [in Finnish]. Skitsofrenian hoito, konsensuskokous, 26–28 October. *Suomen Akatemian julkaisuja, 6*.

Virtanen, H. (1991). *Family- and Environment-centred Geropsychiatric Treatment* [in Finnish, with English summary]. *Annales Universitatis Turkuensis, Ser. C*, Vol. 85 (Turku, Finland).

Volkan, V. D. (1981). Transference and countertransference: an examination from the point of view of internalized object relations. In: S. Tuthman, C. Kaye, & M. Zimmerman (Eds.), *Object and Self: A Developmental Approach* (pp. 429–451). New York: International Universities Press.

Volkan, V. D. (1987). *Six Steps in the Treatment of Borderline Personality Organization*. Northvale, NJ: Jason Aronson.

Volkan, V. D. (1990). The psychoanalytic psychotherapy of schizophrenia. In: L. B. Boyer & P. Giovacchini (Eds.), *Master Clinicians on Treating the Regressed Patient* (pp. 245–270). Northvale, NJ: Jason Aronson.

Volkan, V. D. (1994). Identification with the therapist's functions and ego-building in the treatment of schizophrenia. *British Journal of Psychiatry, 164* (Suppl. 23): 77–82.

Volkan, V. D. (1995). *The Infantile Psychotic Self and Its Fates. Understanding and Treating Schizophrenics and Other Difficult Patients*. Northvale, NJ: Jason Aronson.

Vuorio, K. A., Räkköläinen, V., Syvälahti, E., et al. (1993). Integrated treatment of acute psychosis [in Finnish]. *Suomen Lääkärilehti, 48*: 466–471, 582–588, 689–693.

Watt, D. C., Katz, K., & Shepherd, M. (1983). The natural history of schizophrenia: a 5-year prospective follow-up of a representative sample of schizophrenics by means of a standardized clinical and social assessment. *Psychological Medicine, 13*: 663–670.

Waxler, N. E. (1979). Is outcome of schizophrenia better in non-industrial societies? The case of Sri Lanka. *Journal of Nervous and Mental Diseases, 167*: 144–158.

Weinberger, D. R. (1987). Implications of normal brain development for the pathogenesis of schizophrenia. *Archives of General Psychiatry, 44*: 660–669.

Weinberger, D. R. (1995). From neuropathology to neurodevelopment. *Lancet, 346*: 552–557.

Weinberger, D. R., Berman, K. F., Suddath, R., & Torrey, E. F. (1992). Evidence of dysfunction of a prefrontal-limbic network in schizophrenia: a magnetic resonance imaging and regional cerebral blood flow study of discordant monozygotic twins. *American Journal of Psychiatry, 149*: 890–897.

Weinberger, D. R., Torrey, E. F., Neophytides, S. N., & Wyatt, R. J. (1979). Lateral cerebral ventricular enlargement in chronic schizophrenia. *Archives of General Psychiatry, 36*: 735–739.

Weller, M. P. I. (1989). Mental illness—who cares? *Nature, 339*: 249–252.

Wender, P. H., Rosenthal, D., & Kety, S. S. (1968). A psychiatric assessment of the adoptive parents of schizophrenics. In: D. Rosenthal & S. S. Kety (Eds.), *The Transmission of Schizophrenia* (pp. 235–250). New York: Pergamon Press.

Werner, H. (1948). *Comparative Psychology of Mental Development.* Chicago: Follett.

Whitehorn, J. C., & Betz, B. (1960). Further studies of the doctor as the crucial variable in the outcome of treatment with schizophrenic patients. *American Journal of Psychiatry, 117*: 215–222.

Wiesel, F.-A. (1994). Neuroleptic treatment of patients with schizophrenia. Mechanisms of action and clinical significance. *British Journal of Psychiatry, 164* (Suppl. 23): 65–70.

Will, O. A., Jr. (1961). Process, psychotherapy and schizophrenia. In: A. Burton (Ed.), *Psychotherapy of Psychoses* (pp. 10–42). New York: Basic Books.

Williams, J., Spurlock, G., McGuffin, P., et al. (1996). Association between schizophrenia and T 102C polymorphism of the 5–hydroxytryptamine type 2a receptor gene. *Lancet, 347*: 1294–1296.

Winefield, H. R., & Harvey, E. J. (1994). Needs of family caregivers in chronic schizophrenia. *Schizophrenia Bulletin, 20*: 557–566.

Wing, J. K. (1960). A pilot experiment of long hospitalized male schizophrenic patients. *British Journal of Preventive and Social Medicine, 14*: 173–180.

Wing, J. K., & Fryers, T. (1976). *Psychiatric Services in Camberwell and Salford.* London: MRC Social Psychiatry Unit.

Winnicott, D. W. (1960). The theory of the parent–infant relationship. *International Journal of Psycho-Analysis, 41*: 585–595. [Also in: *The Maturational Processes and the Facilitating Environment* (pp. 37–55). London: Hogarth Press & The Institute of Psychoanalysis, 1965; reprinted London: Karnac Books, 1990.]

Wolkowitz, O. M., & Pickar, D. (1991). Benzodiazepines in the treatment of schizophrenia: a review and reappraisal. *American Journal of Psychiatry, 148*: 714–726.

Wong, D. F., Wagner, H. M., Tune, L. E., et al. (1986). Positron emission tomography reveals elevated D2 dopamine receptors in drug-naive schizophrenics. *Science, 234*: 1558–1563.

World Health Organization (1979). *Schizophrenia—An International Follow-up Study.* Chichester: John Wiley.

Wynne, L. C. (1965). Some indications and contraindications for exploratory family therapy. In: I. Boszormenyi-Nagy & J. L. Framo (Eds.),

Intensive Family Therapy: Theoretical and Practical Aspects (pp. 289–322). New York: Hoeber Medical Division, Harper & Row.

Wynne, L. C. (1978). Family relationships and communication. Concluding comments. In: L. C. Wynne, R. L. Cromwell, & S. Matthysse (Eds.), *The Nature of Schizophrenia. New Approaches to Research and Treatment* (pp. 534–542). New York: John Wiley & Sons.

Wynne, L. C., McDaniel, S., & Weber, T. (1986). *Systems Consultation: A New Perspective for Family Therapy.* New York: Guilford Press.

Wynne, L. C., Ryckoff, I. M., Day, J., & Hirsch, S. (1958). Pseudomutuality in the family relations of schizophrenics. *Psychiatry, 21:* 205–220.

Wynne, L. C., & Singer, M. T. (1963). Thought disorder and family relations in schizophrenia. I–II. *Archives of General Psychiatry, 9:* 191–206.

Wynne, L. C., Singer, M. T., Bartko, J. J., & Toohey, M. L. (1977). Schizophrenics and their families: research on parental communication. In: J. M. Tanner (Ed.), *Developments in Psychiatric Research* (pp. 254–286). London: Hodder & Stoughton.

Wynne, L. C., Singer, M. T., & Toohey, M. L. (1976). Communication of the adoptive parents of schizophrenics. In: J. Jorstad & E. Ugelstad (Eds.), *Schizophrenia, 75. Psychotherapy, Family Studies, Research* (pp. 413–451). Oslo: Universitetsforlaget.

Zubin, J., & Spring, B. J. (1977). Vulnerability—a new view of schizophrenia. *Journal of Abnormal Psychology, 86:* 103–126.

INDEX